Zep Tepi
The Conclusion

HENDRIK G DIRKER

First published in South Africa 2003
Zep Tepi ~ The First Time
ISBN 0-620-30310-7

Limited edition Cape Town Book Fair 2006
Zep Tepi ~ The Conclusion
eBook ISBN 978-0-620-36782-0

BookSurgeAmazon edition 2007
Zep Tepi ~ The Conclusion
ISBN 978-0-620-36781-3

CreateSpace revised edition 2010

Hard cover with colour illustrations
ISBN 978-0-620-47721-5

copyright © Hendrik G. Dirker (all rights reserved)
P.O. Box 316, Simons Town, 7995, South Africa
hendrikdirker@yahoo.com

Governed by its complex nature and new findings, this work evolved into the current cohesive thesis. Every edition was the best I could muster under circumstances and progressive on its predecessor. This imprint is the culmination of experience gained and data gathered during a decade. I hope the reader will enjoy it, yet realise the gravity of the matter. Cover art is from a collection inspired by my research into ancient Egyptian mythology and astronomy -it interprets the purpose of the pyramids through geometry and reflects the division of Upper and Lower Egypt, in resonance with day and night on planet Earth.

Acknowledgements

Foreword 11

Controversy 13

Introduction 15
Claims and findings
The adventure begins 20

PART I
THE OVERVIEW

Chapter 1   ASTRO-ARCHAEOLOGY   32
Chambers and shafts

Chapter 2   PYRAMIDOLOGY   44
(-) Fourth Dynasty (+)

Chapter 3   MYTHOLOGY   52
Time & history
Golden era of the gods
Star gods
Rebirth cult
Decline & legendary dispute
Mystical places and events

PART I epilogue 79
More adventure

PART II
THE DISCOVERY

Introduction	91
DIAGRAMS & IMAGES	93
Chapter 4 CORRELATION	96
Orion	
Celestial Rostau	
Terrestrial Rostau	
Two Lands division	
Chapter 5 UNIFIED SCHEME	114
Giza hub & circle	
Survey grid & co-ordinates	
Wider plan	
Sacred geometry	
Adventure update	130
Chapter 6 GEOMETRICAL ASTRONOMY	134
Pyramids = stars	
The Duat	
Perspective views	
Mysterious symbolism	
Orion & the netherworld	
Chapter 7 ESOTERIC GEOMETRY	148
Celestial pyramids	
Pi (π) in the sky	
Duat obelisk	

Chapter 8 SKY CHARTS & ANECDOTES 154
Planetary paths
Celestial dome
Celestial globe

Chapter 9 THE SECRETS OF ORION 164
Orion pyramid
Secret chambers

Adversity and update 169

Chapter 10 THE CONCLUSION 176
Earth gyration
Precession phases
Climate change
Fabled mystery

PART II epilogue 207

Appendix 218

Index 222

Glossary 224

Dedicated to the memory of my father, who showed me the Southern Cross and how to find the way…

This work spawned a wonderful journey of discovery, yet at times presented a struggle and quest for survival, on which I ponder whether circumstances could have been different or if destiny determined it to be... none-the-less, facing adversity demands determination and perseverance. Challenges present opportunity to build or test character and alliances but faith in a calling and belief in self is vital. The reward is a widened spectrum of the kaleidoscope of experience that comprises human life. There were several individuals along the way, to whom I wish to give acknowledgement:

In the Western Cape:- Catherine and Werner for providing opportunities in Camps Bay and Hout Bay; Ingrid for support and sharing a place of belonging during emotionally charged times; the late Professor Fairall of UCT for reviewing my thesis; Herschel Mair at the Cape Town Planetarium for his assist with sky software; Reinhardt Buys for legal advice; my cousin Karel and Marianne for their invaluable generosity when I was destitute; the Simons Town Museum and Board of Trustees for the panoramic reprieve from my nomadic existence; Diana Reekie for proof reading; Andre Smit for promotional material. The *zip print* team of Fish Hoek for their friendly and efficient service.

In Gauteng:- Rory and Nikki in Pretoria for compiling my astrolink website; Jaco Brugman for interim hosting; my cousin Helgard for his hospitality; my sister Christina for unwavering support and belief in me; my sister Marietjie, to whom I am indebted for backing my first publication; Dave Henderson for my stay and continued writing on the farms; Davey for his companionship and dogs, Maximus and Frikkie, who eagerly accompanied me on walks; Ivica for mentorship on Universal guidance and protection; Gerry in Vereeniging for admin consultation.

In Kwa-Zulu Natal:- Warren and Sally in Durban, for their enthusiasm in processing my first book; the company of my friends Dayne, Mike, Pierre and dog Zulu, who walked the green hills and sugar cane plantations with me on the north coast; the Beach Bums crew for a great 'distressing venue' overlooking the Indian Ocean; Mark and Duval of Ballito, who salvaged my old pc from corrosion.

In England:- the Stevensons and my 'old army buddy' Tim, for their kind integration into the family , which made it possible to further the cause.

To others elsewhere, although unnamed, who gave encouragement, alleviated solitude or provided meaningful input and reference material, I wish to express sincere gratitude. Lastly, to my adversaries: check mate.

Foreword

'In the original concept behind the solar religion, the chief god was associated with cosmic forces, though it later acquired other, political connotations through association with the royal house. …the cult of the sun-god was bound up with laws about the inheritance of power and property; it explained the political order of the present world'

(**Veronica Ions**, *Egyptian Mythology*)

Astronomy, archaeology, mythology, philosophy, spirituality, science and time are all complex, cross cultural, fascinating and intriguing phenomena of which the common denominator is cosmology -relating to how the world came into being.
Politics, on the other hand, defined as the 'art' or 'science' of government is also a complex, cross cultural, fascinating and intriguing phenomenon of which the common denominator is *power* -relating to how the *end* of the world can come to being…
This work relates to the former, more productive phenomena. I felt a certain sense that a moral issue was at stake and that this esoteric knowledge cannot become the source for a bureaucracy, or if that had been the case, time has come for change. Evidently anti-establishment, I believe fulfillment is attainable in doing what one would have done, had it been in heaven, or here and now. The establishment however proves to be a hindrance -evident in the dire state of the world we live in, which is a consequence of the behaviour of humankind and not the evolution of the Universe.
This is a quest for the truth, for once and for *all*, and a tribute to the sacrifice of campaigners such as Dr. Giordano Bruno, who in the spirit of enlightenment, resolutely pursued that passion –only to be brutally persecuted by the establishment.

'...making aggressive use of pseudo-scientific methods and the Internet, the 'New Agers' (including Graham Hancock, John Anthony West, Robert Bauval) are changing the way Egyptian Monuments are seen by hundreds of thousands of tourists...'

(*New Yorker*, 10 February 1997)

Controversy

'The lure of a 'secret chamber' or Hall of Records at Giza has fired the imagination of the general public and has drawn into this history-long quest a horde of unusual seekers. Ranging from sedate scientists to armchair speculators, from eminent academic institutions to dubious psychic societies, from reputable archaeologists to innocuous Walter Mitty characters, and from staunch sceptics to New Age Gurus, a bedazzling assortment of followers rubbed shoulders at Giza. I meet hundreds of individuals who are utterly convinced that they have a major role to play as well as 'something important to contribute' to this archetypal, quasi-mythical human drama. The majority of these characters turn out to be gentle and harmless people who are seekers of enlightenment and peace. Sometimes it is a refreshing and even rewarding experience to exchange ideas with some of them...But there are one or two who, wittingly or unwittingly, end up causing an incredible amount of trouble and confusion.'

'...I wanted others to know what I had found, and academic articles do not bring discoveries to a wide audience. Egyptologists had a reading backlog of ten years, in some cases twenty, with hundreds of articles, theses, dissertations and papers all waiting to be reviewed...

...The more I investigated, the more it drew a mixed reaction from academics. Some felt that they could not comment on the "mathematical" or "astronomical" aspects of my theses, others were nonplussed and most, at least in the early stage, simply could not be bothered to reply...'

'...access to the site, and knowledge about it, has been monopolised by members of the archaeological and Egyptological professions who have agreed among themselves as to the origin, and age, and function of the monuments ...new evidence which does not support this scholarly consensus, and which might actively undermine it has been overlooked or sidelined, ...sometimes even deliberately concealed from the public.'

(**Robert Bauval,** *Secret Chamber*)

Introduction

'...In all ages of which we have any literary records we find the tradition of a recondite *knowledge which could not be disclosed* to any save those who had undergone the severest tests as to their worthiness to receive it.
This knowledge was generally known under the term of the mysteries, and it was *concerned with the deepest facts of man's origin, nature, and connection with the super-sensual worlds of beings,* as well as with the 'natural' laws of the physical world.
It was no mere speculation; it was *real knowledge of 'the things that are'*, a knowledge that gave its possessor powers which at one time or other have been regarded as *pertaining only to the gods...*'

(William Kingsland - *The Gnosis or Ancient Wisdom in the Christian Scriptures)*

The purpose of this work is to resolve elusive riddles of the pyramids and to reveal the uncanny knowledge of an ancient civilization. The Orion correlation theory is based upon a concept where the stars of Orion's Belt were duplicated on the ground, in the layout configuration of the three pyramids at Giza. This book will show the association of specific stars with Egyptian mythology and a wider correlation of stars mapped out in pyramids. The focus is chiefly on the fabulous pyramids of the Old Empire and with particular interest in the Giza plateau. The mystery regarding planning is resolved in an unprecedented and multi disciplined breakthrough. Astonishing new discoveries, that relate time to the pyramids and stars, are unveiled through geometrical philosophy, celestial and terrestrial association and a bit of *methodical* magic. The thesis is graphically demonstrated and supported by unique and tangible evidence. These findings conform to conventional astronomy, contemporary Egyptology and unravel the motive of an ancient stellar cult.

Claims and findings

The anthropomorphic gods of legend are unequivocally identified through a notion of stars being gods and associated with pyramids. This tantalizingly evokes the issue of who the real title holders are to the pyramids. The location of Rostau is shown with duality in celestial and terrestrial topography.

I demonstrate how linear, angular and diagonal measurements were applied over formidable distances to determine the settings. The surveyors' grid, co-ordinates and hub of the Giza plateau is defined. It validates a unified concept of trans-generational planning, which contradicts mainstream Egyptology belief.

The Memphis necropolis is a map derived from a configuration of stars and substantiates that a wider plan of pyramids indeed exists. The 'sacred geometry' of a stellar and solar cult is exposed and eradicates any doubt regarding the possibility of coincidence.

The 'hidden circle' referred to in the *Book of the Duat* and symbolism related to the ulterior significance of obelisks is depicted. This takes on a fascinating dimension that reveals the identity of Horus, the sun-god. The cosmic source and icon for the missing capstone of the Great Pyramid is thereby clarified.

Most significant in culmination, these findings reveal the radical purpose of the pyramids as a blatant warning of a momentous event that will shake the global scientific establishment. Compelling evidence accentuates the profound genius of the master composers and their grand scheme of pyramid construction in antiquity. Contention that they were from a doctrinal advanced civilization, capable of technological wizardry is bolstered, yet they disappeared as mysteriously as they materialized and the haunting question lingers: who were they?

Illustrated interpretation of important relics:

Papyrus Westcar
(item No.303, Antiquities Museum, Berlin)

The advanced astronomical science of a mysterious culture is embodied within ancient oracles. It becomes evident that the Great Pyramid cannot be attributed to Khufu. Celestial blue prints are detailed, complete with secret chambers –a principal chamber is located in the Great Pyramid and has yet to be breached.

Shabaka Stone
(exhibit no.498, British Museum, London)

Intriguing tales, difficult to fathom, are fascinatingly deciphered and schematically depicted. Geometry and archaeo-astronomy is employed as the major medium to interpret esoteric connotation. The concept of the Duat, alluded to as the mythical 'after-world', where the gods of the First Time established a cosmic kingdom, is unraveled in context. The legendary division and unification of the 'Two Lands' -Upper and Lower Egypt -is illustrated in cosmic and terrestrial duality by pyramid-star association. Revolutionary textual interpretation vividly echoes the event and clarifies the expression: "as above, so below". These domains are identified in celestial topography and transposed on the world globe, where it is shown to extend beyond Egypt and to incorporate the complex motions of planet Earth.

The pyramid age reveals a multi dimensional *magic* that discloses the cryptic key to an archaic riddle. This emphatic evidence will lead to a turning point in human destiny. It has direct bearing on one of the prevailing contentious issues of our era, namely climate change but introduces an unexpected twist -a dire situation, almost too fantastical to comprehend and for which, our society is utterly unprepared…

New discoveries also require the formulation of a description and it should be remembered that these are pioneering times, in a field that is not yet defined or academically established. The combination of mythology, astronomy and ancient structures has destined the script to be of technical nature. I have however, attempted to simplify it as much as dictated by articulate ability. Scientific content automatically restricts readership, although the desire is to present it to a diverse an audience as possible. The theme requires the reader to be patient, as unambiguous and concise expressions are not easily attainable in this stampede by a multitude of disciplines, through virgin territory. Several 'hold that thought' instances may be encountered en-route to the remarkable discoveries, which are revealed in Part II of the book. Part I sets the scene and is not an attempt to provide a comprehensive overview of historical or chronological events in Egypt but rather a brief, relevant background to take us to the real purpose of the work: an investigation of texts and monuments that have otherwise defied rationalization. Certain passages, from various sources, are intentionally quoted in a context where deemed appropriate in conveying a stimulating message.

It should be pointed out that titles and tags attached to the pyramids, their interior chambers, passages and shafts do not necessarily date back to their absolute origin, or reflect their original intended purpose. Typical examples of these misnomers are the King's and Queen's chambers. To some, they may give the impression that the chambers were occupied by a King and Queen, such as in a medieval castle, which of course is false. In fact it is doubtful whether they served an actual purpose as burial chambers at all. To add to the confusion, Egyptian cities have been renamed throughout the ages and Deities, Pharaohs and even pyramids bear a multitude of names. Sometimes, the same identity, by another name, is present in various mythologies. Certain stars have a proper name, while others within the same constellation are differentiated by brightness and labeled by a catalogued object number. This 'pick & mix' exhibit an array of spelling found in various sources –the English version typically derived from Arabic, Greek or Roman origin. For the general demonstrative purpose of this work and to minimise confusion, common names and decimal rounding is used as far as conceivable. Repetition of elementary detail, which has been well documented in numerous publications, is avoided. In order to emphasise context of words, or sections that occur in pyramid texts, *italics* are used where pertinent. The intention is not to maliciously discredit other theories but in view of the importance of the matter, it should be pointed out that the matching of pyramids with stars, as presented in *The Orion Mystery*, beyond that of the Orion's Belt stars, present a defective layout.

Accreditation of ownership, or who was responsible for building the pyramids has been questioned and remains a contentious issue. Whether the general consensus is correct or not, at this stage, is irrelevant as this is an analysis of the visual and tangible, first and foremost. Initially, one is obliged to humour conventional history, however, as the investigation progresses it evidently becomes necessary to question everything that we have ever been told. My discoveries provide irrefutable scientific proof that will launch Egyptology into a new dimension, albeit per the rate of change expressed by Albert Einstein: 'one grave at a time'. Some answers are obscured in myth, which is not so tangible. The pyramids are classified as wonders of the ancient world and their perplexity escalates with the passage of time. Their purpose lead us to a nail-biting conclusion. Let's journey to where it began…

The adventure begins

8 August 2001
The telephone call was made around noon;

"Believe me I am quite sober... and sane." (I added in case he thought the altitude had got to me)

"At first, you're not going to realise the significance or consequences... probably the biggest of all time!" I blurted out.

"Henri slow down, I believe you -now, what exactly are you talking about?"

"I've made an incredible discovery... *I have deciphered the ancient code of the gods!*"

The Journey

Friday 16 March, almost five months earlier.
I had been travelling along the M1 for the last 120km, heading South from Pretoria via Johannesburg then Easterly in the direction of Durban. These are all big, modern hustle-bustle type cities with probably the best infrastructures in all Africa. Even so, I was happy to leave the traffic behind me and see the smog fading away in the rear view mirror as the vast open spaces of the Highveld were unfolding ahead of me. The vintage resembling a 'jeep' was packed with the last shopping from civilisation and had seen better days. I was listening to Chris Rea, or what was audible above the noise from a leaking exhaust and rattling door. The song: 'Road to Hell' was quite apt to my experience... how I missed my microbus!

The weeks leading up to this had been a blur of activity and upheavals. I needed to raise some capital to commence with phase one of my dream venture and had sold the vehicle. I was in good spirit, as it was the start of a great adventure. The warm Indian Ocean was not my destination, although unknowingly at the time, future events would lead to the shores of the Zulu Kingdom. The 'roof of Africa' -the Maluti Mountains in the Kingdom of Lesotho, some 400km distant, was where I was headed -beautiful, primitive wilderness, inhabited by the friendly Basotho and their sure footed horses. During the past ten years I had been conducting adventure tours -wildlife safaris in the bush and pony treks in the mountains –in all aspects of logistics and execution. Living for adventure and *on* adventure, some friends called me names like 'Indiana Jones' or 'Crocodile Dundee'. I had planned to establish a permanent base and infrastructure: a lodge with facilities that would, in addition to tourism, accommodate the corporate market. During initial site preparation and collection of material, I stayed a couple of weeks at a time but commencement of construction required my permanent presence there. My journey was interrupted by a broken tie rod that sheared off the front wheel and I had to spend the night in the small town of Ladybrand. Mercifully I had reduced speed in a last minute decision: push on before night fall, or stop for fish & chips supper. The following day, after temporary repairs to the Nomad, I crossed over the border, with 60km still to go before I was to reach my destination. The last 40km was mountain country -winding, twisting and climbing. After having negotiated Bushman's Pass, it was the descent to the security checkpoint where the guards, who normally recognised the Kombi with the 'Adventures Unlimited' logos, walked around the vehicle, shook their heads and showed gleaming teeth. After a long day, which by then had made way for night, it was a relief to be back, although I had to get a ride for the last 2km with the driver of the Molimo N'Thuse Lodge, where the Nomad remained, immobile.

In the mountains

Breathing the mountain air again was an invigorating experience. To marvel at an awesome star-studded sky, set in absolute blackness with the absence of the Moon, was a reminder of one's own insignificance. Most of all, appreciating the almost 'deafening silence'... after the journey in the 'machine from hell' -a home coming to humble accommodation amongst friends. Friends like Salang, an expert horseman, who together with Joseph, had been my local guides for the past ten years and with whom I'd shared many a magical moment in those magnificent mountains. Sometimes subjected to the unpredictable forces of the elements or discussing our dreams around a fire, under the spectacular African sky, always looking out for each other and always getting the job done -negotiating the terrain, trekking, guiding and catering for our groups and ensuring our guests had a memorable experience... He named his second son after me and calls me H. Our *other* associate Philip, the 'Lone Ranger' with his scout hat; no ordinary guy -practical and resourceful, a teacher by profession, a liberal at heart with a passion for the outdoors. When Philip arrived on Roll Over (his horse with short-cropped mane), with three donkeys carrying six bags of potatoes and sometimes also with two oxen, it's like the cavalry arriving!
Life at the 'God Help Me Pass' was very basic; we used candles for lighting and heated water on an open fire. Until we could take occupation of our site, situated next to a spectacular waterfall, our operations centre was based at the Basotho Pony Trekking station, some 2330m above sea level. With mountains in all directions, invigorating spring water, the ever present Basotho Ponies, inexpensive beer at the local shop, peace and tranquility prevailed, until about five thirty in the morning when Julius, our neighbour, awakened. Julius grew up in the mountains, which he got to know very well as a herd boy while looking after goats, sheep or cattle. It's quite a mundane life so herd boys do things to entertain

themselves and to pass the time. Singing is one such pastime and singing is Julius' forte'. Not only did he pursue it with great gusto, but with a variety of accompanying whistles, jumping and stomping while washing and cooking in the morning. I figured it was probably a way of getting warm on a cold day but this theory was no longer valid with the advent of summer. In any case in winter, with snow abound, Julius would be washing himself outside in the snow! An avid storyteller with hilarious experiences to share, the ever present radio dangled around his neck announcing his approach from afar. This was our source of local news retold by Julius amid much of his own chuckling. One such recent bit of information was of a political party, in the hope of canvassing support, which had promised would be voters across the air waves that they would arrange for a train to collect them. This all seemed like a good gesture except, for the small oversight that there was no railway line! Many other colourful characters and interesting stories would fill volumes, another time…

The moods of the mountains, their sheer size an omnipresent testimony to a traumatic conception in pre historic time -twisted, convoluted lava, earth and rock moved by immense energies. Weathered over vast time, they now exude a picture of peaceful tranquility and timeless beauty. Great sentinels over rolling hills and slopes, that transform from intense greens to autumn yellows and white winters. Cascading waterfalls transform to meandering crystal streams and rejuvenate fertile valleys below. Evolving weather introduces time and motion to formidable elements that take their toll. Equipment, clothing, man and animal are all subjected to the severest tests but enjoying our space and freedom, we were the 'mountain cowboys' -riding on big-hearted, even-tempered Basotho Ponies, taking in the sweeping vistas and panoramas, crossing streams and the Makhaleng River before arriving at the site some 5km distant. Nestled in a remote and truly unspoilt mountain environment of great scenic and natural beauty, access is on horseback along a contour path, with dynamic views of gorges and waterfalls. From there excursions can be made on horseback to remote villages scattered throughout the mountains, where one can become part of a community for an evening and experience the unique culture of the Basotho and their way of life. The day spent constructively in natural surroundings left one physically tired, with some respite in sharing of humour and content that a dream was materialising in stone timber and thatch, slowly but surely. Riding back, with a setting sun casting a golden glow on towering cliffs, briefly halting for the ponies to drink from a crystal stream with small rapids, one's questions were few and conversation unnecessary -looking forward to a cool beer upon returning. Then, bathing from a bucket, by candlelight and surrounded by silky white Angora goat skins while listening to classical music, became my ritual. Donning clean clothes afterwards, one felt a tremendous sense of belonging, meaning and ultimate well-being.

Other times there was nothing to do but wait. Those were times to 'get lost', daydream, contemplate life and philosophise. To lose track of time was an amazing experience. Not knowing what day it was, sometimes even the month was uncertain. I would go on walks in search of my other friends; a pack of Grey Rhebok antelope, which I dubbed 'the magnificent seven'. I had struck up some kind of trusting relationship, albeit over long distance. They were a very alert and skittish group and would only be seen if they wished to be. Their survival assets were agility and camouflage that blended them cunningly with their habitat. I didn't see them for some time and was beginning to get concerned, then, one day while on a walk I spotted them. Their long ears pointed skyward, white short fluffy tails arched up, with the ever weary flank and rear guards at their posts, raised snouts to test the air and locked gaze upon me. The cows in the centre lay on their bellies, legs folded beneath like a coiled spring in a cocked rifle, ready to launch instantly at the distress signal. But they stayed put, as though wanting to share something. Out of habit I counted them and instead of stopping at seven, counted up to nine -that's why they'd been so scarce! I missed observing the larger game and greater variety of species that inhabit the bush and other regions in Southern Africa, so too the soothing, ceaseless motion and beauty of the oceans that wash the coastal shores. Wanting it all, I guess -to feel, breathe, smell and taste, explore and discover, wonder and dream -to live and be one with it, to belong. Romance was not a chapter in that episode as aspects such as economics and security would have to pave the way first. In the past there'd been wonderful episodes, varied like the moods of the weather: enriching and sustaining the total picture, yet leaving a void... in the meantime there's a mission and objective to pursue and fortunately I get along well with myself!

With winter looming, I thought it a good idea to get a book to pass some idle time and occupy my mind especially on those days when it would not be possible or pleasant to venture out. On the next excursion to town, while getting a newspaper, I scoured the small bookshelf at the CNA in Maseru. I was not in the mood for fiction adventure as enough of the real thing was coming my way. Under the handful of other titles, one grabbed my attention. The idea was to read it slowly and to make a study of it. Graham Hancock's fascinating book: *The Sign and the Seal*, which traces the intriguing path of the lost Ark of the Covenant, is a masterful investigation and gripping eye opener and I couldn't put it down.

On 30th April I was up early in anticipation as both the Hubble Space Telescope and the International Space Station were due over those latitudes from a South-Westerly to North-Easterly direction, between 05h50 and 06h10. With little diversion or social activity in our remote location, other interests and pastimes became big events! Looking out the window when I first got up, I was greeted by a dark, clear and star speckled sky. There was time to fix a cup of coffee and after doing so, I, returned with the intention of getting comfortable in front of the window. From there I would have a reasonable view, without having to venture out into the pre-dawn chill. But a bank of cloud had rapidly moved in and obscured any hope of seeing anything. Lesotho is also known as 'the Kingdom in the sky', the terrain and weather is comparable to that of the Scottish Highlands –four seasons can occur in one day although the climate is generally more temperate. After all, it is Africa! Five days later an early bout of snow transformed the landscape into a fairytale. The following day broke with blue sky of incredible clarity and glorious sunshine. Trudging a solitary trail in the virgin snow, I spotted a Bearded Vulture (a large and endangered species), then another! The pair effortlessly rising on a thermal, spiralling elegantly upwards without flapping a wing, clearing the snow covered peak of Machache, skillfully manipulating the forces of nature and continuing their upward journey into a perfect unblemished sky. I watched them until they disappeared in the blue yonder, and experienced that primordial desire; the ability of flight.

I enjoy observing the world from another perspective, when travelling on board an airliner. Those passing overhead are oblivious of life below, likewise the sensation and lifestyle of those 'up there' are beyond the scope of a herd boy tending his goats, cattle or sheep. Yes, there still exist places where seeing a white man or a vehicle is a novelty. How does one reconcile a child growing up in those mountains and in a lifetime never sees the ocean? Hunger takes priority; freedom, pleasure and well being can only be truly appreciated for value in context of a broad spectrum of consciousness. Adventure also has other elements to deal with and aspects to overcome. It is sustenance for the spirit that in turn will enrich the soul through perspective and balance. The spirit of adventure drives us to search for W's; whatwherewhywhowhen? Some don't have the urge or perhaps there is nothing to be discovered! The weather warmed again and the snow disappeared almost as suddenly as it had appeared. Winter proper was yet to come however, and another book was required -a thick one...

In the stars

I have been blessed with wonderful, eventful life-experiences and a variety of talents for which I am truly grateful. Although put to the test in the past, felt that I had endured the challenge, observed, learned and shared, yet wondered whether all life was such a trial? With this thoughtful frame of mind and while browsing through the newspaper, bought on the last trip to town, some time ago (time there has another dimension!) I came across the astrology section, which at other times I wouldn't have paid much attention to, but read 'your stars forecast' in any case;

Libra:
'Contract negotiations could get held up by details -or egos. Don't fight it. This is the cosmos at work, telling you now is not the time, and these are possibly not the people. Still, it won't be long before your energies are back on track, or even creating a new one. The worst is over, and you're still looking as good as you did when it started. Hold out your hand and wait.'

(***The Star*** news paper 22/04/2001)

It had a nice ring to it, so I cut it out and kept it! Once a month, we would make the 60km journey (which, by local transport, was a challenging experience to say the least) in order to replenish our stores of supplies and on the next excursion to town, the thick book, once again the only copy, virtually jumped from the shelf at me. The front cover displayed a great pyramid captured in golden sunset, the title: *Secret Chamber* by Robert Bauval. I was armed with reading material for winter. Little did I suspect what lay ahead. Once again a fascinating work and a riveting subject: the ancient Egyptian star cult and unexplained mysteries of the pyramids. The common factor in the subject and my curiosity was the stars. The unfathomable distances, time dimensions and innumerable celestial objects of the unexplored Universe intrigued me endlessly, although my interest exceeded my knowledge by far. I became entirely engrossed and while digesting the information and making notes, again realised that there are many unanswered questions about mankind's history. Reference was made to stars in a particular region of the sky with which I am familiar and where most of the brightest stars are located. This region is host to, among others, the familiar constellation of Orion, the legendary hunter, who according to Greek mythology was severely punished for his arrogance by Scorpio. These stars have played a significant role in navigation throughout the ages. I was attempting to 'see' mythical legend uttered in spells of the ancient Pyramid Texts. The location of the pyramids is in the northern hemisphere –a long distance from where I was but the sky provided a mutual element, although it appears 'upside down' for a viewer in the southern hemisphere. Perhaps these very factors would count in my favour. Experiencing Egypt in the sky and dealing with orientation calls for some unorthodox approaches - food for analytical minds. Some problems were the Moon 'getting in the way' and the cold temperatures. It was not a very inviting prospect to get out from under two duvets before Sunrise. At that time (Southern hemisphere winter) the constellations of relevance would only rise shortly before daybreak above Thaba Putsoa (the Blue Grey Mountain) in close proximity from where I was making observations. This allowed short periods of visibility only and having a photograph of the sky was a real blessing. Previous experiences seemed to strangely come into play as part of a chain of unfolding events. During childhood my father had showed me the Southern Cross and how to determine the four cardinal directions in the absence of the Sun: by extending ones right arm outward to this constellation and looking straight ahead, one will face east. This had evoked an interest in star gazing. The South Pole of the axis, around which the Earth spins, is determined by a point at the intersection of a line drawn perpendicularly between the 'two pointers'; alpha and beta Centauri, up to where it intersects a line extended through Crux.

On Saturday 21st July, while reading my treasured book, by then in several pieces, I noticed two Herons fly by as they headed for shelter, indicating significant weather change. They don't migrate, opting for the ample supply of rats in the fields. Later, the 'snow that divides the year in two' as the Basotho refer to it, came down gently and in eerie silence. I was alone and lit the small fire. The following day I ventured out and using a shovel, built a giant Mutlanyana (snow rabbit) while keeping the cold at bay with ample sherry. The thirty young ponies, sheltered in their stable - anticipating the pending snow, they had long winter coats and round bellies.

In the early morning hours of 4th August, with Orion in the East, I observed the planets Venus and Jupiter in the vicinity of the 'Grand Gallery of the Duat,' Saturn was near the Hyades. I watched Venus for quite some time, so bright and visible even after daybreak and decided that the time to act had come. Searching for the signs in the sky had brought results. I had located the 'missing capstone' and unaware at the time also the 'navel of the Globe'.

During the past few weeks I had become entirely engrossed in star gazing and in an obsessive frenzy making notes, drawing and reading while Salang and Philip, not knowing what I was up to sensed it was important and let me be. Another reason for being in Lesotho had been revealed mysteriously. Being there on another purpose altogether, whether by coincidence or consciously, a new energy was guiding me as though by *magic*. Perhaps part of a bigger plan and for reasons unknown to me but if I could make a contribution, I'd be honoured. Four days later, on my next visit to the capital, Maseru, I made the telephone call to Cape Town.

19th August
In the company of three French tourists, who appeared at just the right time in the Malutis, I was travelling the 1100km from Lesotho via the vast barren Karoo to the Southern tip of Africa…

PART I
THE OVERVIEW

Chapter 1
ASTRO-ARCHAEOLOGY

Chambers and shafts

'There is nothing more awesome or provocative than the sight of the Giza necropolis. Home of the Three Pyramids and the Great Sphinx, Giza personifies the mysteries of our remote past. To many, Giza also symbolises that universal yearning and age-old expectation that one day a great discovery will be made, one that will totally alter our perception of who we really are and where we came from.'

(**Robert Bauval,** *Secret Chamber*)

The Great Pyramid remains one of the oldest and largest of all stone constructions on Earth. It was the world's tallest structure for millennia and surpassed only in the late 19th century with the construction of the Eiffel Tower. The pyramids of ancient Egypt are shrouded in mystery and even today we do not understand how they were built, let alone why. The secrets of their messages defied interpretation. Orthodox belief is that the pyramids of Giza were built for the entombment of three Egyptian kings and of course, that each could only commence with construction once they came to power, as trans-generational planning is considered taboo by Egyptology. The complexity and vastness of the structures for the purpose of burial sites have led to much speculation about their apparent hidden purposes. From this was born a proliferation of theories on their origins; ranging from an earlier and more developed but now lost civilization to extra-terrestrial contact. It is difficult to believe that the Great Pyramid could have been used only for the burial of King Khufu and then sealed up forever, as no mummy or remains were discovered.

The architectural and technological feat of building the pyramids is mind-boggling. The three at Giza -the most famous of the Egyptian pyramids -are thought to have been built in a time before the invention of the wheel, the development of the pulley and iron tools. The Great Pyramid at Giza consists of more than 2 million limestone blocks, each weighing at least 2.5 tonnes. In order to put them into place during King Khufu's 23 year reign, would equate to positioning one block every 5 minutes! The complex internal features, of course, had to be contended with as well. Then the four faces still required casing with finely polished limestone from quarries in Tura. These slabs were much larger than the blocks used for the core, and set closely together with the greatest precision. Testimony of this can be seen in the Second Pyramid, which still bears remnants of cladding on its apex. All the material required being cut and transported from the quarry to the site, which alone would have been a time consuming operation with considerable manpower requirement.

Regarding selection of Giza as the site, we reach a conclusion later. Prior to any earth works, certain geological and engineering considerations would have been necessary: the ability of foundations to resist dead and live loads, such as the vertical mass of the structure itself exerting tremendous downwards force, as well as other powerful forces, like ground pressure due to seismic activity, or temperature changes which could shear foundations. Preceding commencement of construction, an extensive survey would have been required. The focus now is not on the actual methods employed in construction, but rather on the origination of plans –that would be the logical sequence. Meticulous architectural planning, not only for Giza but involving pyramids across the entire Memphis necropolis and beyond, was required. All indications are that *long term* provision had been made from the outset and on a grand scale! (this is conclusively supported by my findings in Part II).

Each of the three pyramids at Giza is set in a manner by which the squares of the base face the four cardinal directions; each set on a meridian of its own and not as a group. The Great Pyramid is at the centre of the Earth and aligned to the cardinal directions with uncanny accuracy. It is believed that stellar alignment was the means by which this could be achieved. Accurate correspondence with a precise terrestrial meridian supports this. Designed for a dialogue between Heaven and Earth, the pyramids reflect a cosmic ambience. Their perfect geometrical abstract forms exhibit harmonious architectural design -the precision of angles and dimension ratios is evidence of highly evolved technological ability. It is a fact that their design and relationships in layout incorporate sophisticated knowledge of geometry and observational astronomy.

The internal features of the pyramids are as impressive and even more mysterious. The passages run perfectly North-South and were positioned by the same means. Similarly, the causeways are integrated with the overall geometry of the Giza complex and are in line with the equinox Sunrise and the two 14 degree cross quarters, North and South of East respectively -the equinox being due East. Summer and winter solstice sunrises occur at 28 degrees north and 28 degrees south of East respectively. The two 14 degree cross quarters thus being the points in between, when the Sun passes over the equator and when day and night is of equal length, in the two respective hemispheres, twice per year.

The Great Pyramid boasts a unique arrangement of internal passages, portcullis blocks, chambers and shafts that are unparalleled anywhere. The presence of the granite plugs blocking the ascending gallery cannot be denied, but it is uncertain when the pyramid was sealed. Caliph Abdullah Al Ma'mun, a 9th century ruler of Egypt, first entered the Great Pyramid by chopping a passage below the sealed original entrance in the North face. The ascending corridor is a narrow tunnel, upward inclined and due south oriented, deep within the core of the Great

Pyramid. It starts as a branch from the descending corridor (the original access to the pyramid) and runs up to the level of the Queen's Chamber, where it transforms into a 8.5m high corbel-vaulted passage, known as the Grand Gallery. Comprising seven courses in corbel fashion, it continues upward at the same angle to the level of the King's Chamber and is said to be the most elaborate architectural feature of the whole interior of the Great Pyramid. Ascending the Grand Gallery brings one to the King's Chamber, which is regarded as being the finest structure of all. Inside the chamber, at the Western end, is the mysteriously empty granite sarcophagus, cut from a solid piece of granite. Some alternative historians believe it to have been made employing technology surpassing even that of modern time.

It should also be noted that the narrow star shafts (complete with bends and angles) were not drilled or cut through the masonry, but built into the structure of the Great Pyramid, as part of the design specifications. Without elaborating on technical aspects, it can be said that this required phenomenal engineering prowess and sophisticated construction techniques of high precision, not contemporary with the time. The star shafts were at first thought to be for the purpose of ventilating the internal chambers of the pyramid. An 'accepted consensus' today is that they served a religious purpose of passageways for the ascent of the soul of the dead King. It could be argued that both hypotheses might be a possibility in the Kings Chamber, although from an engineering perspective, it has been proven that far more practical methods and angles could have been implemented for ventilation purposes. The shafts in the Queen's Chamber, unlike those of the Kings Chamber however, do not pierce the pyramid throughout, but instead stop within the core of the structure. This was an original design feature and deliberately concealed. The shafts of the Queen's Chamber were closed from both ends for over 4000 years. The Southern one has been determined to be 64m long, ending in a limestone 'door' with about 17m to the outside face of the pyramid, which leaves ample space for a chamber. Engineers from a Boston firm, several years subsequent to its discovery, determined the door to be a 7.5cm thick slab by drilling through it with the aid of a robot. The other end of this shaft originally stopped some 13cm short of piercing the Queen's Chamber, once again by design. The two ends of the shafts, which connect the interior of the Queen's Chamber, were first opened in 1872 by the British engineer Wayman Dixon and his colleague Dr. Grant. The probability that they ever could have served as ventilation does not even warrant consideration.

The two Northern shafts, one each from the Queen's and King's Chambers respectively, deviate westward and at different points, away from the Grand Gallery which is aligned North-South. The deviations would appear to be deliberate design features, as there is no apparent obstacle to necessitate their change in course. The shafts measure approximately 20cmx20cm. A German team explored the narrow shafts in 1992 with a high tech robot for the first time. The robot was provided with remote control that feeds a miniature video camera, as well as a laser guidance system and a sensor capable of measuring the angle of the shafts to one tenth of a degree. The robot was unable to explore in the Northern shaft, as the shaft makes a sharp bend to the West after rising relatively straight. Although attempts at probing it with rods have been made by early explorers, it is unknown where this shaft leads to.

Archaeologist Sir William Flinders Petrie, who is fondly referred to as 'the father of British Egyptology', made a detailed survey of the Great Pyramid in the early 1880's. Using the most sophisticated technology available at the time, he also measured the slopes of the shafts.

source: *The Orion Mystery*

Shaft:	Gantenbrink:	Epoch:	Petrie:	Epoch:
KC south	45°00'00"	c.2475BC	44°30'00"	c.2600BC
KC north	32°28'00"	c. 2425BC	31°00'00"	c.2600BC
QC south	39°30'00"	c. 2400BC	38°28'00"	c.2750BC

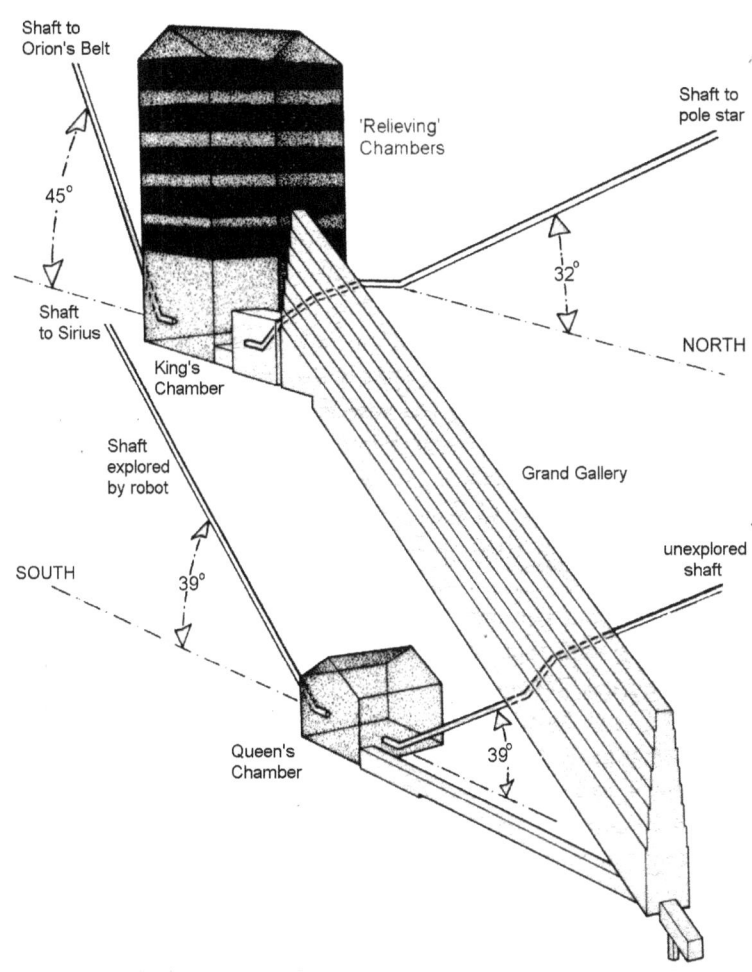

FIG. II. Upper chambers & star shafts

'For the whole of 1997 the Great Pyramid was officially closed, rumour ran wild, the Internet was rife with stories of secret explorations, of secret chambers being found, and most of all, that the Egyptians were trying to see what was behind the 'door.'

A closed 'door' inside one of the world's largest, oldest and most mysterious of monuments is powerful stuff and it has triggered a sense of immense expectation in the collective subconscious. These expectations range from 'nothing will be found' to the most outrageous claims such as the remains of a UFO or an extra terrestrial being. It is one of those issues that has entered the mass psychosis of the new millennium and will be remembered as such in decades to come. One of the main problems that Gantenbrink (a robotics engineer) faced was that he did not belong to the Egypt logical profession... In the short term, there still remains his exploration of the northern shaft- possibly before Christmas 1993 - and of course, the climax of his work when the little door is opened in the southern shaft in February or March 1994.'

(Robert Bauval, *Secret Chamber*)

By August 2002 the door had still not been opened...

This was an original design feature and deliberately concealed for over 4000 years. Finally, after a year was spent planning the project, the door in the Southern shaft of the Queens Chamber, within the Great Pyramid was penetrated. This event took place almost a decade since its rediscovery was made public and was broadcast 'live' by National Geographic Television in September 2002. All that this mission revealed was another obstruction, its purpose unclear. What may be found beyond it is still a mystery. As far back as 1964, the Egyptian architect Dr. Alexander Badawy and the American astronomer Dr. Virginia Trimble, proved that the so called air shaft in the King's Chamber of the Great Pyramid were orientated to the stars of Orion's Belt. Further evidence of a stellar correlation of Orion's belt and the Giza pyramids came with the studies of Robert Bauval around 1990. The Southern shaft of the Kings Chamber, angled at 45degrees, had been directed to the star zeta-Orionis (Alnitak) in Orion's Belt. The Northern shaft of the King's Chamber is believed to have been directed at the circumpolar stars. Bauval has also demonstrated that the Southern shaft of the Queens Chamber was directed to the star Sirius, which the ancients identified with the goddess Isis.

'Thy protector is the star-god... thy soul passeth on... they body is equipped with power... The doors of the hidden land are opened before thee... Osiris, conqueror of millions of years, cometh unto thee...'

(Book of the Duat, **E.A. Wallis Budge**, *The Egyptian Heaven and Hell*)

While the general consensus among Egyptologists, that the star shafts served the religious purpose of a rebirth cult, it may not have been the *original* purpose (aspects in Part II of this book substantiates other insights). According to tradition, the first Kings of Egypt were the gods themselves. Egyptologists seem to agree that the mythology could not possibly have developed overnight, but would have required a long process of evolution. When the process started, however, is unclear. The ancient Egyptians attributed their civilization to 'the gods' who came to the Nile Valley in Zep Tepi - the First Time, a remote epoch thousands of years before the era of the Pharaohs. The Egyptian stellar cult is rooted in the belief that the gods were born in the sky. The Neteru, or gods, were four children of the sky goddess Nut. They were Osiris, Isis, Seth and Nephtys. Horus, the son of Osiris and Isis, was believed to be the first man-god to rule Egypt. The Greek name for the star Sirius (Sopdet to the ancient Egyptians) is Sothis, which was used in the translation of the Pyramid Texts. It was also believed that the King was linked via ancestral lineage and through reincarnation to the gods.

'Behold he has come as Orion, behold *Osiris has come as Orion*... O king, the sky conceives you with Orion, the dawn-light bears you with Orion...you will regularly ascend with Orion from the Eastern region of the sky, you will regularly descend with Orion in the Western region of the sky... *your third is Sothis...*'

{Pyramid Text 820-2}

'O King, you are this Great Star, the Companion of Orion, who traverse the sky with Orion, who navigates the Netherworld with Osiris; you ascend from the east of the sky, being renewed in your due season, and rejuvenated in your due time. The sky has born you with Orion...'

{Pyramid Text 882-3}

In *Discussions in Egyptology* no.13, Robert Bauval argued that the three Giza pyramids were constructed to a unified plan. This is widely referred to as OCT (the Orion Correlation Theory) and basically means that the three pyramids at Giza were modeled on the stars in Orion's Belt. Furthermore, that a symbolic match in the relation of the Nile River to the Giza pyramids and the Milky Way to the stars in Orion's Belt is part of the concept. The religious motive of the plan was to represent the central region of the Duat sky -the starry kingdom of Osiris-Orion defined by the three stars of Orion's belt: **z**eta-Orionis (Alnitak), **e**psilon-Orionis (Alnilam) and **d**elta-Orionis (Mintaka). It was also suspected that other pyramids may be involved as part of a greater, so-called 'wider plan'. That there is a resemblance between the layout of the three pyramids at Giza and the three stars in Orion's Belt cannot be denied, although it is enthusiastically and hotly debated.

'The Genesis date indicated by astronomy for the site as a whole is 10,500BC. That is what the layout of the pyramids says, even if they themselves are younger.'

(*Keeper of Genesis,* **R. Bauval & G. Hancock**)

This suggestion is based on precession and an attempt to achieve a ground-sky image match. Astronomer's charts have to be adapted periodically, due to continually changing co-ordinates of star positions. The change is a consequence of the wobble of the Earth, performed over a period of approximately 26,000 years. It is known as precession and the observable effect, over long periods, is an ever so slow pendulum motion of the horizon against the background of the sky. What *actually* takes place during this cycle is unknown however, as we have not been around long enough for a first hand experience of the event, or have we? This phenomenon was first noted by the Greek astronomer Hipparchus, around 120BC and many centuries later, only during the time of Isaac Newton, was it considered to be sufficiently understood. There are, however, signs of a primeval knowledge regarding this phenomenon, that exceeds our own. The Hermetic Texts, a body of Greek writings, compiled in Alexandria, encapsulates wisdom of the Egyptian god Thoth. It expresses astronomical events in mythical terminology and with a strong esoteric flavour of precession:

'...Heaven will not support the stars in their orbits, nor will the stars pursue their constant course in Heaven... But when all this has befallen, Asclepius, then the Master and Father, God, the first before all, the maker of that god who first came into being, will look on that which has come to pass and will stay the disorder by counter working of his Will... He will call back to the right path those who have gone astray, he will cleanse the world from evil... Those gods who ruled the Earth will be restored...'

(Corpus Hermeticum- *Asclepius III*, **HermesTrismegistus**)

We recall how the Southern shaft of the Kings Chamber aligned with Alnitak (z-Orionis) in Orion's Belt, the celestial counterpart of the Great Pyramid, when it transited the astronomical meridian in c.2500BC. At the same time, the Southern shaft of the Queens Chamber aligned with Sirius, when it transited the astronomical meridian. This shaft was originally blocked at two ends, by sophisticated concealing design. For the three belt stars to match the three Giza pyramids, Professor Tony Fairall calculated that it would require time regression to the epoch 12,000BC. This epoch is also believed to equate to the 'First Time' -when Sirius, the bright star of Isis would be resting on the horizon -an event that could be witnessed from Giza, 30 degrees North latitude.

The question to consider, is whether it is imperative to wind back time - for the terrestrial & celestial meridians to align -and the Nile River to mirror the Milky Way before a master plan can be seen? The answer is emphatically, *no!* Before attempting to get a match, we first need to identify a correct visual, which will be revealed and demonstrated in sections to follow. Regardless of alignments of shafts on stars at meridian transits, the presence of a particular pole star or the Sphinx 'gazing at its Zodiacal counterpart', what we should ask, first and foremost is: **what-where-why-who?** then only **when?** and **how?** By aligning the aforementioned features, specific dates are fixed in time, which can be regarded as four-dimensional geometry. The effects on the relation between the constellation of Orion and other constellations would be barely perceptible because such relations involve numerous 'fixed stars'. The progression of time is important, as we'll discover, however, we need to first observe two-dimensional geometry to determine **where what is.** *The geometrical map/plan was visible then, as it is now, and will be till the end of time...* I substantiate this in great detail in the Discovery section, where the wider correlation of other pyramids and stars are illustrated. Therefore, the next two chapters will look at other pyramids and Egyptian mythology.

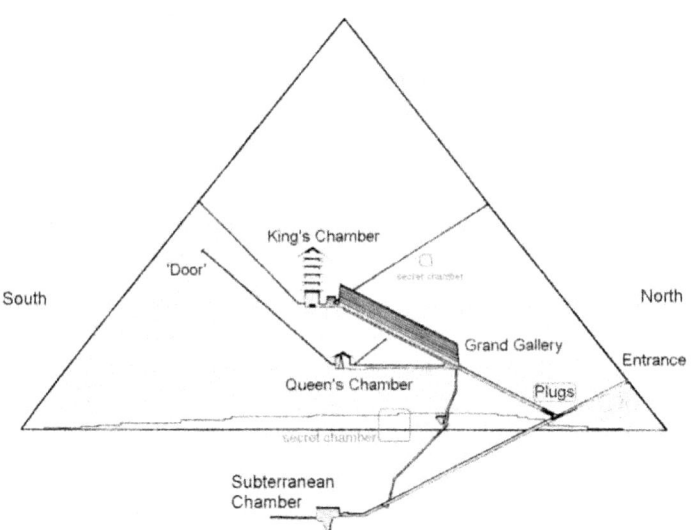

FIG. I. Great Pyramid N-S cross section (East elevation)

Chapter 2
PYRAMIDOLOGY

(-)Fourth Dynasty(+)

The civilisation of the ancient Egyptians thrived in the Nile Valley for thousands of years, until their conquest by the Roman Empire in 30BC. This era has been divided by historians into long periods called Kingdoms: the Old Kingdom, Middle Kingdom and the New Kingdom. These in turn comprise early, intermediate or late periods; in all some thirty shorter periods called Dynasties. The archaic period precedes the Dynastic era and is regarded by Egyptologists as mythical only.

The foundation of Egyptian history is that Egypt was made up of the 'Two Earths' (hieroglyphic translation) that were united. Based on archaeological and chronological evidence, Egyptologists date the unification of the Two Lands at *circa* 3,100BC. This is generally regarded as the beginning of the Dynastic Period, when King Menes joined Upper and Lower Egypt by force. The 1st and 2nd Dynasties are called the Early Dynastic Period. The Old Empire (3rd to 6th Dynasty) was essentially the period of the pyramids, but the order of events is difficult to establish due to the many breaks that occur in chronology and the lack of historical facts.

The earliest pyramid was the Stepped Pyramid, near Saqqara, Memphis. It was built during the reign of King Zoser (Djoser), who was the second ruler of the 3rd Dynasty. It is the world's oldest preserved monumental structure and reported to employ some 850,000 tons of material (Dr. Kurt Mendelssohn). This architectural innovation is attributed to Imhotep, vizier to Zoser and a high priest of Heliopolis. His achievements became legendary –a genius architect, astronomer, the father of medicine and magician healer whom the Greeks equated with Asclepius, their god of medicine, whose emblem is the entwined snake. Regarded as the greatest wise man he was later deified. The step pyramid builders were succeeded by the celebrated Kings of the 4th Dynasty, to whom the building of the true pyramids are accredited. No two of these pyramids or their internal features are identical. The most common denominator is that access is generally from the North face and by means of a descending corridor. These passages are aligned with the North Pole.

The Meidum Pyramid has not been investigated sufficiently, and allocation of ownership is uncertain although Sneferu is considered to be the eventual owner. The two stelae in the mortuary temple on the East of this pyramid have no inscriptions - massive and mysterious, this pyramid some 45km South of Dahshur, is believed to have been originally built as a seven-stepped structure. It was subsequently altered to eight steps and supposedly converted into a smooth-faced pyramid. The original core represents a quadrangular tower, but incorporates other features of a general pattern to be found in subsequent pyramids: a smooth outer casing, entrance shaft from North leading to a chamber, a causeway, as well as a valley temple. The Meidum Pyramid is also known as the 'collapsed pyramid', due to piles of sand and rubble that lies at the base of this structure. It leaves a number of questions unanswered: *Why is this pyramid so uniquely different from the other pyramids? Was this to draw attention to a specific function? Does the smooth outer casing indicate that the quadrangular tower was indeed the only intended shape?* Traditional belief is that Huni, the last King of the 3rd Dynasty and father of Sneferu, may have initiated its erection.

The first King of the 4th Dynasty was Sneferu, father of Khufu. Egyptologists have been at a loss to explain what made it possible and indeed imperative at the opening of Sneferu's reign, for this dramatic technological upsurge in architectural and engineering ability. One theory suggests that it could be the inspiration of Imhotep; perhaps he was still alive even when Zoser's pyramid was completed and Sneferu came to power. Another hypothesis suggests that the Stepped Pyramid was a later, rudimentary attempt at mimicking the achievement of the builders of the true pyramids. Sneferu must have been significantly influenced to abandon the step pyramid design and embark on construction of the two enormous, smooth-sided pyramids at Dahshur, in the Southern Memphite Necropolis. *Two* pyramids accredited to him, although, not without skepticism. The Southern pyramid at Dahshur, commonly referred to as the Bent Pyramid, is actually rhomboidal in shape, the sides having a curios double slope; approximately 54.3 degrees at the base, then changing to 43.2 degrees from the middle, with a slightly raised intersecting line. It is not known what necessitated the shift in inclination by 11.1 degrees and abundant hypotheses surround the issue. This pyramid would have been the largest in Egypt, however, due to the altered slope it is the fourth largest. The Bent Pyramid is unique in having a shaft high up in the West face, in addition to the North face entrance. The interior is described as complex and sophisticated, with two chambers (one above the bedrock) and portcullis blocks. *Was the change in angle of the slope an error adjustment, or intentional and with specific purpose?*

The Northern pyramid at Dahshur is known as the Red Pyramid and has a slope of 43.2 degrees -the same angle as the upper part of its nearby companion. The Red pyramid is the third largest after the Great Pyramid and its cardinal alignment is said to be somewhat lacking. This Pyramid features three chambers, all above the bedrock. Traditional belief has it that these two pyramids were built by Sneferu. The reader will recall the statistics of moving and positioning blocks that was required for Khufu to complete the Great Pyramid during his 23 year reign. His father, who ruled for 24 years, would have exceeded that performance in erecting *two* massive pyramids! Archaeological evidence suggests that the Bent and the Red Pyramid were built before the three great Giza pyramids. The First Pyramid at Giza (G1) is attributed to King Khufu (largest pyramid in Egypt), the Second Pyramid (G2) to King Khafre (second largest pyramid) and the Third Pyramid (G3) to King Menkaura.

South-East of Giza is the site of Zawyat el Aryan and the remains of two 'unfinished' pyramids; the smaller Layer Pyramid, which has been attributed to King Khaba of the 3rd Dynasty; and to the North-West the incomplete remains of a great pyramid. A sarcophagus of unusual form was found embedded in the floor of the large 'abandoned' infrastructure, cut into the natural rock. Although there is much doubt among Egyptologists, ownership is thought to belong to a King of the 4th Dynasty.

Approximately 7.5km to the North-West of Giza is the site of Abu Ruwash, an important administrative centre during the Old Kingdom. Here there are old tombs that date to the pre-dynastic era and the incomplete remains of a great pyramid, the superstructure being in ruined condition. General consensus among Egyptologists is that it belonged to King Djedefra, a son of Khufu, who followed him to the throne. This pyramid was supposed to have been as large as the Second Pyramid at Giza. Recent archaeological findings revealed that the lower casing of the structure was of red granite and the upper part white limestone, which concords with the two Egyptian crowns.

Heights of primary (-)4th(+) Dynasty pyramids:

Location	Name	Original Height (m)
Meidum	'Collapsed' Pyramid	93.5 m
Dahshur South	Bent Pyramid	105
Dahshur North	Red Pyramid	104
Giza	The Great Pyramid (G1)	146
Giza	The Second Pyramid (G2)	143.5
Giza	The Third Pyramid (G3)	65.5
Zawyat el Aryan		(unknown)
Abu Ruwash		(unknown)

Source: *Atlas of Ancient Egypt* - **John Baines** & **Jaromir Ma'lek**

If we are indeed to *assume* that archaeological evidence is correct in as far as dating, sequential construction and accreditation of the ownership of these tombs, the Great Pyramid is the result of just over a century of architectural and construction evolution. The oldest (*c*.2630BC) believed to be the step-pyramid of King Zoser at Saqqara, followed by the 'converted' one at Meidum and the two true pyramids at Dahshur. Followed the Great Pyramid, when Khufu ascended to the throne (2551BC) -a sequence in which the Great Pyramid is seen as having evolved from and was preceded by the four earlier pyramids. It has been alluded to that if it could be proven the other way round, the technological mastery of the Great Pyramid should not be attributed to Khufu. The wisdom of the old adage 'where there is smoke, there is fire' comes to mind. The French Egyptologist Auguste Mariette found a stela close to one of the subsidiary pyramids of the Great Pyramid in 1858. Known as the 'Inventory Stela,' it consists of a list of items found by Khufu when he restored the temple of Isis.

'...Long live... the King of Upper and lower Egypt, Khufu, given life... He found the House of Isis, Mistress of the Pyramid, by the side of the hollow of Hwran [the Sphinx]... and he built his pyramid beside the temple of this goddess and he built a pyramid for the King's daughter Henutsen beside this temple. The place of Hwran Horemakhet is on the south side of the House of Isis, mistress of the Pyramid...He restored the statue, all covered in painting, of the guardian of the Atmosphere who guides the winds with his gaze...'

Modern belief is that the stela, due to its poor form of execution and style of the inscription, is a forgery dating from the 26th Dynasty around 600 BC. In our own era such practice is common but for want of satisfying historical chronology it is not a sound argument. Chiseling stone is not as easy a feat as embezzlement of documents and motive actually counts against the celebrated 4th

Dynasty Kings. Based upon it being a forgery, we cannot then either surmise that Khufu built *the* Great Pyramid. The principal argument concerning the above text is generally centered on the Sphinx and whether Khufu could have restored it or not, since his successor, Khafre is supposedly the builder of it. I wish to shift the focus to Isis instead of the Sphinx in this inscription. If, according to the text, Khufu did indeed 'find' and restore the House of Isis, then it stands to reason that this temple dates from antiquity. An important question that comes to mind is; *when* did Isis become known as the 'Mistress of the Pyramid' and does it necessarily imply Khufu's pyramid? She could only have become the mistress of such when it was built -in the time of Khufu or otherwise. If she was known as such and had acquired this title *before* the time of Khufu, was she then the mistress of another pyramid? *Could she have been the mistress of Osiris, or of his pyramid for that matter?* This hypothesis is further substantiated in Part II.

Mainstream Egyptological belief is that the chronological evolution of pyramid technology originated in the two stepped pyramids (Saqqara & Meidum) and culminated in the three Giza wonders, supposedly during the 4th Dynasty period. Bauval and Hancock suggest that "the Giza necropolis may be the result of a long period of architectural development, based on a unified master plan that started in 10,500BC and came to an end 8,000 years later in 2,500BC". Whichever of the two options (or any other for that matter) one supports, what has defied explanation however, is the nagging question of *how* this was possible. The pyramids were built before the 'official' Bronze and Iron Ages (conceding meteoric iron may have been known to the ancient Egyptians). By the beginning of the 4th Dynasty, technology was suddenly available to cut, move and raise large blocks of stone, some weighing several tons, to a height of nearly 100 meters. In all, an estimate of 9 million tons (Dr. I.E.S. Edwards) of limestone blocks in the space of perhaps two decades. The 4th Dynasty pyramid construction has been calculated to involve some 25 million tons of stone blocks, said to be more than 75% of all the stone that was quarried and shaped into pyramids during the pyramid age. The Sicilian historian, Diodorus Siculus' comment sums up the gigantic enterprise remarkably well:

'...they do not have the appearance of being the slow handiwork of men but look like a sudden creation, as though they had been made by some god and set down bodily in the surrounding sand.'

(**Diodorus Siculus,** *Book 1* –c.60BC)

The pyramids accredited as belonging to the 5th and 6th Dynasties exhibit material evidence of a drastic turnabout in construction enthusiasm or lack of skill. Their masonry was of much poorer quality, and also became smaller in size. During the 4th Dynasty, the Egyptians were master builders, then suddenly, within a generation or so, there was a radical decline in proficiency. (The Old Kingdom entered a period of feudalism during the 23rd century BC and fell into decline.) The pyramids from the 5th Dynasty are described as resembling huge piles of stone rubble. Conventional reasoning cannot explain the visual evidence. It is almost as if Egypt experienced a technological exodus. Dr. Jaromir Malek of the Ashmolean -Museum in Oxford compared it to 'the handing over of the state's authority to a less experienced government after a large-scale event'. We should question *what* became of this sophisticated architectural competence and the ability or initiative behind it after the 4th Dynasty. Since the 4th Dynasty Kings did not glorify their achievements by inscriptions, it has been questioned whether they actually regarded themselves as individual owners of the pyramids. Another question raised is whether the 4th Dynasty pyramids are part of a single unified scheme, which required the building of *different pyramids at a specific location?*

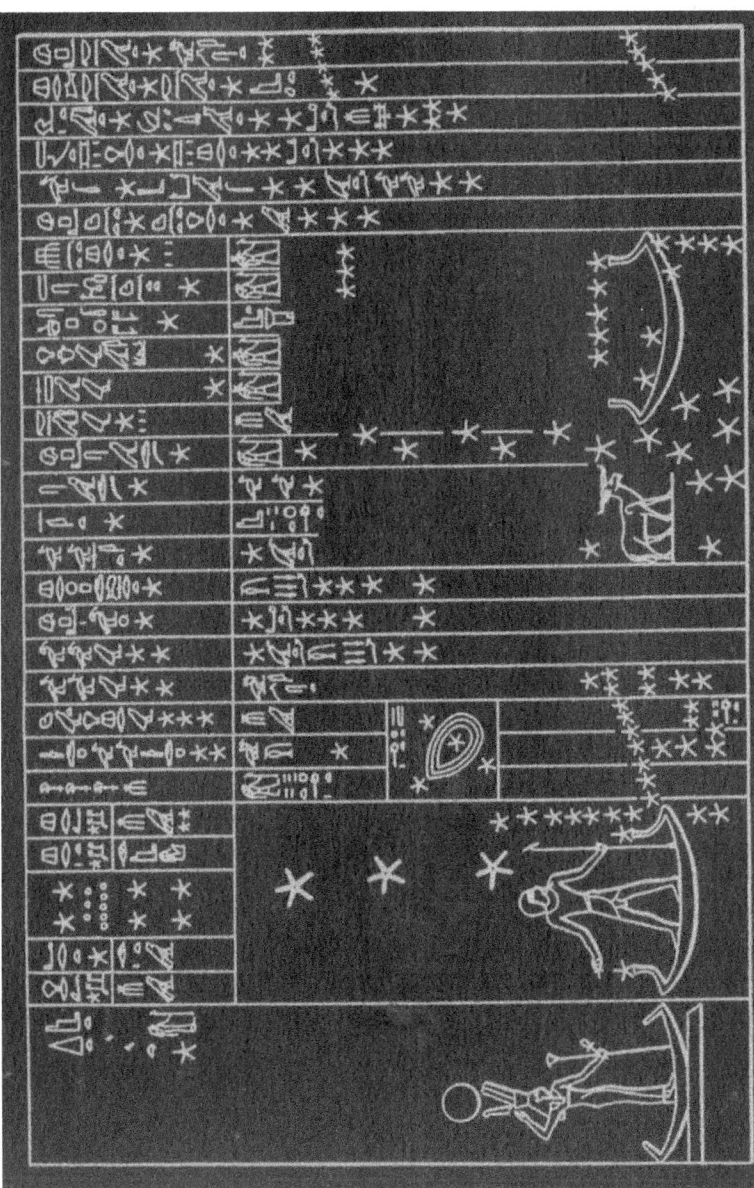

FIG. IX. Mnemonic message?

Chapter 3
MYTHOLOGY

Time & history

The Pyramid Texts remained secret for nearly 5000 years and are considered among the oldest writings in the world, followed by the Coffin Texts, The Book of the Dead, that of the Ptolemaic Period and shortly thereafter, the Christian and Gnostic writings. They mysteriously appeared only at the end of the 5th Dynasty and during the 6th Dynasty, after which they were no longer used. A factor which merits close scrutiny is that the pyramids of Sneferu and those at Giza do not bear any inscriptions. Ironically the later, more inferior pyramids that are inscribed with texts containing many elements of astronomy do not incorporate any elaborate internal features or star shafts –only the burial chambers that entombed their owners. It is in these chambers that the bulk of Pyramid Texts were found. The most recent inscriptions were found in four pyramids of the 6th Dynasty *c.*2100BC. The first texts discovered were those in the pyramid of Unas, last ruler of the 5th Dynasty, located south of Zozer's Stepped Pyramid. Professor Gaston Maspero, Director of the Services des Antiquities and discoverer of the first texts in 1881, concluded they were written around 3200BC. Although this is deemed to be a conservative estimate, it is more than 3400 years *before* the first Christian Gospels were recorded and two millennia before the Old Testament. The Pyramid Texts constitute the oldest corpus of Egyptian religious and funerary literature now in existence. It is said that they are the least corrupt of all such collections and include very ancient texts, among those regarded as contemporary with the pyramid in which they were inscribed. They assume familiarity with a larger body of knowledge that is not presented in the texts themselves. The few direct statements, concerning the pyramids are contained in one passage known as Utterance 600. Texts are referred to by Line or Spell number. The meaning of many words cannot be translated with exactness and the unusual construction of sentences might also be an indication that the texts themselves were copies of earlier, unknown literature. For detail studies see; *The Ancient Egyptian Pyramid Texts, The Ancient Egyptian Coffin Texts, The Ancient Egyptian Book of the Dead;* R.O. Faulkner / Sir. E.A. Wallis Budge.

Amduat, is the ancient name for 'the book of what is in the other world' and it is believed to be based on earlier writings. Comprised of text and drawings, it was painted upon the walls of burial chambers. It forms the cast of theological compositions of the New Kingdom and comprises twelve chapters. These represent the hours of the night and are separated by vertical divisions. Each hour is further divided into three horizontal registers. Scribes use the words *'Gem Ush'* in places. Translated this means 'found defective' and indicates damaged papyrus or source material used for copying. Since this would imply an antiquated source, the question that comes to mind is *who* compiled the original and when?

'The World was created on 22 October, 4004BC at six o'clock in the evening'
(Arch Bishop **James Ussher**, Annals of the World, 1650)

'...man was created on the 23 October 4004BC at nine o' clock in the morning...'
(Dr. **John Lightfoot** –1859, vice Chancellor, Cambridge University)

According to general world history, Neanderthal man lived around *c.*75000BC and Homo Sapiens x Sapiens were on the scene some 30,000 years later. The last Ice Age experienced a climax around 15000BC and with sea levels rising *c.*11000BC, hunter gatherers were the order of the day. Domestication of plant and

animals took effect c.8000BC; also the early days of basic metalworking. Irrigation was widely practiced by 5000BC. Dating by C14 radiocarbon analysis places the Old Kingdom period of Egypt between c.2800BC and 2200BC. The same method places the 4th Dynasty, the time of the pyramids, between c.2650BC and 2450BC. Tests performed on pyramids turn up satisfactory results within their relative chronology but not according to an absolute.
The Sphinx is said to bear erosion marks from before the Sahara became a desert. The erosion marks are said to imply a time somewhere between 7000BC and 10,000BC –long before the supposed dawning of Egyptian history around 3000BC! Egyptian priests told Solon, the Greek lawmaker, when he visited the city of Sais in Lower Egypt around 590BC that mysterious people from a place called *Atlantis* had invaded much of the Mediterranean basin, including Egypt, some "nine thousand years" ago (Plato, *Timaeus and Critias*). According to tradition, the first Kings of Egypt were the gods themselves, after which Pharaohs ruled as Kings of unified Upper and Lower Egypt for more than 30 centuries. Historians are generally of the opinion that the Stone Age and unlettered cultures preceded the Dynastic Period of Pharaonic rule and regarded as having commenced around 3100BC, at the end of Neolithic times.

'Yet according to present archaeological evidence, we have moved from cave dwellers to space travellers in little more than 5000 years. Could archaeological evidence again be wrong and could Egyptian civilisation be much older than modern scholars concede?'

(R. Bauval & A. Gilbert, *The Orion Mystery*)

It is quite evident that we don't know who we are or where we came from, never mind when! There simply are not any as yet discovered surviving records or documentation complete enough to provide us with an identity... only blind faith. Then again, other people seem quite certain that they descended from the apes. There is so much uncertainty among Historians and Egyptologists regarding time epochs, it prompts me to avoid specifics, as other issues by far eclipse squabbling over a few years, or a few decades for that matter -the 'when?' issue will be resolved in due course.

The Ancient Egyptian Kings did not see themselves as belonging to Dynasties, but as a continuous line of divine Kings. Jean Francois Champollion, who first deciphered hieroglyphic symbols in 1882, estimated the 1st Dynastic Period at *circa* 5800BC. The modern view among scholars of History and experts of Egyptology would appear to be that the same epoch started with King Menes alias Narmer/Scorpion *circa* 3100BC. The source most commonly used was derived from *commentaries on the work of Manetho*, the Egyptian priest and historian who lived in the 3rd century BC when Egypt was under the Ptolemies. Manetho grouped the pharaohs into 31 Houses or Dynasties and ascribed great antiquity to Pharaonic Egypt. According to the commentary of Eusebius (*c*. AD221), who was the chronicler of Constantine the Great, Manetho's chronology showed three distinct epochs before the 1st Dynasty of King Menes: the rule of demigods followed by the Horus-Kings, together lasting 15,150 years and then a predynastic line of kings lasting a further 13,777 years. This meant 28,927 years before King Menes. *The epochs preceding that of King Menes are regarded by Egyptologists as religious fictions and mythical kings only.* Another archaic (*c*.1400BC), original Egyptian papyrus, preserved at Turin in Italy and on which the third epoch before King Menes cannot be deciphered due to damage, lists two other epochs as 13,420 years and 23,200 years, a total of 36,620.

Epochs relevant to this work:
Pre Dynastic: Neteru-Gods followed by Horus Kings.
Early Dynastic: 3100BC (1st-Dynasty-2nd) 2686BC
Old Kingdom: 2686BC (3rd-Dynasty-6th) 2181BC

FIG. III Ennead of gods + Horus

Golden era of the gods

The ancient Egyptians attributed their civilization to the gods, who came to the Nile Valley in Zep Tepi, which translates as: the First Time -a remote epoch thousands of years before the era of the Pharaohs. Set in a region south of the apex of the Nile Delta, the domain of the gods is the terrestrial counterpart of the Duat, which is the cosmic land of the souls. In the *Book of What is in the Duat (Shat Ent Am Duat),* as well as other ancient Egyptian funerary and rebirth texts, numerous references are to be found to Zep Tepi, the First Time. This time was emphatically believed by the ancients to be an historical time during which the gods had lived on Earth and fraternised with humans. All ceremonies, doctrines, laws, temples and tombs of the Pharaonic theocracy were based on the immutable conviction that the king was linked via his divine lineage, instigated by the birth of Horus, to the distant golden age of the gods called Zep Tepi, the First Time. A system of cosmic law and order, known as Maat, had been established by Osiris during this golden age of the gods and it was the duty of his son Horus and all succeeding kings to ensure that Maat was upheld throughout the ages. Maat translates as 'Truth Justice' and is represented by a winged goddess with feather headdress. It is the code of practice to which a human must adhere to, but this alone is not sufficient for achieving immortality of the soul; Heka must be acquired through initiation into the magical knowledge of Thoth to overcome a journey of ordeals and tribulations through the Duat. Immortality is attained through the fusion of quality of character and knowledge -Maat and Heka. The mortal, yet divine line of Pharaohs, were the custodians of these laws that were established in a distant time by a race of gods, who ruled Egypt for many millennia. Every decree and action had to be justified in terms of the First Time. The rule of Osiris was seen as unmistakably real and Egypt's happiest and most noble epoch. The Great Ennead of gods, according to the Pyramid Texts, was recognised everywhere. This great pantheon was composed of nine deities and ruled by Atum-Ra, the ubiquitous *sun*-god. Atum-Ra is said to have arrived in a capsule on the dark and watery nothingness, referred to as the Nun.

The modern day cosmological account of the origin of the universe, the 'Big Bang theory', is that all matter was contained in compact volume and high temperature. An explosion resulted in separation and the expanding universe. Careful cognisance will reveal similarities of the mythical interpretation! According to ancient Egyptian cosmological mythology, Atum-Ra, created Shu (air god) and Tefnut (moisture goddess). These two united into atmosphere and in turn created Geb (earth/soil god) and Nut. The action of Geb and the sky goddess Nut resulted in the conception of four anthropomorphic gods -the Neters who inhabited the Earth. These were two brothers, Osiris and Seth, and their two sisters, Isis and Nephtys. Osiris and Isis were the first sovereign couple of ancient Egypt. Isis gave birth to a divine son, Horus, after miraculous conception, achieved through powerful charms.

Although several poetic variants of cosmogony existed, the myths seem to be easily reconcilable. Heliopolitan cosmogony is based upon the so-called Ennead of Heliopolis and was a well established tradition in the Egyptian religion (detail studies; Prof. R.T. Rundle Clark, *The Legend of the Phoenix, Myth & Symbol in Ancient Egypt;* Mythologist Jane B. Sellers, *The Death of Gods in Ancient Egypt*). It is generally accepted that Heliopolis or On, as it was referred to in the Bible, long pre-dated the pyramid age, but how long is not certain. From prehistoric times, there was a Heliopolitan doctrine to the glory of the sun-god, Ra.

The Osirian cult preceded Christianity by at least 3000 years and survived alongside it as a serious opponent until emperor Theodocius outlawed its practice in AD391 and when the systematic destruction of its temples was ordered by the Church. The ancients had no concept of religion as such, only Heka, a magical equilibrium of spiritual consciousness and cosmic ambience. A great paradox exists wherein Egyptologists are at a loss to explain why there is no mention of Osiris in inscriptions that predate the Pyramid Texts. The earliest known reference to Osiris is found in Pyramid Texts which date from *c.*2300BC. Egyptologists seem to agree that the mythology could not possibly have developed overnight, but would have required a long process of evolution. When the process began, is also uncertain. It is as if the cult suddenly materialised out of nowhere and was adopted with great conviction by the pyramid Kings as the principle tenet. The question has been raised whether the sudden introduction of the Osirian cult was the result of a 'messianic' display of stars? *Was it a precedent for Christianity?*

FIG. IV. Orion / Osiris-Horus Kings

Star gods

The Egyptian stellar cult is rooted in the belief that the gods were born in the sky. These gods are associated with stars in an area of the sky that hosts the constellation of Orion. To interpret the legend I introduce the notion that the gods are stars, *literally*. The birth is a consequence of action between the sky (the goddess Nut) and the horizon of Earth (Geb). The gods are the four children *(stars)*: Osiris, Isis, Seth and Nephthys (the fifth god being Horus, *'the Sun'* of Osiris and Isis). Their numerical birth contains the 3:4:5 Pythagorean characteristic, a precessional connotation (multiplied by 72 respectively, these three numbers produce 216: 288: 360). The gods are born in the Eastern horizon at dawn during the five days of the year also referred to as the five intercalary days. The ancient Egyptian calendar consisted of 360 plus the 5 days before summer solstice. 'Regular ascend' and 'regular descend' refers to daily rising and setting of stars, due to the rotation of the Earth. Where stars are below, or become visible above the horizon after longer periods, is seasonal due to the tilt of Earth's axis, in conjunction with orbiting the Sun. The Greek name for the star Sirius is Sothis, which was used in the translation of the Pyramid Texts. The texts make explicit reference to celestial conception and birth. In certain instances the same text can be interpreted with dual meaning i.e. gods or stars. Other texts refer to mounds (pyramids) of the gods. This concept will be detailed further on, with the aid of diagrams.

Birth/conception terminology:
'...behold Osiris has come as Orion... O king, *the sky conceives you* with Orion, *the dawn-light bears you* with Orion... you will regularly *ascend* with Orion from the eastern regions of the sky... your third is Sothis...'

{Pyramid Text 820-2}

Mythical terminology:
'Your sister (Isis) comes rejoicing for love of you. You (Osiris) have placed her on your phallus and your seed issues in her, she being ready as Sothis, and Horus Sopd has come forth from you as Horus in Sothis.'

{Pyramid Text 632}

Stellar terminology:
'Your sister *(the star Sirius)* comes to you rejoicing for love of you. You *(the star Alnitak)* have placed her on your phallus and your seed issues into her, she being ready as Sothis, *(Sirius)* and Horus *(Sopd)* has come forth from you as 'Horus who is in Sothis.'

{Pyramid Text 632}

Ground-sky duality (pyramids=stars/gods):
'Thoth and Horus then come to help Osiris to the sky; Horus comes, Thoth appears, they raise Osiris from upon his side and make him stand... Raise yourself, o Osiris, Isis has your arm, o Osiris; Nephtys has your hand so go between them. The sky is Given to you, and the Fields of Rushes, the Mounds *[pyramids]* of Horus, and the Mounds *[pyramids]* of Seth...'

{Pyramid Text 959-61}

If these gods are taken to be stars, literally, then the passage we recall from the Hermetic writing describes an astronomical occurrence that insinuates precession.

'...He will call back to the right path those who have gone astray, he will cleanse the world from evil...Those gods who ruled the earth will be restored...'

(*Corpus Hermeticum- Asclepius III*, **HermesTrismegistus**)

It is believed that the Phoenix came to Heliopolis to mark important cycles and the birth of a new age. The first coming seems to have produced the cult of the Benben -a mysterious stone credited with cosmic origins. In Ancient Egyptian art the Phoenix was usually depicted as a grey heron. The apex stone, or pyramid ion on top of a pyramid or obelisk, is also known as a Benben Stone and said to be symbolic of the Phoenix. Part II provides a feasible interpretation, associated with precession. The Phoenix brought the life-giving essence, the magic *hike* (Heka) *'from beyond the limits of the world -the Isle of Fire, the place of everlasting light, where the gods were born in the Duat...'*

In the pyramid age, the fabled Bennu was the symbol of eternal return. After a long period of absence, it opened a new golden age. It was housed in the Temple of the Phoenix, possibly where there stands today the obelisk of Sesostris I of the 12th Dynasty. Sesostris I (*c.*1970BC), who succeeded Amenemet I (*c.*1990BC), restored the sacred city of Heliopolis and erected the obelisk at Heliopolis. It is believed that where this great obelisk stands, once stood the sanctuary of the Phoenix, which housed the sacred Benben during the Pyramid Age. The two obelisks of Alexandria, dubbed Cleopatra's Needles, had originally stood in the great sun temple of Heliopolis. Annu, the ancient name of Heliopolis, was apparently derived from a sacred pillar which stood at a temple dedicated to Atum -the Complete Executive One -father of the gods and the creative power behind the *sun* and everything else in the world. The position of Heliopolis is on a line that extends from the Great Pyramid at Giza. *see* map[X]a.

Rebirth cult

'I stand before the masters who witnessed the genesis, who were the authors of their own forms, who walked the dark, circuitous passages of their own becoming...
I stand before the masters who witnessed the transformation of the body of a man into the body in spirit, who were witnesses to resurrection when the corpse of Osiris entered the mountain and the soul of Osiris walked out shining...when he came forth from death, a shining thing, his face white with heat...
I stand before the masters who know the histories of the dead, who decide which tales to hear again, who judge the books of lives as either full or empty, who are themselves authors of the truth. And they are Isis and Osiris, the divine intelligences.
And when the story is written and the end is good and the soul of a man is perfected, with a shout they lift him into heaven...'

(*Egyptian Book of the Dead* -Normandi Ellis translation)

According to Plato: "the demiurge made souls in equal number with the stars and distributed them, each soul to its several star... and he who should live well for his due span of time should journey back to the habitation of his consort star..."

In Egyptian mythology, Osiris is the god of resurrection. After he was killed by Seth, he departed into the sky to establish a cosmic kingdom of the *first time Duat* among the *stars* of Orion, on the banks of the *Winding-Waterway*; the celestial Nile. According to legend, the body of Osiris was cut into fourteen pieces and that, over the place where each was buried, Isis caused a sanctuary to be built. The tombs of Osiris on Earth had their counterparts in Heaven. Text on the stellar rebirth cult is to be found in the various versions of the 'Book of the Dead', inscribed on papyri and in New Kingdom tombs and Temples.

'The writings of the hidden chamber, the places where the souls, the gods and the spirits stand. What they do. The beginning of the Horn of the West, the gate of the Western Horizon. This is the knowledge of the power of those in the Netherworld. This is the knowledge of what they do: the knowledge of their sacred rituals to Re; knowledge of the mysterious powers: knowledge of what is in the hours as well as of their gods, knowledge of what he says to them; knowledge of the Gates and the way on which God passes; knowledge of the powerful ones and the annihilated...'

(beginning of *Amduat*)

The Pyramid Texts also speak of rebirth:
'O King, you are this Great Star, the Companion of Orion, who traverse the sky with Orion, who navigates the Netherworld with Osiris; you ascend from the east of the sky, being *renewed* in your due season, and *rejuvenated* in your due time. The sky has born you with Orion...'

{Pyramid Text 882-3}

'Behold he has come as Orion, behold Osiris has come as Orion...
O king, the sky conceives you with Orion, the dawn-light bears you with Orion...you will *regularly ascend* with Orion from the Eastern region of the sky, you will *regularly descend* with Orion in the Western region of the sky... your third is Sothis...'

{Pyramid Text 820-2}

It cannot be certain that the rebirth cult, where departed Kings were associated with Osiris in the after world, was part of the belief system in the 4th Dynasty -the time of Khufu, Khafre and Menkaure of Giza. The Pyramid Texts, which appear only after the 4th Dynasty, are by this time applied as spells in the interest of a departed King.

'The undoubted connection that it has with the Fourth Dynasty is not in dispute, but the precise nature of this connection remains unproven. It could be the case, as has happened elsewhere in the world, that an ancient and sacred site designed and built for one purpose was subsequently taken over and re-used for another rather different purpose. A later adaptation effected by people who were unconnected to the genesis of the site but who sought to be interred in a place that was imbued with ancient prestige and sanctity. The owners of many of the coffins and tomb walls onto which they were copied had not even the faintest inkling that specific astronomical observations and directions were being duplicated at their expense. What motivated them was precisely what the text offered – the lure of immortal life. Yet by taking that lure did they not in fact guarantee a kind of immortality for the texts themselves? Together with the ancient texts and rituals that are linked to them, could the vast monuments of the Giza necropolis have been designed to transmit a message from one culture to another - a message not across space, but across time?'

(**R. Bauval & G. Hancock** – *Keeper of Genesis*)

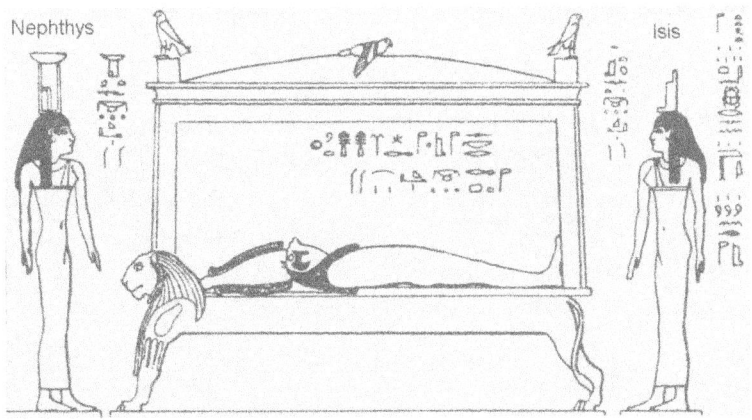

FIG. VI. Osiris-Horus tomb?

Decline & legendary dispute

The course of Egyptian history witnessed three periods of major social breakdown. According to conventional Egyptology, the power of Pharaoh gradually weakened from the 5th Dynasty and there was a collapse of centralised government at the end of the 6th Dynasty (c.2258BC). Feudalism and foreign invasions led to the decline of the Old Kingdom of the 23rd century BC. Provincial governors exploited local cult allegiances to seize power and the office of governance became hereditary. The worship of sacred animals began only when royal power weakened during the decline. The Egyptian insight into divinity was multiform and the characters of animals are unchanging, unlike humans who are continually evolving. Modern scholars increasingly are of the opinion that the Egyptians worshipped the qualities with which they believed these animals to be endowed rather than the animals as gods themselves. During the great centuries, the political, social and economic foundations of Egypt rested on a theological basis wherein Pharaoh had to ensure the triumph of Maat. In the original concept behind the solar religion, the chief god was associated with cosmic forces, though it later acquired other, political connotations through association with the royal house. The 5th Dynasty Pharaohs gained divine ancestry and from then onward, were worshipped as sons of Ra (descendants of the Sun). According to Dr. I.E.S. Edwards and other Egyptologists, this was an indication of cultic change and when the golden age of Osiris's reign came to an end. Was there a dispute over the throne of Egypt at the end of the 4th Dynasty? According to legend, Osiris was brutally killed by his brother Seth. Seth however accused Osiris of instigating the rivalry (*'he attacked me'*).

'It was *he* (Osiris) who *attacked me* (Seth)...when there came into being this his name of Orion, long of leg and lengthy of stride...'
{Pyramid Text 959}

Why would Seth accuse Osiris of instigating the fight? Was Seth the wicked conspirator he is made out to be, or was he defending himself?
After their jealous brother Seth cut Osiris into fourteen pieces, Isis recovered all of the pieces except the phallus. Through magical rites she had learned from Thoth, she became pregnant with the seed of Osiris and gave birth to their divine *sun*/son Horus. *Does this marvel imply artificial insemination or surrogate manipulation?* This event has a familiarity in Christianity where Jesus Christ, the son of God, was born from the womb of the Virgin Mother, Mary - the surrogate wife of the Biblical Joseph. The stellar Horus was born from the 'womb of Sothis' -the union between Isis and Osiris. Horus is believed to be an historical person who became the first man-god to rule Egypt. Pharaoh comes from *Per-Aa* meaning "Great House", from which the kings of Egypt came. All subsequent kings were deemed to be the reincarnation of Horus. *Could it be DNA cloning?*

'Horus cried out because of his eye, Seth has cried out because of his testicles, and there leaps up the eye of Horus, who has fallen on yonder side of the Winding Waterway... Thoth saw it on yonder side... the eye of Horus fell on Thoth's wings on yonder side of the Winding Waterway, on the eastern side of the sky...'

{Pyramid Text 594-6}

Khem, also known as Assim, later called Letopolis, was the site of a temple which outdated the pyramids and was closely connected with the Falcon god of the sky, Horus. He engaged in an epic battle that went on for several years, with his uncle Seth over the throne of Osiris, during which Horus lost his left eye and Seth lost his testicles. Thoth persuaded them to put their case for arbitration before the council of gods, the Great Ennead. The trial is said to have lasted for 80 years. Most of the tribunal favoured Horus. He journeys into the afterworld-Duat in search of his father, Osiris, to 'present' him with the eye.

> 'Geb, (earth god) commanded the nine gods to gather...
> He judged between Horus and Seth;
> he ended their quarrel.
> He made Seth king of Upper Egypt,
> upto the place where he was born, which is Su...
> and made
> Horus king of Lower Egypt,
> upto the place where Osiris drowned...
> -which is *the 'Division-of-the-Two Lands'*.
> Thus Horus stood over one region and Seth over one region...
> They made peace at Ayan.
> Then it seemed wrong to Geb that the portion of Horus
> was like that of Seth.
> So Geb gave to Horus his inheritance,
> for he is the son of his first born...
> Then Horus stood over the Two Lands...
> He is the uniter of the Two Lands...
> who arose as King of Upper and Lower Egypt...'

(**Shabaka Stone**, *British Museum* –Miriam Lichtheim, *Ancient Egyptian literature*)

The land in question was not all of Egypt as we knew it, but a region with a cosmic duality and which specifically contained the House of Sokar. Veronica Ions, in her publication *Egyptian Mythology*, points out that this trial was the subject of one of the few consecutive stories connected with Egyptian mythology that have survived. The cult of the sun-god was bound up with laws about the inheritance of power and property. The dispute centred on Horus and Seth -descent versus seniority -involving land tenure in the political interpretation of Upper Egypt subjected to Lower Egypt. With the passing of time, these two gods had become the personification of good and evil, with Seth being cast as the wicked one and Horus, through avenging his father, representing righteousness. Seth however, accused his nephew of being a bastard and only the *alleged* son of Osiris.

Were The Shemsu Hor "Companions of Horus" -the line of reincarnated Kings -the beneficiaries of a masterminded Dynastic coup? After a seemingly fair verdict, the earth-god Geb retracted it and awarded all to Horus. Was the battle that raged for ages the archaic history of another civilisation, or a cosmic event? Could it be a component of intricate science encoded in a vague star cult?
Was it a battle of time -a geometric expression in the configuration of pyramids that demarcate light and dark geographically -whereby it divides the Globe and continents? Who owns the World?

'...the gods will return from Earth to Heaven; Egypt will be forsaken, and this land which was once the home of religion will be left desolate, bereft of the presence of its deities. This land will be filled with foreigners... O Egypt, Egypt, of thy religion nothing will remain but an empty tale, which thine own children in time to come will not believe; nothing will be left but graven words, and only the stones will tell of thy piety...'

(Thoth/Asclepius-The Lament)

FIG.VII. Sokar ship –departure of gods?

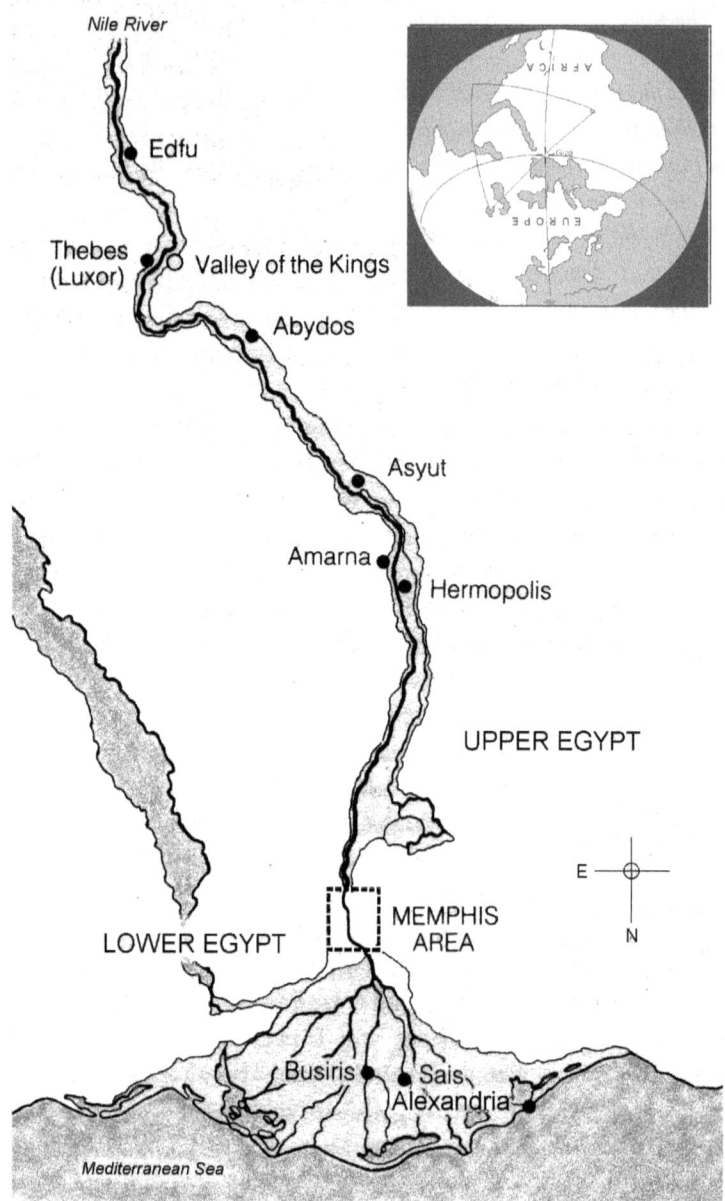

FIG. V. Nile Valley, Delta

Mystical places and events

If we were dealing only with the mythical issue, it could easily be put down to fertile imagination or tales of fantasy. Even a crude sky map could be entertained and the stellar cult can be practically explained as the gods only being stars. *If* the only surviving evidence were the pyramid ruins of the 5th Dynasty, time epochs and architectural ability would not be questionable issues but how does one explain away the un-inscribed pyramid groups of the 4th Dynasty at Giza and Dahshur and as we shall discover, the geometrical aspects of the Duat?

'I shall not be turned back at the *gates of the Duat*. I ascend to the sky with Orion... I am one who collects... his efflux in front of Rostau...'

{Coffin Text 236}

The Duat is the cosmic land of the souls in the 'after world' -a region in the 'deepest most central' part of celestial topography in Aker and accessed via Rostau, in the region of Orion. (*Aker* could be interpreted as the Galaxy within the encompassment of the Universe). The terrestrial equivalent of the Duat, where the gods of the First Time established their kingdom, occupies a tract of land across Memphis -South of the Nile Delta, between Heliopolis, Giza and Saqqara. According to iconographic and textual evidence, the god Sokar precedes Osiris. Saqqara is believed to derive its name from Sokar, who was also identified with Ptah, god of the Memphite Necropolis and the Duat. In Memphite cosmogony he was regarded as creator of the Universe and considered the greatest of craftsmen. Imhotep, the renowned vizier and architect of the Step Pyramid at Saqqara, is thought to be an offspring of Ptah. The central region of the Memphite Necropolis was Rostau, closely identified with the Giza pyramid field. In ancient times and throughout the Pharaonic era, Rostau was considered the main entrance to the after world. The House of Sokar is situated in the 5th Hour division of the Duat. The narrative in the 5th Hour states that:

'...the image is in utter darkness. The egg which belongs to the God Sokar is lighted up by the eyes in the head of the Great God, his flesh shines, his legs are inside in coils. Noise is heard inside the egg after the Great God has passed by it, like the sound of roaring in the sky during a storm.'

The *BOAT* of Sokar, the *Hnw-BARQUE*, features prominently in text of the Duat; *it carried the king to heaven*. Numerous passages from Pyramid Texts contain elements of space flight:

'There shall be brought to you the *Hnw*-bark and the... of the *Hn* - bird. You shall fly up therewith... You shall fly up and alight'
{UTT. 669}

'The King is a flame, moving before the wind to the end of the sky and to the end of the Earth... there is brought to him a way of ascent to the sky...'
{UTT. 261}

'I am this one who has escaped from the coiled serpent, I have ascended in a blast of fire having turned myself about. The two skies go to me.'
{UTT. 332}

'...the gate of Aker is opened... may you remove yourself to the sky upon your iron throne...'
{Pyramid Text 1014}

The starry world of Osiris was called the Duat and Professor R.O. Faulkner, after meticulous analysis and translation of the Pyramid Texts, concluded that: "the Duat was not a part of the Sun, but often considered a part of the visible sky".

'I am Osiris, I have come to Rostau in order to know the secret of the Duat... I live on white emmer, filling the Winding Waterway...'

{CoffinText 241}

Egyptologists are in agreement that although the Book of what is in the Duat is a New Kingdom text, it is an edited version of an older text that would have had a different emphasis during the Old Kingdom. (*Shat Ent Am Duat -The book of the Duat*, E.A. Wallis Budge translation; *The Egyptian heaven and Hell*) In this 'book', reference is made to an area in the sky known as the *'hidden circle of the Duat'* in the body of Nut (the sky) -a district in the Duat 440 cubits x 440 cubits. This is identical to the square base of the Great Pyramid and relates to a dimensional icon of one half of the Globe. *Could the Duat have multiple celestial and geographical connotations? Where exactly could this area be located in celestial topography? Can it be identified within the realm of conventional astronomy?*

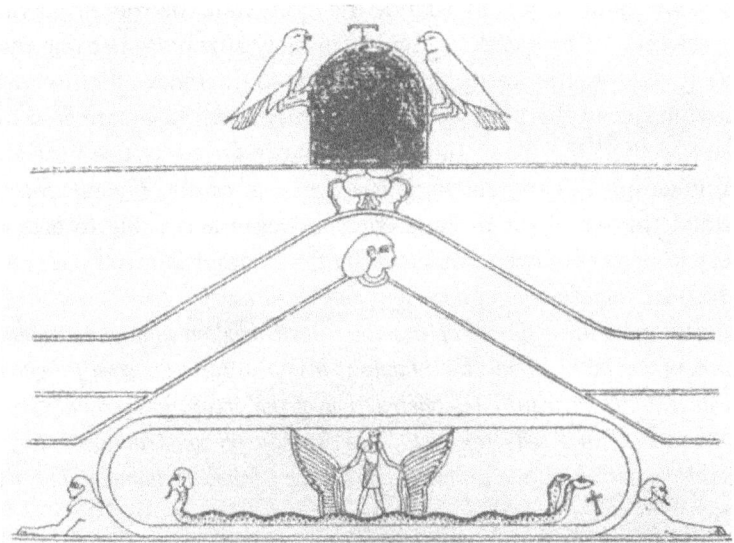

FIG. VIII. Hermetic cycle of Duat?

We recall that Egyptian priests told Solon about mysterious people who invaded the Mediterranean basin and that records of them still survived in Egypt. The Edfu Building Texts are the only surviving reference to the *'Seven Sages of the First Time'*. They are inscribed on walls of the Edfu Temple in Upper Egypt, portions of which are believed to date to the Pyramid Age. According to the texts, "Words of the Seven Sages" were recorded by Thoth in a book entitled: *Specifications of the mounds of the early primeval age.* The 'Sages' were the only divine beings who knew how the temples and sacred places were to be created and it was they who initiated construction at the Great Primeval Mound. An edifice specified as **nwt-vtp** '*Speedy of construction,* the sanctuary within it -Great Seat', by name. With these works completed, the *owp udw* magical protection of the site was made by the Sages. They appear as survivors of a cataclysm, who set about a recreation of a former world (*detail study;* E.A.E. Reymond, *The Mythical Origin of the Egyptian Temple, 1969*). According to the Edfu Texts, the Sages originally came from an island, the homeland of the Primeval Ones, which met its end suddenly. The few survivors became the gods in Egypt -the Lords of Light who could renew themselves and who raised the seed for gods and men. The Sages are said to have specified the plans and designs that were to be used for all future temples. This *esoteric knowledge* was of the *highest order;* deemed too secret for profane eyes and only accessible to a few *chosen initiates* -not even possessed by the Pharaoh himself (George Hart, *A Dictionary of Egyptian Gods and Goddesses*).

Just who were these divine beings with such wisdom and phenomenal powers of creation? What exactly does it mean to 'raise the seed for gods and men'? Did they initiate construction of the great pyramids at Giza with a device that was referred to as 'speedy of construction'? Is it concealed somewhere in a sanctuary? Was the island, the homeland of the primeval ones –the survivors of the cataclysm, located in space?

Could it have been Mars, or is there a 'missing' planet, or perhaps a missing continent – does Atlantis lie beneath the Antarctic ice?

'...the development of, as well as the origins of written language, remains mysterious'.

(**Lucie Lamie,** *Egyptian Mysteries*)

Depicted as an Ibis, Thoth is the highly revered Egyptian god of wisdom and magical words, who *gave Egyptians knowledge to write by picture symbols, which he received from the Gods*. According to legend Thoth has written a book of forty two volumes that contains all the mysteries of the world. The texts were the clues to all religious mysteries and in this is the association with magic. He held the highest office in the Pantheon, that of scribe and magician to Osiris. He was the recorder of time and of the stars, *navigator of the celestial ship of a million years* in which supreme God Atum Re and retinue travelled *across space and time.* He was the *messenger* of the Gods and *instituted worship* of the Gods. He was also associated with mathematics and geometry. In the Biblical account, this figure is identifiable with Enoch, who was taken up into the heavens and received instruction by angels. To the Greeks, who attributed the building of the Great Pyramid to him, he is known as Hermes, the 'Thrice Great'.

'Ye holy books written by my perishable hands,
they have been anointed with the drug of imperishability
by Him who is master over all,
remain ye undecaying through all ages,
and undiscovered by all men
who shall go to and fro on the plains of this land,
until the time when the heavens grow old,
shall beget men worthy of you.
...accurate knowledge of the truth...
the secret things of Osiris...
these holy symbols of the cosmic elements...
those Gods who ruled the earth will be restored...'

(Prophecy of **Thoth**: Hermetic writing - *Kore Kosmou*)

'This is the *word* which is in darkness. As for any spirit who knows it, he will live among the living. *Fire is about it,* which contains the *efflux* of Osiris. As for any man who shall know it, he will never perish there, since he knows what shall be in Rostau. *Rostau is hidden since he fell there,* for he is one who has come down from upon the desert, and he possesses *writing material*... Rostau is for Osiris. As for any man who is there, he will see Osiris every day, his breath will be in his nose, and he will never die...'

{Coffin Text 1087}

'Myth is a deliberately chosen means for communicating knowledge... To make sense of the myth, we must first convert it into a form the intellect will accept... Myth works directly upon the understanding... the symbols in ancient Egypt is a scrupulously chosen pictorial device designed to evoke an idea or a concept in its entirety. It is a means of bypassing the intellect and communicating directly with the intelligence of the heart, the understanding. The heart synthesizes the mind analyses. A true symbol is neither primitive nor subconscious. It is a deliberate means of evoking understanding, as opposed to conveying information...'

(**John West,** *Serpent in the Sky*)

What was the mysterious roaring 'egg' that belonged to the god Sokar?
Did the gods arrive by 'celestial' ship, capable of traversing a Galaxy?
How did they introduce language, science, astronomy and geometry?
Did they have experimental partaking in the creation of human-kind?
Were they stranded, lived and died here, and if so, did they procreate?
Or, was the evolution gap too great and their own gene pool too small?
Was their progeny absorbed into Earth's population, and if so, where?
Could the vessel of Sokar still be concealed somewhere in a sanctuary?
Was it a purposeful visit, to impart knowledge and then depart again?
Did the visit provide the catalyst for the evolution of our civilisation?
Is there a looming cataclysm that will impede our existence on Earth?
Did they leave a warning and directions in case we attain the means?

'on the day of *concealing the mysteries* of the deep place in Rostau... I am he who sees secret things in Rostau... O you who open up ways and open up paths for the perfected souls in the House of Osiris...'

{Coffin Text 314}

Terrestrially, Rostau translates as the Giza plateau and is counterpart of a celestial equivalent in the constellation of Orion. Rostau, according to legend (Coffin Texts c.2000-1800BC), is the *the gateway* to access the Duat after-world where the House of the god Sokar is situated. An inscription on the New Kingdom stela situated between the paws of Sphinx states that 'the Location of the Sphinx is beside the House of Sokar' (*Ancient Records*, James H. Breasted).

'For I am Sokar of Rostau, I am bound for the place where dwells Sokar...'

{Pyramid Text 445}

Although Egyptologists do not dispute Rostau being on the ground in the Giza area and with a counter part in the sky near Orion, it has never been defined. Egyptologist and archaeo-astronomer Jane B. Sellers (*The Death of Gods in Ancient Egypt*) points out that the scriptures *(Egyptian Book of the Two Ways)* strongly indicate Rostau to be located in the sky...a celestial Rostau in the Milky Way region.

'I have passed over the paths of Rostau, whether on water or land... they are *at the limit of the sky*. As for him who knows the spell for going down into them, he himself is a god in the suite of Thoth, he will go down to any sky he wishes to go down to...'

{Coffin Text 1035}

Where exactly in the Milky Way region, near Orion, could the limit of the sky and the gateway to the after-world be? Can it be identified within conventional astronomical topography? Yes!

An artifact associated with King Shabaka for its preservation during the 25th Dynasty, c.700BC is referred to as the Memphis / Memphite Theology or the Shabaka Texts. It relates to the Pyramid Age and gives the following Osirian account:

'This is the Land... *the burial of Osiris in the House of Sokar*... Isis and Nephthys without delay, for Osiris has drowned in his water... Horus speaks to Isis and Nephthys: "Hurry, seize him... "Isis and Nephthys speak to Osiris: "We come, we take you..." They brought him to. He *entered the hidden portals* in the glory of the lords of eternity... *thus Osiris came into the Earth at the Royal Fortress, the North of... to which he had come... There was built the Royal Fortress...*'

(Shabaka Stone, British Museum)

Was Osiris physically buried?
Does this equate to starlight from Alnitak, at meridian transit, entering into the southern shaft of the Kings Chamber in the Great Pyramid?
Was this the astronomical observation and projection for the surveying of the Giza plateau and the Great Pyramid —is it the the Royal Fortress or is there another interpretation?

PART I epilogue

Part I contained condensed documented knowledge, with specific extracts and some thought provoking questions. This potent mixture of mythology and archaeology contained elements of astronomy, which in part two will be manifest. The Pyramid Texts are generally accepted to be transcripts of several archaic compositions and that the original sources of the literature are long since lost. Translations were compiled from often damaged, incomplete or vague inscriptions in an alien language with symbols, all enshrouded in the cloak of time. This has been to a large extent the extremely challenging situation faced by students and researchers of the ancient Egyptian relics, making it virtually impossible to place them into coherent context without speculation and postulation.

'The Pyramid Texts are full of difficulties of every kind. The exact meanings of a large number of words found in them are unknown… the construction of the sentences often baffles all attempts to translate it, and when it contains wholly unknown words it becomes an unsolved riddle.'

(**E.A. Wallis Budge,** *From Fetish to God in Ancient Egypt*)

This has also been the grounds on which Egyptologists discard texts as religious and mythical fictions. That is about to change! With pioneering insight, comprehension of astronomy and vivid interpretation, the star gods, as well as the locations of Rostau, the Duat and the Two-Lands, can now be vividly depicted as real, within celestial and terrestrial duality. Numerous texts are now graphically and literally interpreted… for the first time!

'We have reached this fascinating point in our evolution... we have reached the time when we can talk to each other across the distances between the stars...'

(Dr. **John Billingham,** NASA Ames Research Center, 1995)

More adventure

Big discovery, big dilemma

I have uncovered compelling evidence to solve a controversial puzzle that has haunted man for centuries. The pyramids are descendant from the stars... If it were coincidental, it would be the most incredible coincidence in the Universe, but substantiated in meaningful context it is the Big Bang of compelling evidence that will obliterate many historical untruths. The academic establishment has failed to come forward with plausible explanations regarding the pyramids or their origin. The fact that they remained an unsolved mystery for thousands of years is testament to the perplexity of the matter. The expected norm would be for an acclaimed brainiac from the 'right community' to make this breakthrough. However, the generations that will implement this knowledge are yet to be born, so who ought to be informed that can comprehend it and how does one go about it? When the dust has settled, scientists and academics should be encouraged, in fact obligated, to respond ethically to the relevant technological as well as theological components and to the benefit of all mankind.

The work, *Zep Tepi*, was not about me, I was just enthusiastic to make the right connections. I was not an archaeologist or Egyptologist, neither an astronomer, nor an established author for that matter but merely in awe of nature, with an analytical, inquisitive mind and sense for proportion —perhaps instinct in my DNA, or inspiration by a vision that as a species we *can* coexist harmoniously on our beautiful planet and indeed in the Universe. The key, I believe, lies in knowledge and truth -knowledge *of* the truth. Before we can hope to achieve that however, something needs to transcend our evolutionary path, which is on a headlong course to self destruction! On Tuesday 11 September 2001, barely a few days later, this sentiment was clearly re-emphasized with the horrific events and senseless act involving the World Trade Center in New York. I had never really been an avid scholar, then, suddenly found myself researching astronomy and mythology along with a myriad of related and unrelated subjects, hoping to clarify one of the oldest archaeological mysteries of this world. These findings have inadvertently created a big dilemma for me and, ironically, this knowledge proved difficult to impart. For lack of an insightful definition it is broadly brushed as 'pseudoscience'. What is the right protocol and who is responsible? We, the inhabitants of this planet, should ultimately manage our own destiny. My lack of 'proper' credentials would prevent opportunity to present my findings to the scientific world with any credibility. After careful consideration and unsure of friend or foe, the 'illuminati' et al, I set about matters in a manner where it would count eventually and avoid abuse or misuse. I had to be resourceful and opted for the Trojan Horse -by the time of realising what's going on, 'they' will be besieged...

I was staying in Cape Town and had presented to a local Publisher, where concerned parties signed non-disclosure agreements. Preparations were underway to introduce the greatest discovery of all time to the world!

Cape of Good Hope

It might seem bizarre, doing such a remote study of the pyramids of Egypt. The entire length of the African continent lies between the Cape and Cairo, yet that was the reality of the situation. The Cape of Good Hope was dreaded by early sailors for the notorious conditions that can be encountered on rounding the Southern tip of Africa, where the Atlantic and Indian oceans meet. With a European heritage and abundant architecture that exhibits Victorian charm from a bygone era, among a diversity of other colourful and multicultural influences, Cape Town is the Mother

City. With the fierce South-Easter gales being the antonym, her most famous geographic claim to fame is the mountain with its conspicuous flat top contour. With its Northern slope softly illuminated at night and reaching up to a starlit sky, Table Mountain is a sight to behold. Frequently capped by cloud - referred to as the 'table cloth', it is the only geographic feature on Earth after which a constellation has been named: Mensa, or Mons Mensae -the (Mountain of) stars over which hang (a large Magellanic Cloud of) other stars, which are satellite galaxies to our own Galaxy.

Being back in civilisation and in an unfamiliar city, I expected that it could be unsettling. When one is fine-tuned to the tranquility of nature, the up-paced beat and associated distractions is not conducive. Yet I had arrived there fit and confident to face destiny. Content with the thought that the task at hand required me being in that environment, knowing a different lifestyle and circumstances, a different climate, altitude and diet, would all play a role. After a humble existence in the mountains it was good to have electricity for reading at night as opposed to using three or four candles. The downside was poorer conditions for star observation, due to light pollution associated with cities. While still having an uncorrupted perception of my revelation, I knew that the notes had to be processed systematically. During the day I worked on that and at night I would read. There was *The Orion Mystery* and *Keeper of Genesis* to read as both works were referred to in Bauvals' *Secret Chamber* and I had to cross check and research. Indeed, while doing so, my case was strengthening even more. It was comforting to know that there were the Planetarium and libraries, should I need them. The Internet could be useful too and was the stage of a heated debate on the Egyptological and astronomical issues that are *very* relevant to my discoveries. At that stage I was glad not to be a part of it, although probably unavoidable in the future...

Occasional socialising and making new acquaintances was a pleasant distraction. One appreciates it in a different light when you have been in the wilderness for some time, however, the cliché of loneliness in a crowd was a reality. Difficulty in communication arose when being confronted by the usual line of questioning: who are you? Where are you from? What do you do? I couldn't exactly reply that I don't know, yet, getting into a situation of premature debate had to be avoided until the work was formulated. I was elated of course about the discovery, although at times it seemed a great burden to shoulder. Not being able to talk freely about it to anyone, sometimes wondering if my mind was playing a trick on me, I probably would not have persisted were it not for the uniqueness of the diagrams and their reassurance. It felt as though I was pitted in a race against time - knowing the discovery was justified, but the mammoth process of writing about it amounted to sheer frustration. Trying to speedily compile it into a comprehensible text out of the necessity to get it published was a vicious circle. Spiritual harmony was not attainable under such conditions and funds that were intended for the project in Lesotho had to be applied for a different purpose. City living was not cheap and writing a manuscript did not earn an income. Only sales of the book could one day fulfill that dire need. I am normally appreciative of time passing slowly and equate it with quality experience. However at that time, although I knew it was 'the Cosmos at work', it seemed like an eternity but was hopeful all would make sense in retrospect. Cape Town is a very beautiful city and the kind of experience which ought to be shared, but I was 'too focussed to experience it', or so I thought...

The conventional social masquerade led to dinners and introductions, a function at the Royal Cape Yacht Club, drinks at the Radisson Hotel on the Atlantic seaboard, 40th birthday celebrations at the Buena Vista Club followed by Italian food at Mario's Restaurant. Decadence that had been dormant for a long time, rekindled by someone whom I ought to not have taken notice of (because it was unplanned and logically untimely), not a good time -yet emotional eccentricity incited me to buying red roses... Normally I would trust my instincts, but they could have been rusty; was it destined, or was I destined to make a fool of myself? The effects of this could have been very damaging at a sensitive time... riding the emotional roller coaster when I should have been concentrating on the manuscript. Finally, after a couple of weeks, I found myself on an enjoyable evening walk with Ingrid along the Palm lined boulevard of Camps Bay -a strip usually crammed with tourists and diners. We had stopped for drinks on the sidewalk of the Sunset Beach Bar blessed by the presence of a pale crescent Moon in the western sky, tantalizingly suspended over gentle swells of the Atlantic Ocean. Later, over dinner at The Bayside Restaurant, I was looking across the table into sparkling blue eyes, suffused in dancing candlelight... opalescent innocence, a spontaneous glint... a trace of apprehension, perhaps, a veil of a remote disappointment. Her smile exuding the confidence of maturity yet lightly brushed with youthful shyness. I was oblivious to the rest of the world, content with the moment, although impossible to reconstruct. It is strange how certain encounters can have such a great impact on our lives, our emotions, our hearts, our souls and dictate to our minds -perhaps it could be ascribed to the fine bottle of Zonnebloem Chardonnay. If only we could think with our hearts and feel with our minds, for such is life that when our minds perceive circumstances as being suitable, it is often the case then that loneliness is the only available soul mate...

Although lamenting, I cherish the reward of experience, for it hosts the wealth of inspiration to write or to philosophise. The intangible powers of attraction and the complex phenomena of love are as integral to humankind as is the mists of time to the mysteries of the Universe -all will be revealed in due time... and I was supposed to study the latter !

'The foremost duty of a scientist is to check the facts. However science on an inspired level requires more than making and collecting observations; it is also the drawing of conclusions, and possibly the formulation of a theory. At this stage imagination is needed and this involves a much more difficult task... Usually scientists are willing to give any theory, however doubtful, a try provided it shows imagination and it offers new ideas... A scientific theory has to be judged by its credibility, which depends on the supporting evidence. Its value increases with the volume of such evidence...'

(Dr. **Kurt Mendelssohn,** *The Riddle of the Pyramids*)

PART II
THE DISCOVERY

Introduction

Let's continue and *see* if we can create order to resolve some of the mysteries that persist in Egypt. Will 'those gods who ruled the Earth' be restored'? How do we *interpret a message across time* and of the great pyramids (themselves devoid of any inscriptions), of which so much has been recorded, yet after vast time has left more questions than answers? We need to go back to the basics and now, question everything that we've ever been told! Diagrams contained in this section are not dependent on myth for justification but can be subjected to scientific scrutiny. The fact that they integrate remarkably however, provides further endorsement for investigation. Sections that contain major elements of mythology are confusing and not in the conventional boundaries of logical reasoning. This may yield some frustration for the reader who expects instant clarity -no amount of creative writing can fulfill easy comprehension -intellect and reasoning ability would be most useful. A parallel can be drawn with many passages that occur in the Bible and other theological compositions, that cannot be logically or literally interpreted, yet convey a message. The ancient texts have posed many problems to an ensemble of dedicated researchers who have studied them. The texts should be read attentively in conjunction with the icons -the most viable medium to convey information. Sections that deal with astronomical and geographical correlation are more readily understood. The stars are not concealed beneath sand or eroded away by time but visible, mapped and there for everybody to *see* – they are our future and our past. This is, for the first time, an investigation and unequalled clarification of the mysterious monuments and mythology of ancient Egypt. Sky charts are employed to demonstrate tangible and compelling evidence - impossible to ignore and if we do, we deserve to remain primitive and eventually fade away into the abyss of oblivion!

During the Renaissance period, Nikolaus Copernicus, a Polish priest, proposed that the Sun and not the Earth is at the centre of the Universe. For fear of his life, he held back publishing this, knowing that the church would not approve of such ideas. This is a popularly quoted tit-bit of historical antics and a typical example of an establishment that is light years from being accepted into the Galactic village. Speaking of which, stars /suns feature prominently in this work and some data on their typical characteristics will be informative:

Our Sun has approximately one-hundred-thousand-million neighbours… suns (stars) that are *not uniformly distributed* in our Milky Way Galaxy. The Sun is vital to our existence on Earth, which is 149 597 870 km distant (one astronomical unit). In his publication *Night Skies*, Dr. Peter Mack quaintly describes our Galaxy as a gigantic spiral city, in which we live. If we could be a great distance out of this galactic city and look back, what we would see is a flattened disc with a central bulge and one hundred thousand million shining stars, which are all suns. The stars in the bulge are mainly well advanced in their evolutionary cycle and are metal poor. It is assumed that Star formation in the bulge has ceased. Our Sun is situated in a spiral arm of the Galaxy, which also contains approximately 10^{10} solar masses in the form of interstellar matter. The stars in the Galactic disc revolve around the nucleus and our Sun (and us) takes over 200 million years to make an orbit. The reader should take note that the stars that are visible with the naked eye, are not as pronounced or numerous as they appear in the grainy photographs of the diagrams -the reasons are magnification and reproduction. The star maps show the brightest, stars more realistically, such as could be observed in the light polluted environment of a city, or, in the twilight of a rural setting. All the layovers and projections that follow incorporate an identical background that shows a region in the Milky Way and the constellations which I have identified as those that comprise the Duat. I will elaborate on that in a later section.

When we observe the sky by means of unaided sight, our perspective view is illusory. This illusion captures a dimension known as scale –an accurate replica in all aspects, relevant to perception. Thanks to modern technology, we know that the Universe is multi-dimensional, especially if one is to include the notion of time. We know that stars are separated by enormously vast distances and not necessarily in true proportion or relative position from our earthly peripheral. Not withstanding these facts, for functional and illustrative purposes, sky charts, diagrams and photographs are projected as static and with limited perspective onto restrictive two-dimensional paper. In the sections to follow, another concept will be revealed step by step, where pyramids represent stars and are associated with the gods terrestrially and cosmically with simultaneously duality. This is the manner in which the texts are compiled and the pyramids set out accordingly. It is also said that the tombs of Osiris on Earth had their counterparts in heaven.

'It was he who attacked me… when there came into being this his name of Orion, long of leg and lengthy of stride…
Thoth and Horus then come to help Osiris to the sky… they raise Osiris from upon his side and make him stand… The sky is Given to you, and the Fields of Rushes, the Mounds [Pyramids] of Horus, and the Mounds of Seth…'

{Pyramid Text 959-61}

'The king's sister is Sothis, the king's offspring is the Morning Star'

{Pyramid Text 357,935}

# DIAGRAMS

'Behold he has come as Orion, behold Osiris has come as Orion... your third is Sothis...'

{Pyramid Text 820-2}

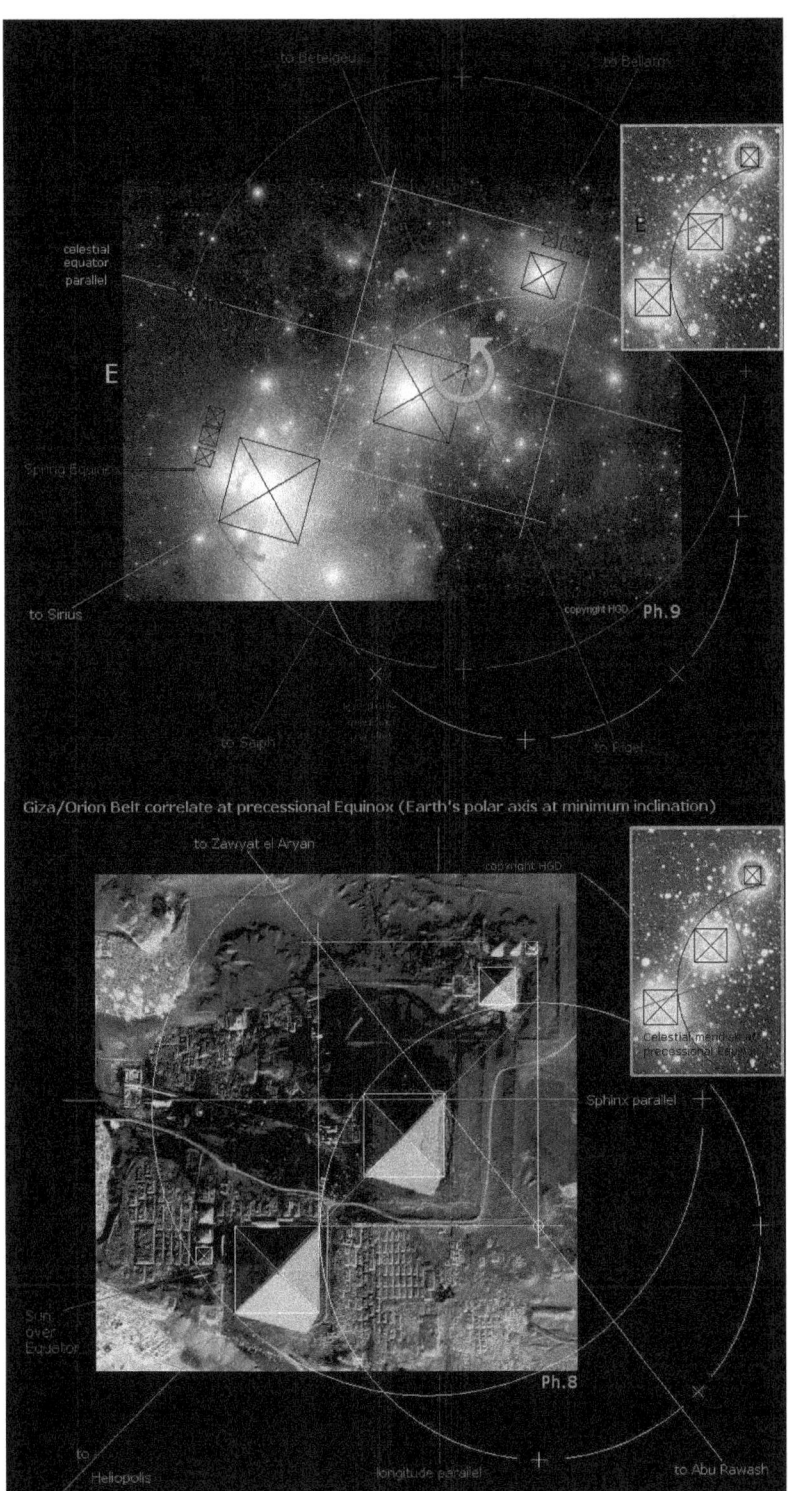

Giza/Orion Belt correlate at precessional Equinox (Earth's polar axis at minimum inclination)

[A]
BETELGEUX
RIGEL

Open Cluster
NGC2169
MEISSA
BETELGEUX
BELLATRIX
MINTAKA =
ALNILAM =
ALNITAK =
D
E
Z
ORIONIS
SAIPH
RIGEL
SIRIUS

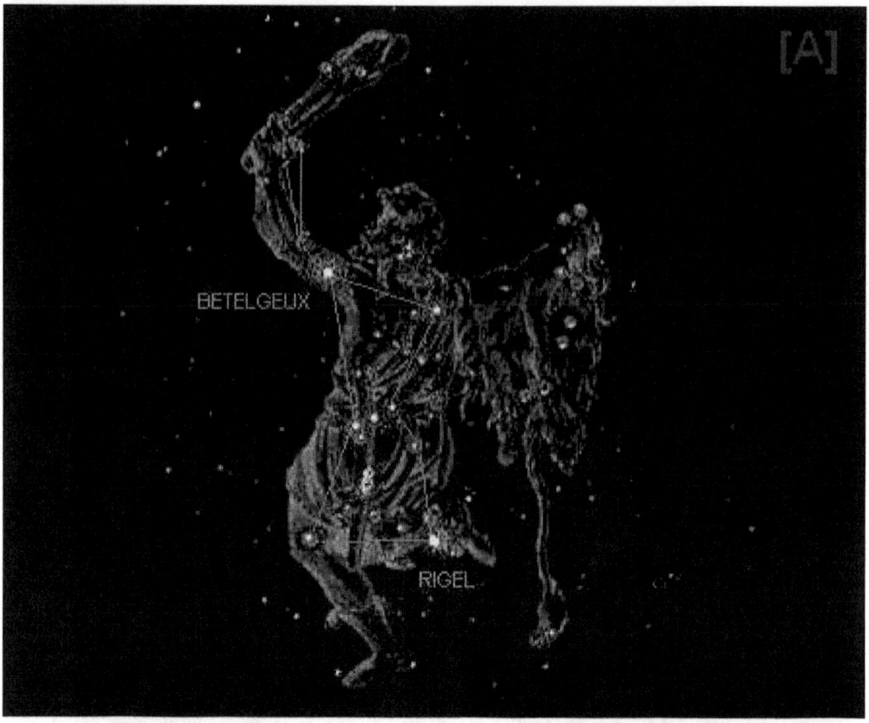

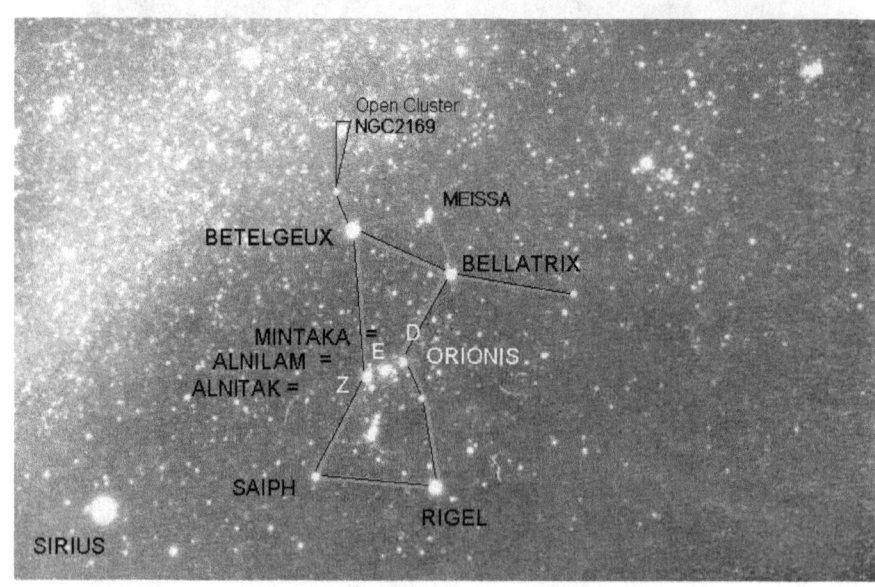

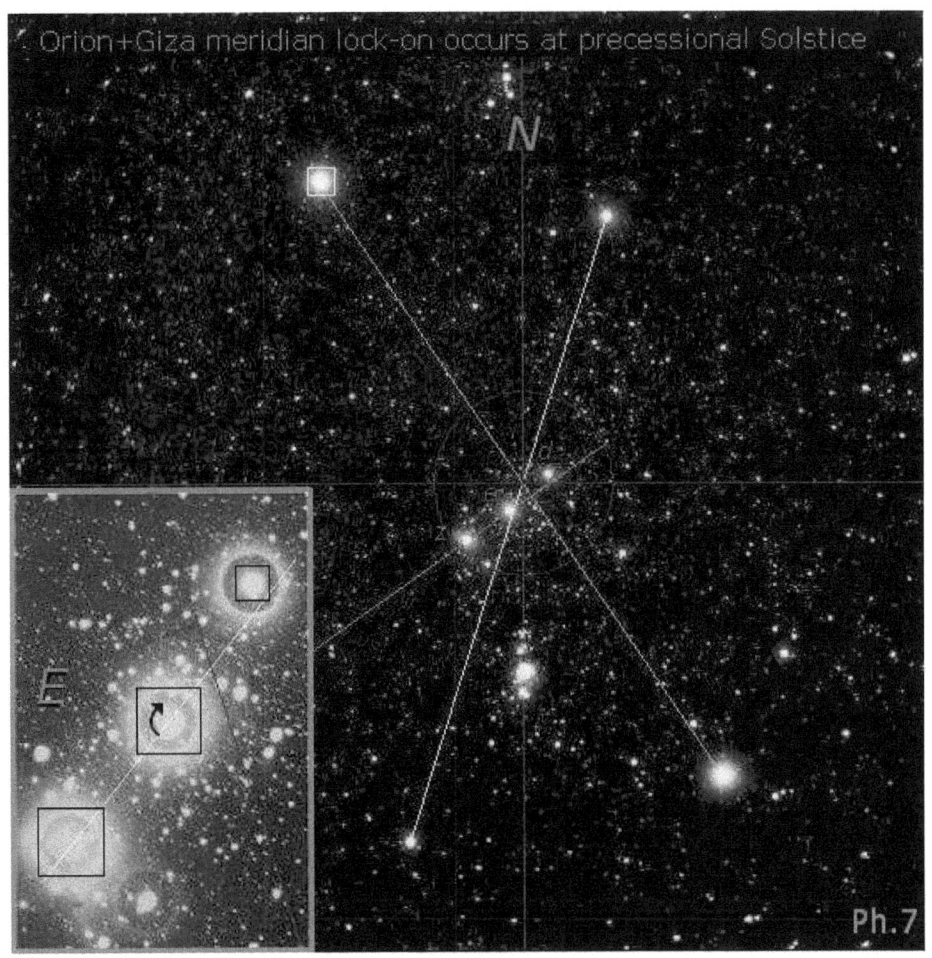

CONSTELLATION of ORION

CELESTIAL ROSTAU diag. [B]

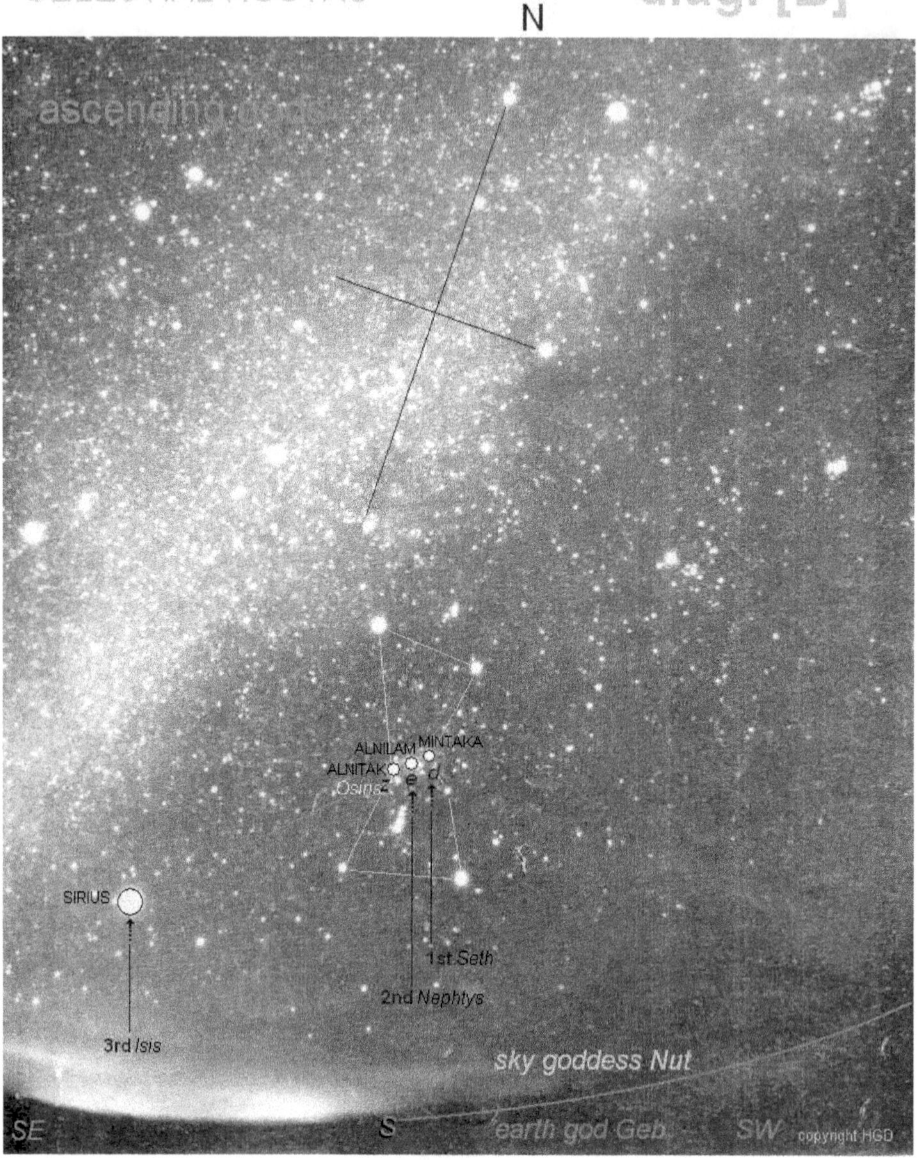

TERRESTRIAL ROSTAU

diag. [C]

Super imposed

Nile River

S (TERRESTRIAL)

E

W

THIRD PYRAMID
SECOND PYRAMID
GREAT PYRAMID

HELIOPOLIS

LETOPOLIS

copy right HGD 2K2

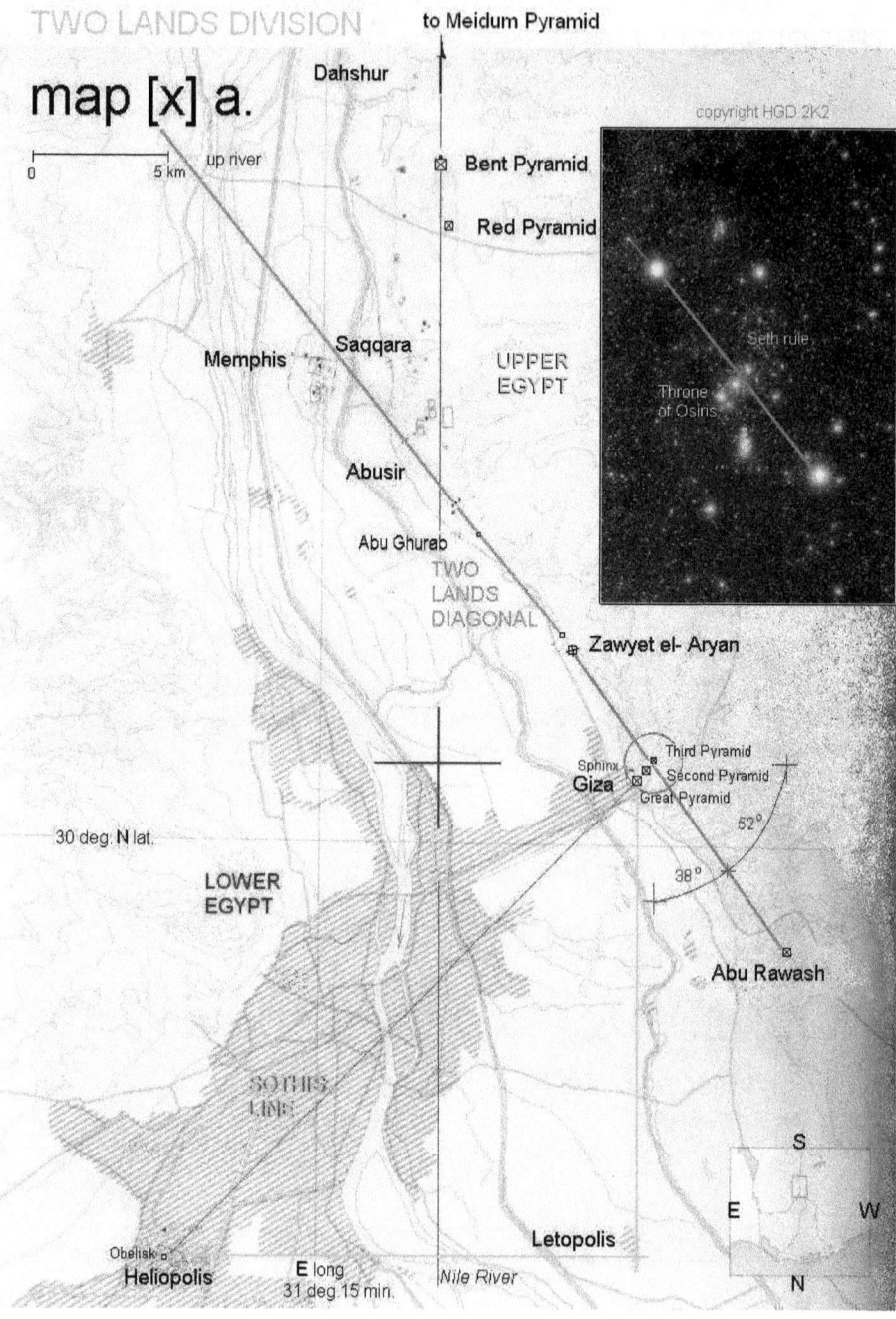

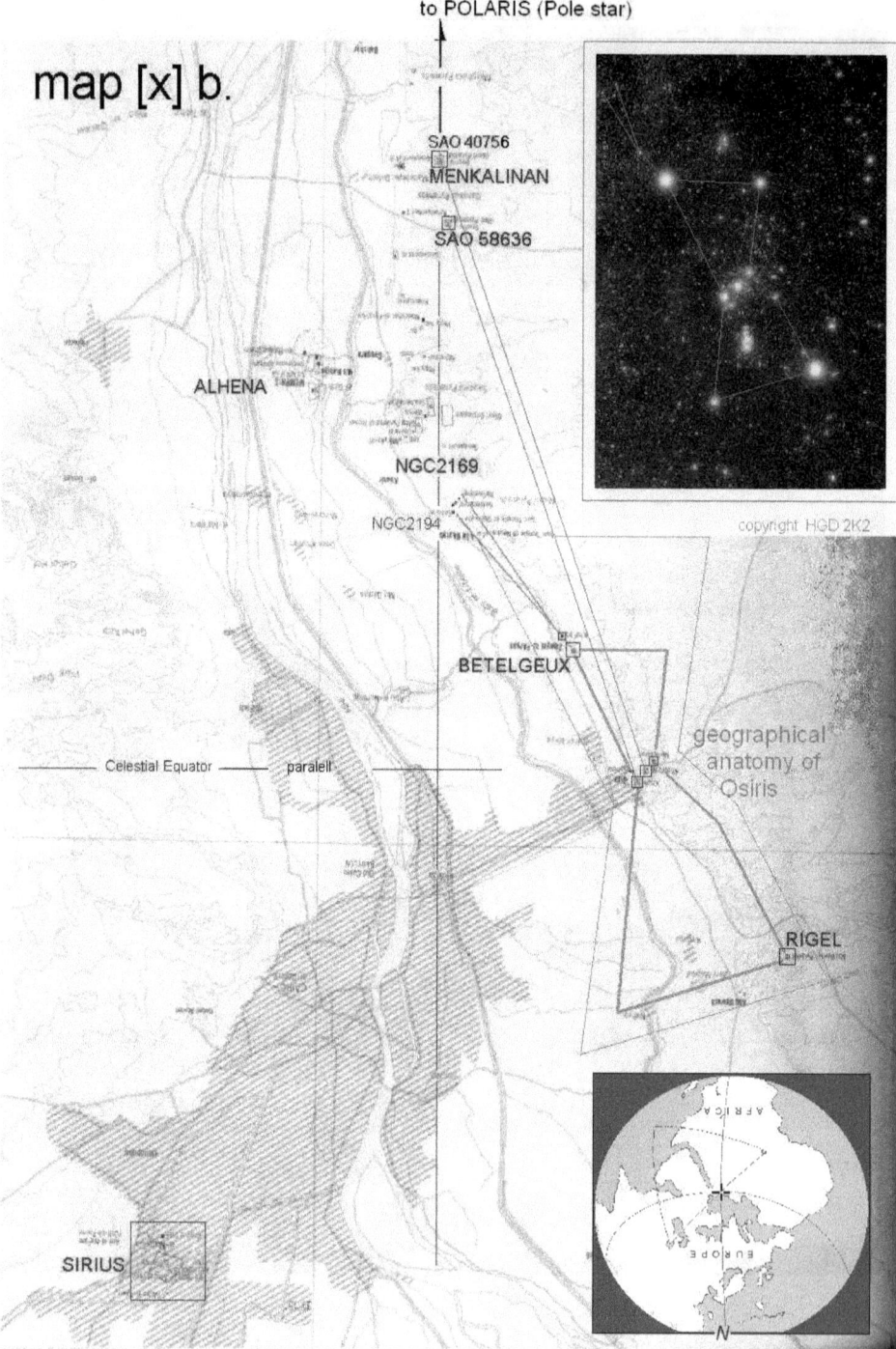

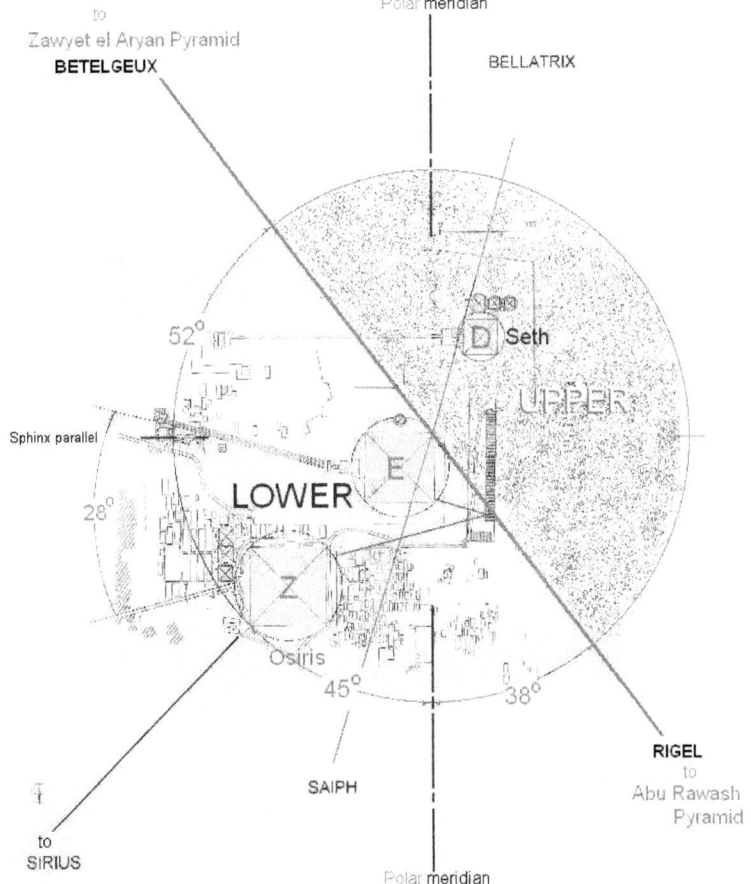

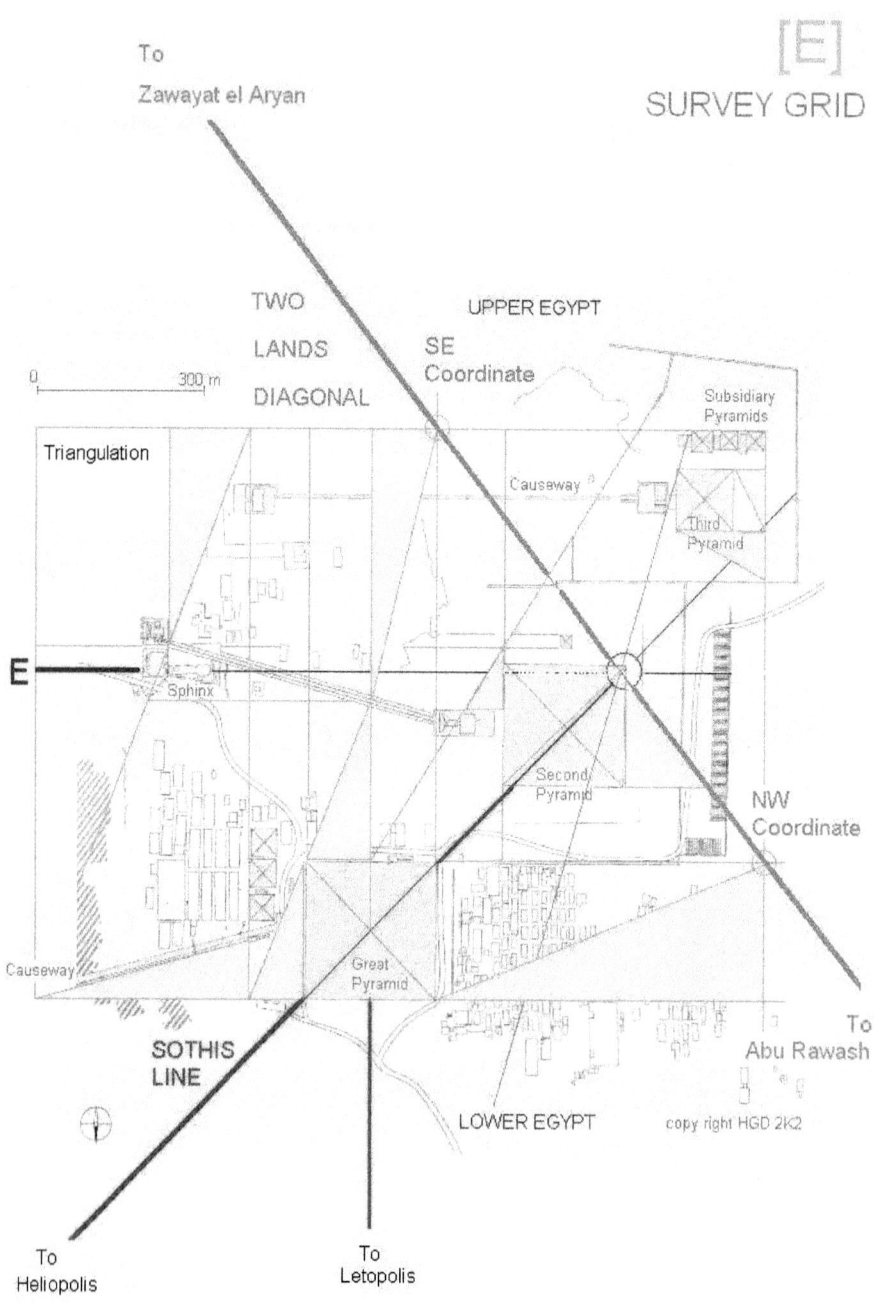

CO ORDINATES

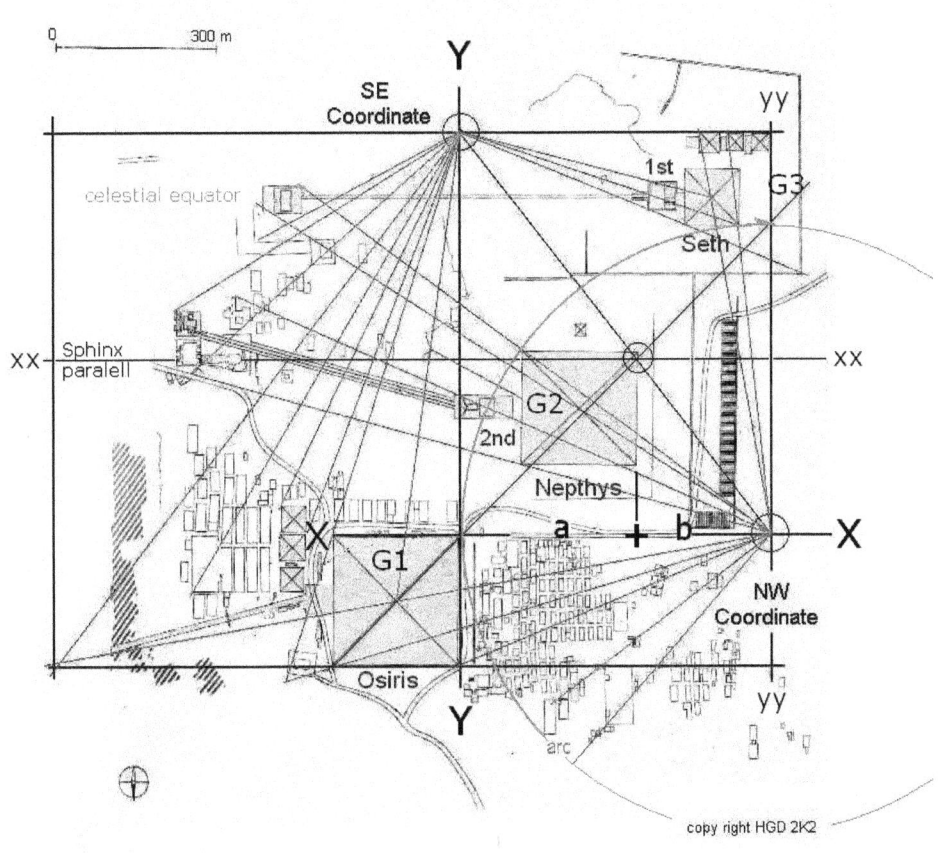

3rd = Sothis
Heliopolis

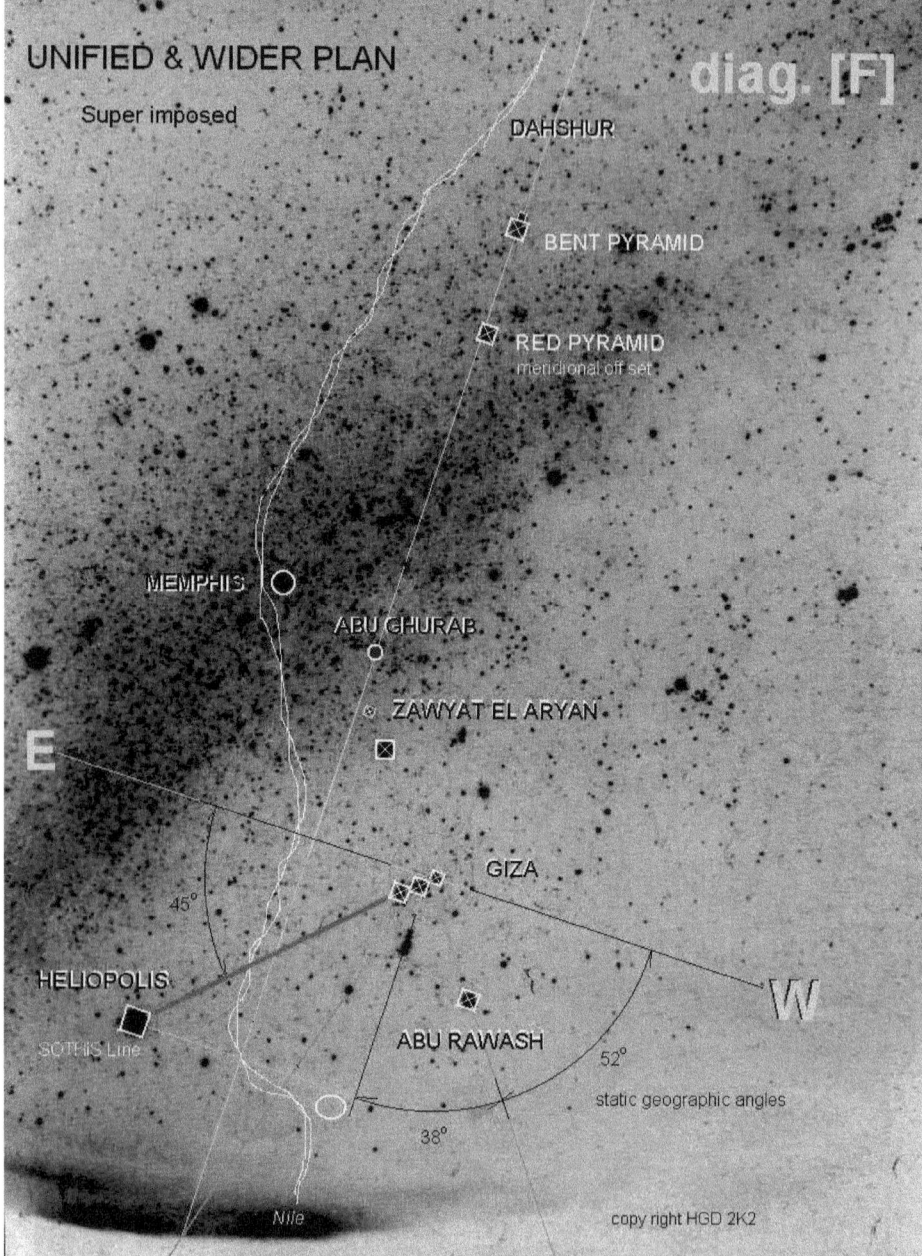

COSMIC MASTER PLAN
ESOTERIC GEOMETRY

diag. [G]

to POLARIS

SAO 40756 — RA 5H 59' 55"
MENKALINAN — RA 5H 59' 30"

SAO 58636 — RA 5H 59' 43"

ALHENA

PLEIADES

Seven Sages

Open Cluster
NGC 2169
SAO 113389

ALDEBARAN

E

BETELGEUX

E D
Z   ORIONIS   UPPER CELESTIAL SPHERE

Declination
measurements

SOTHIS
Line

RIGEL

0°
Latitude

W

SIRIUS

Two Lands
Diagonal

6 Hour
Right Ascension Meridian
from Vernal Equinox
Longitude

LOWER CELESTIAL SPHERE

copy right HGD 2K2

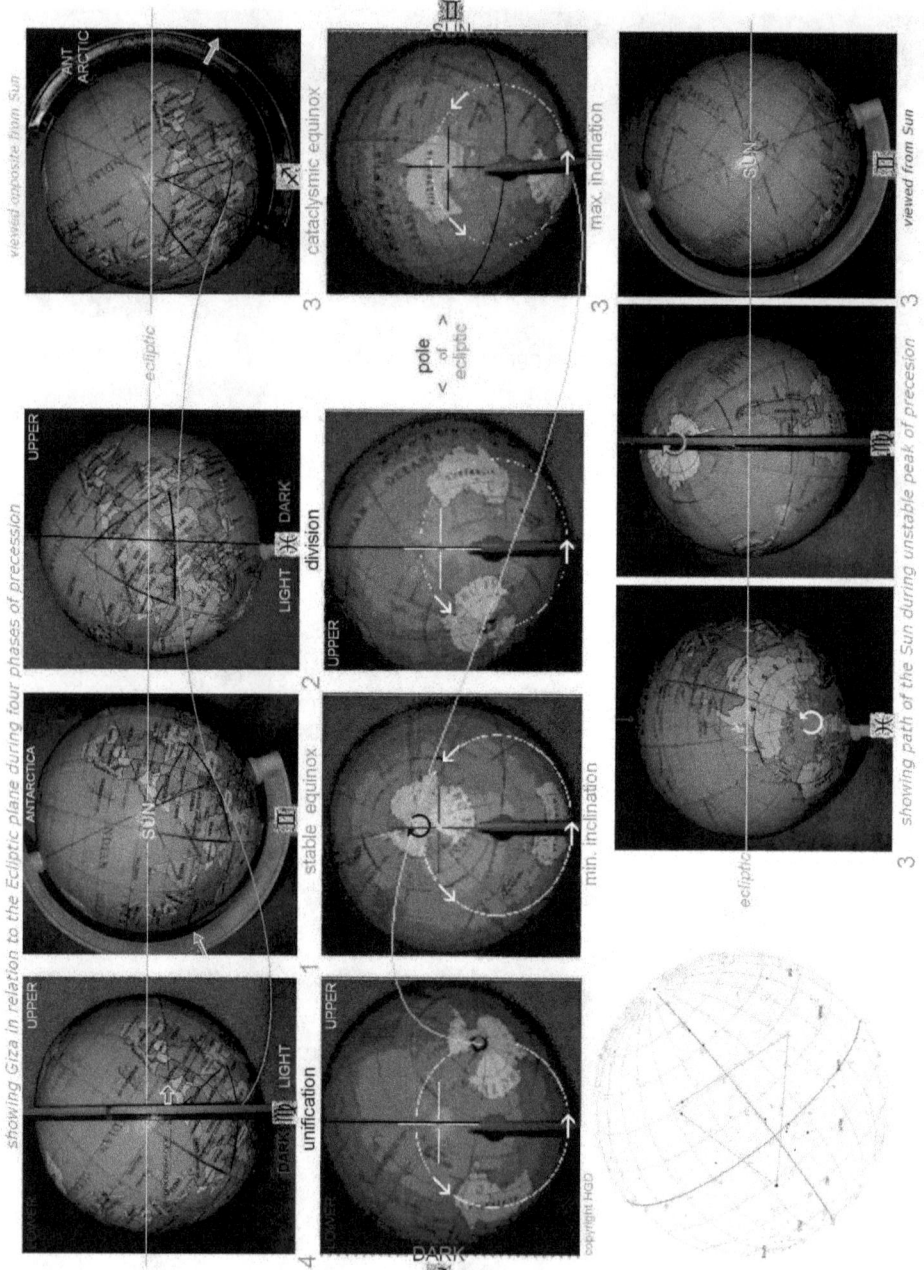

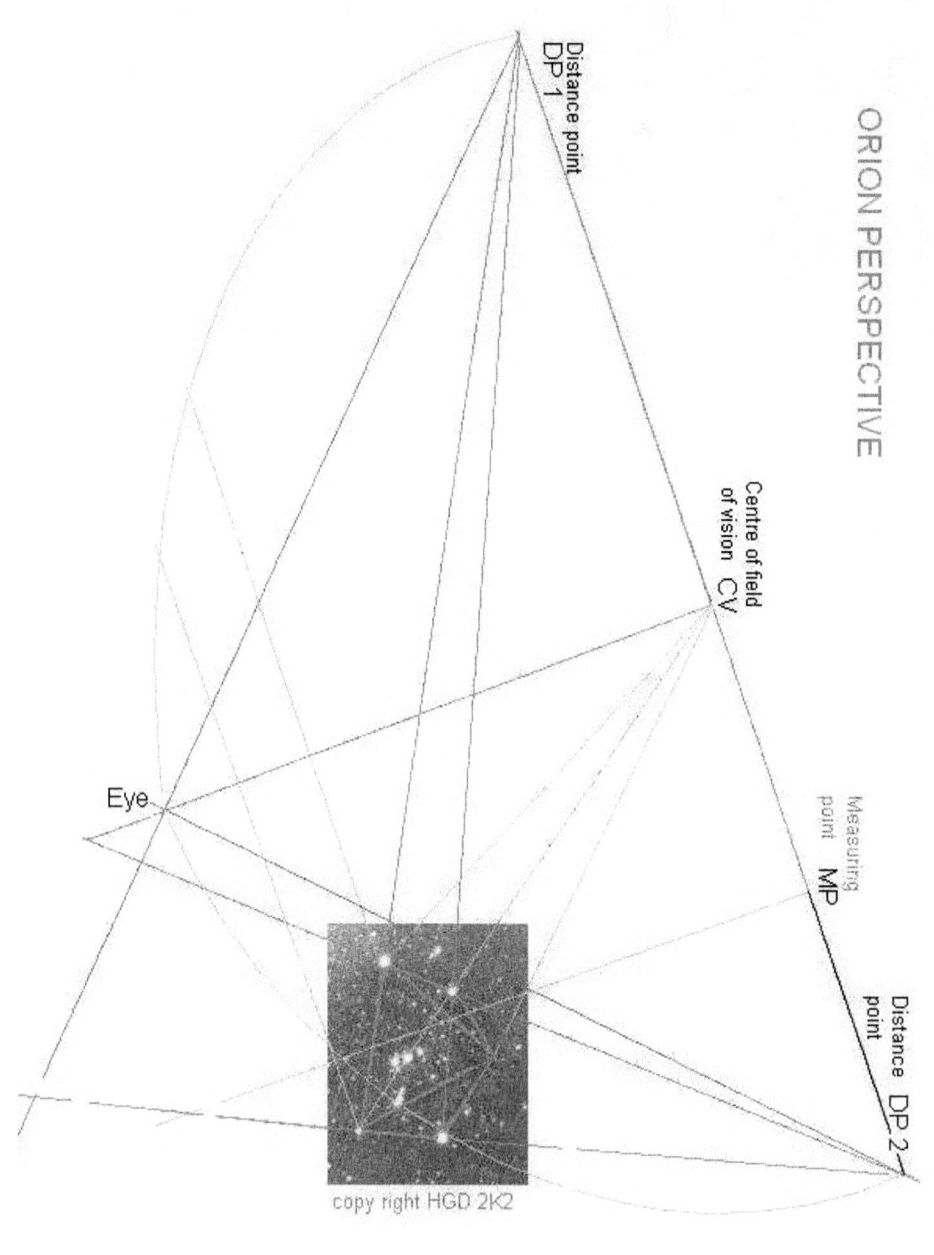

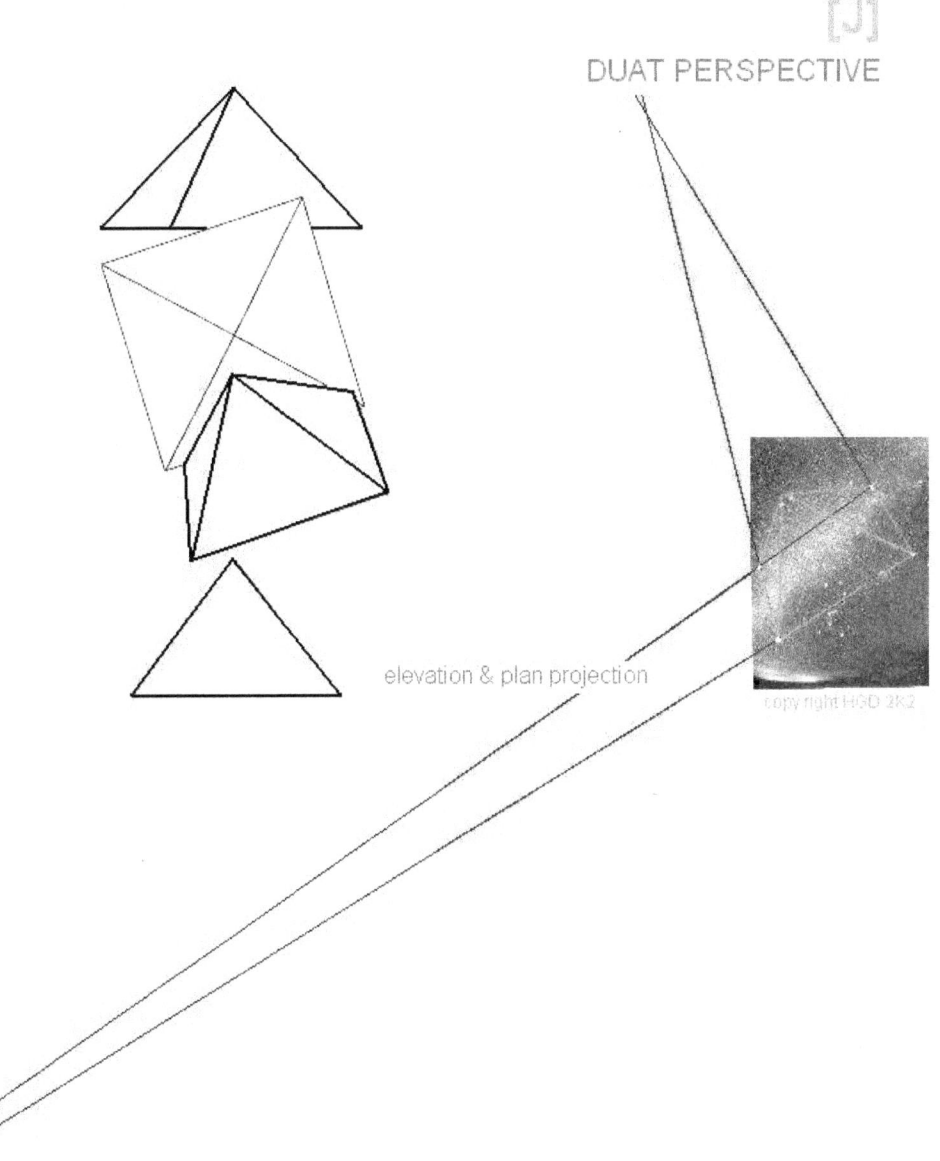

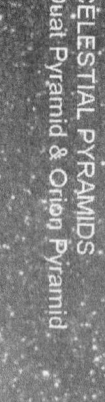

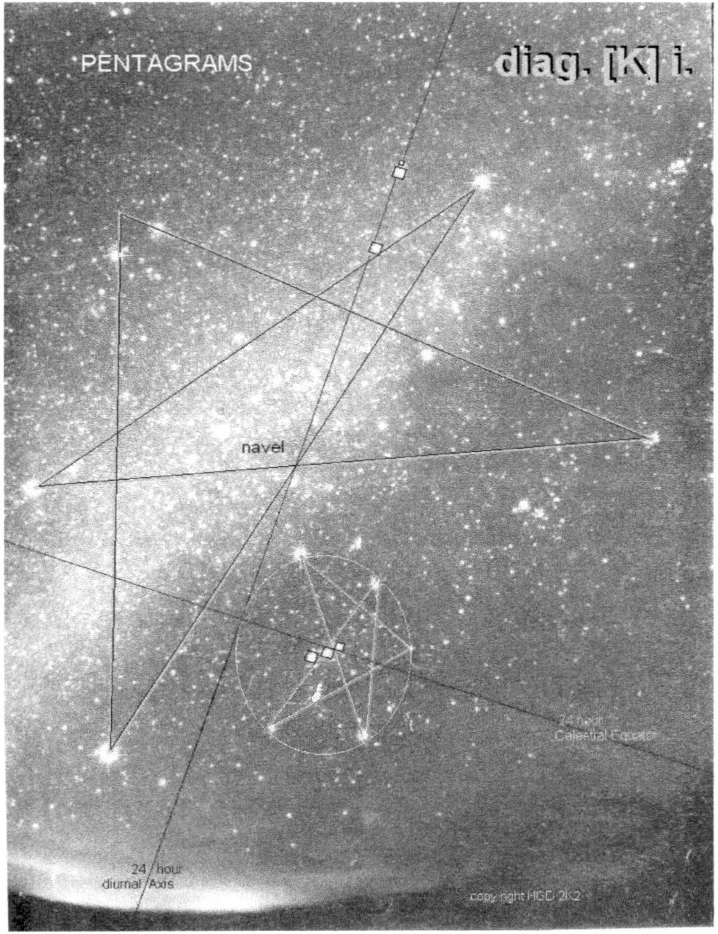

PENTAGRAMS

24 / hour
diurnal / Axis

navel

Equator /
Celestial Equator

copy right HCD 2K2

diag. [K] i.

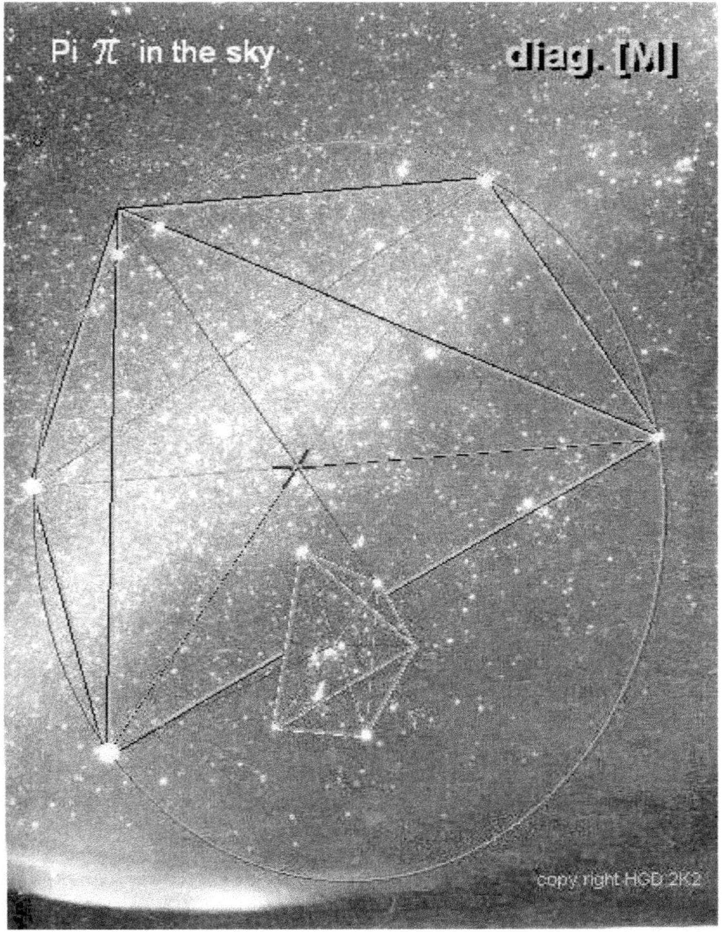

Pi π in the sky

copy right HCD 2K2

diag. [M]

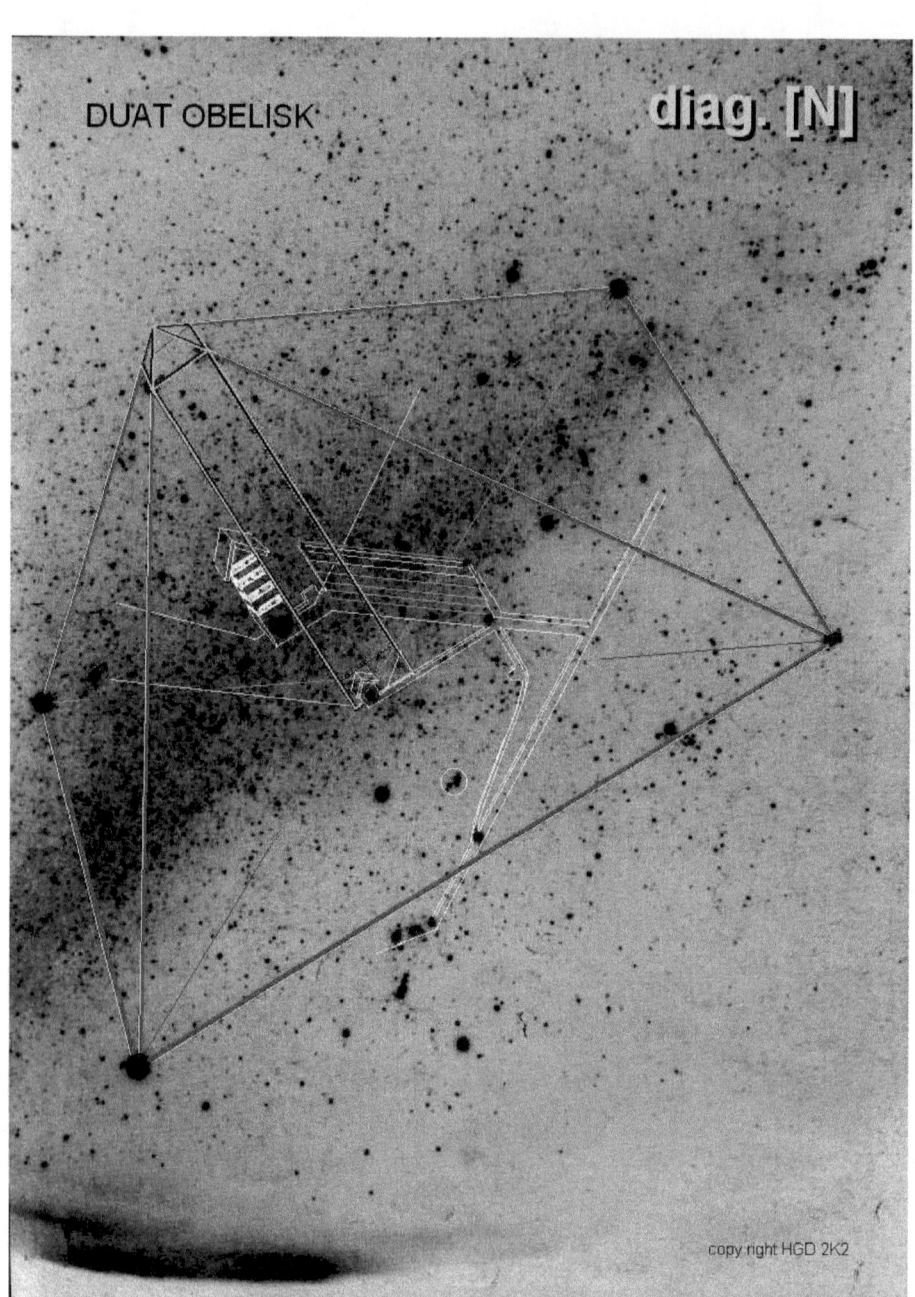

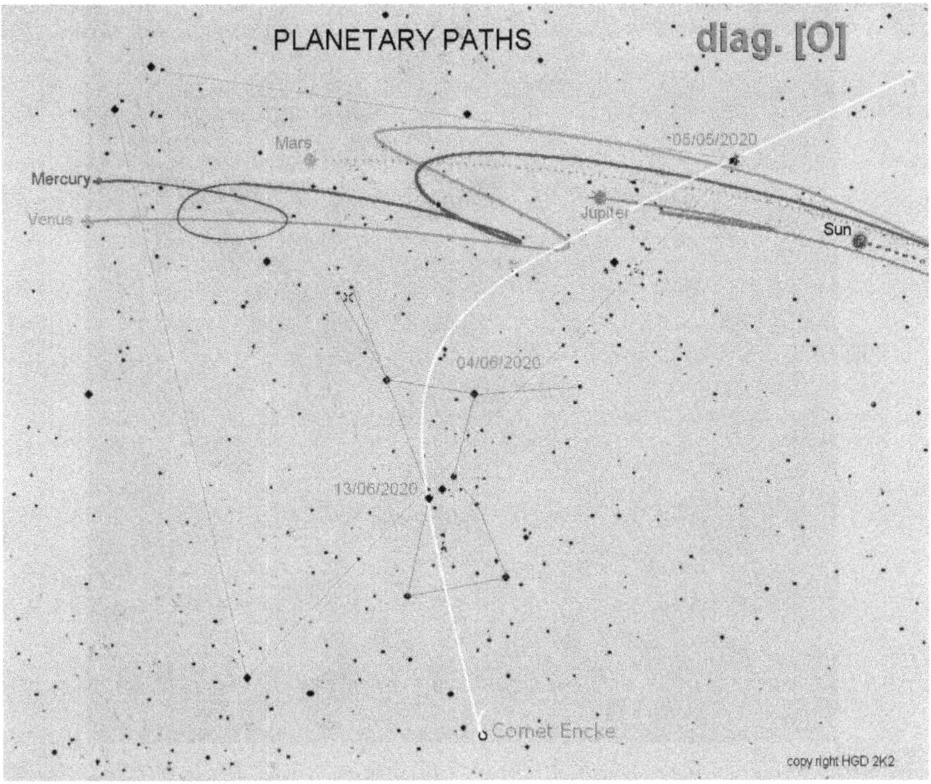

PLANETARY PATHS
diag. [O]
Mars
05/05/2020
Mercury
Venus
Jupiter
Sun
04/06/2020
13/06/2020
Comet Encke
copy right HGD 2K2

Equinox
♓

Solstice
II
CHINA
MONGOLIA

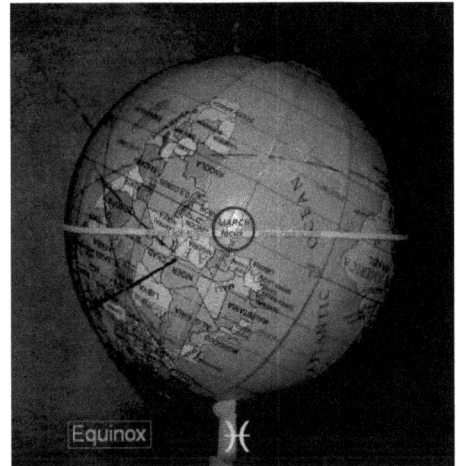

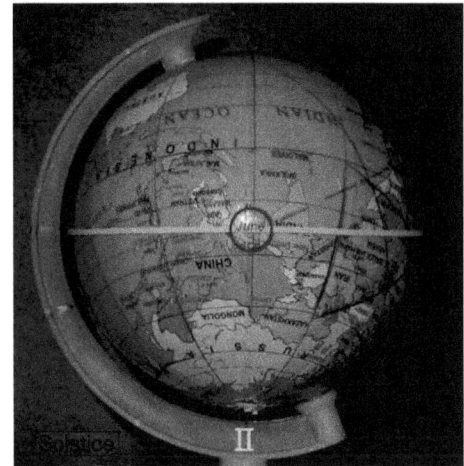

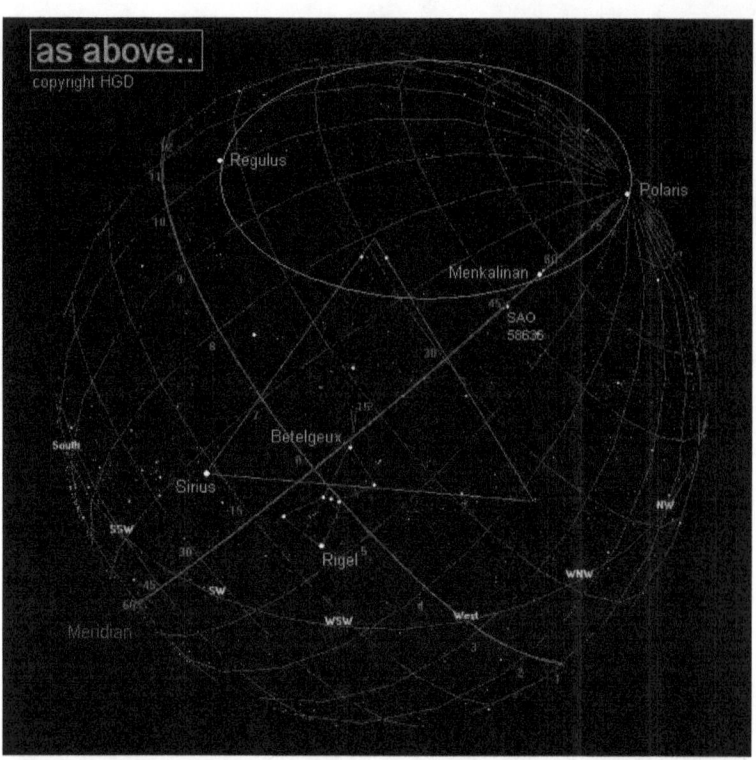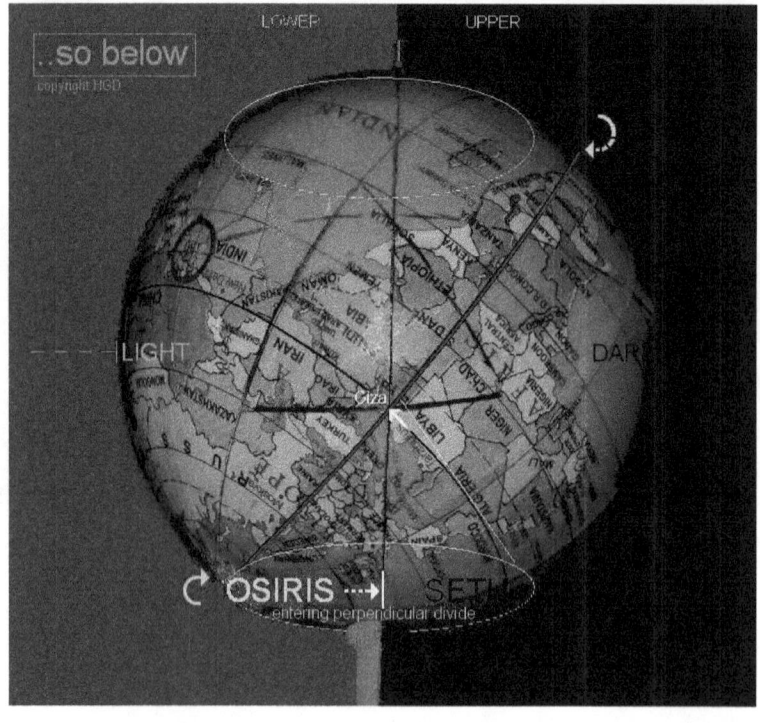

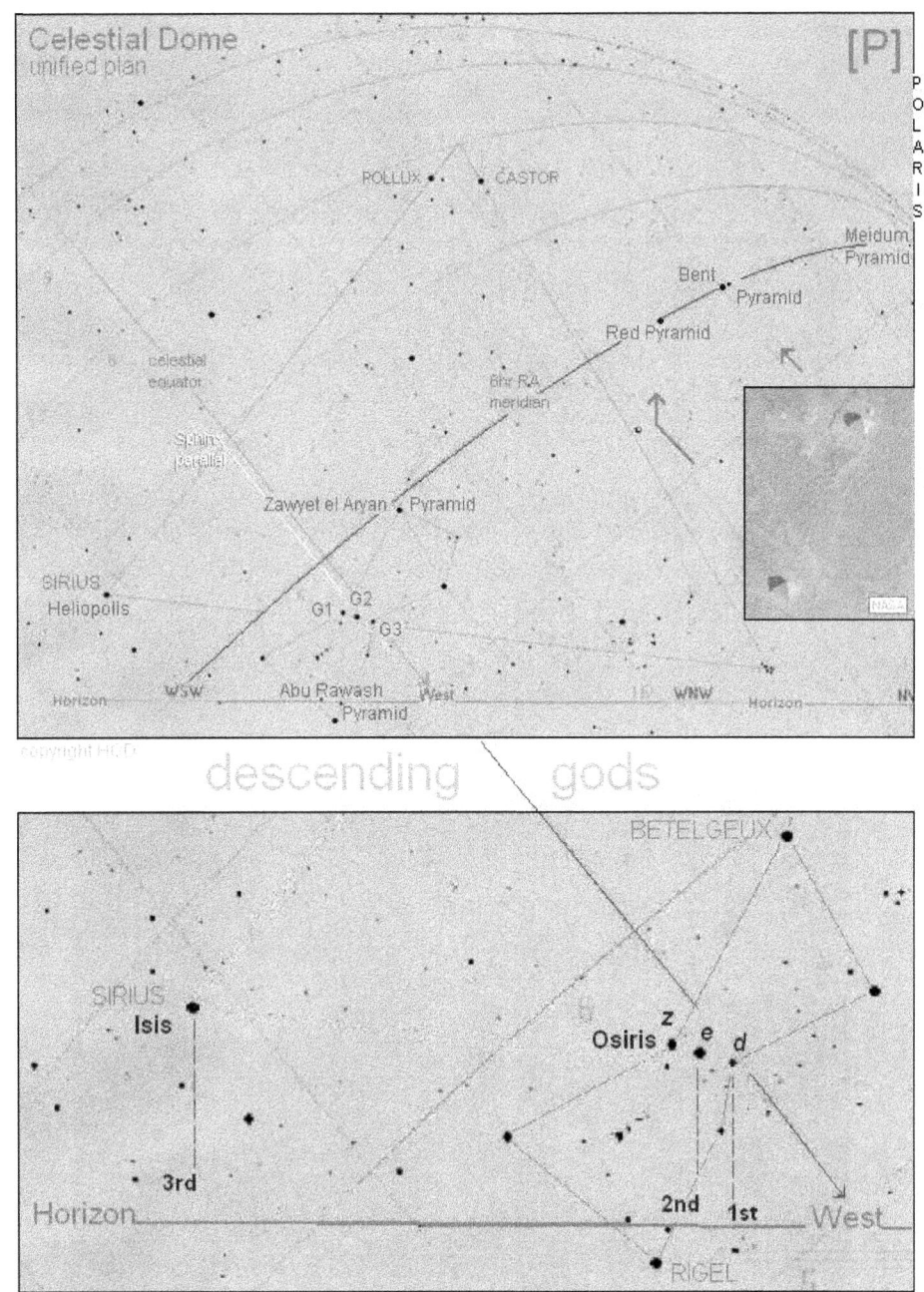

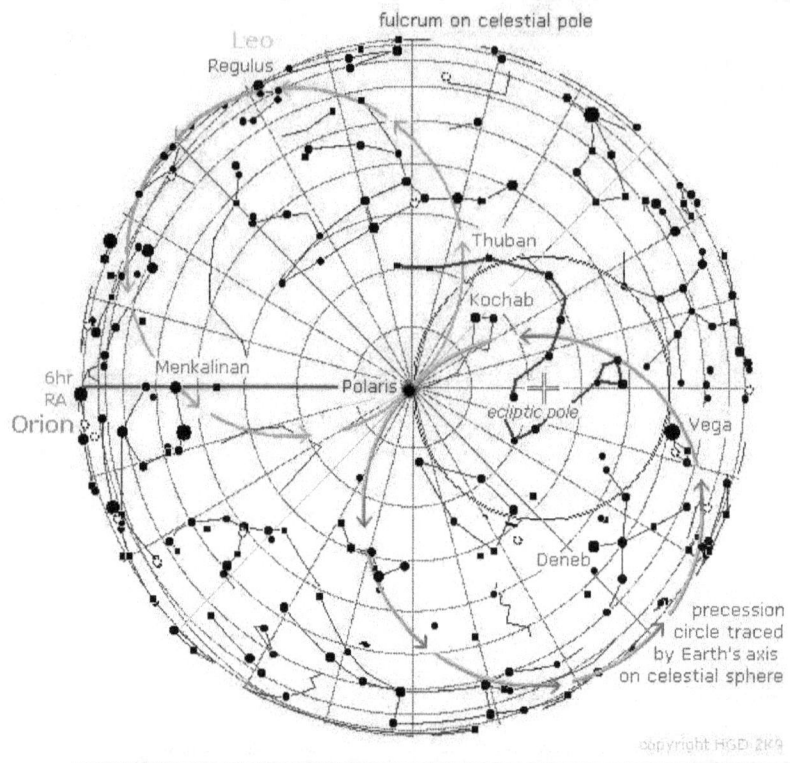

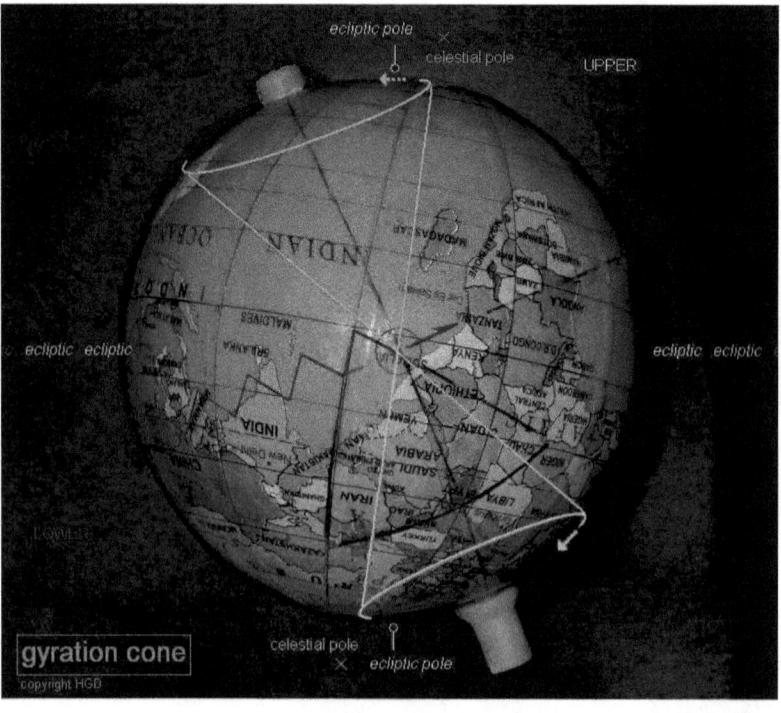

CELESTIAL DIVIDE
copyright HGD
[Q]
UPPER
LOWER
Ursa Minor
POLARIS
Meidum Pyramid
Cepheus
Ursa Major
Camelopardus
Cassiopeia
Lacerta
Leo Minor
Lynx
60
Andromeda
Pegasus
Bent Pyramid
MENKALINAN
Auriga
45
Perseus
Leo
Triangulum
Red Pyramid
SAO 58636
REGULUS
Cancer
Gemini
30
Pleiades
Aries
Pisces
Sextans
Taurus
10
Canis Minor
15
0
BETELGEUX
Zawyet el Aryan
Pyramid
Hydra
Orion
1
Cetus
8
Monoceros
Giza
0
7
3
RIGEL
Abu Rawash
Pyramid
Sculptor
SIRIUS
Heliopolis
6
Pyxis
Canis Major
Lepus
Eridanus
-15
Fornax
Puppis
Columba
Caelum
Horologium

spin
Night
Day
ecliptic pole
'conventional path'
UPPER
'alternative path'
copyright HGD

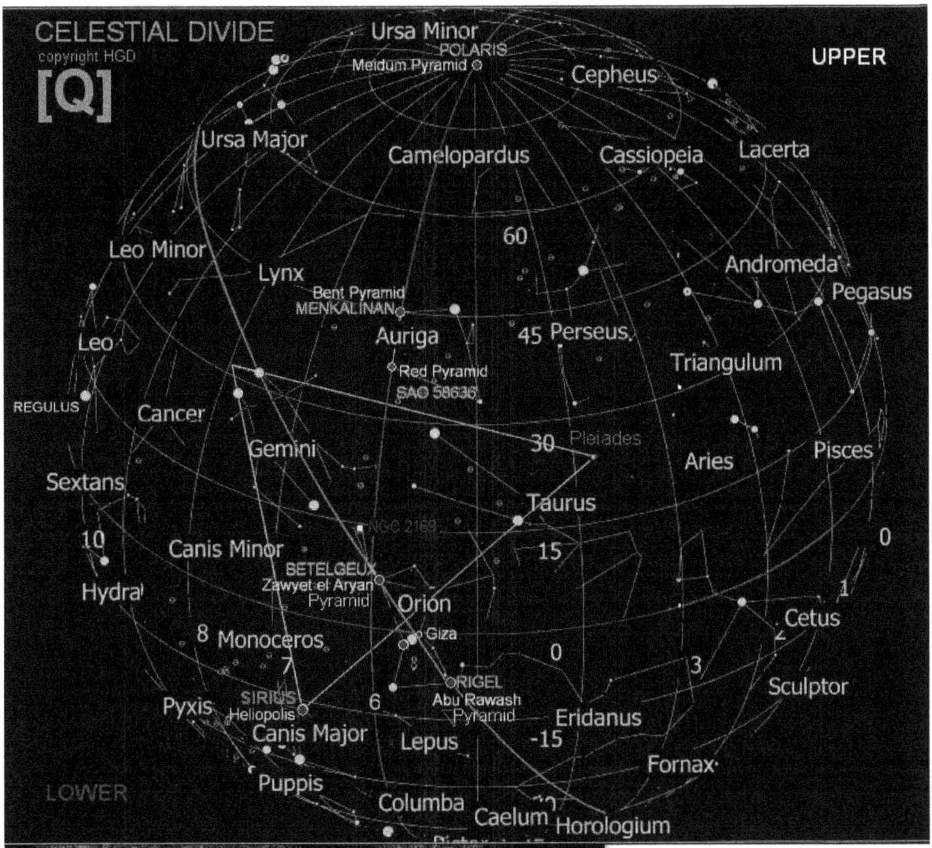

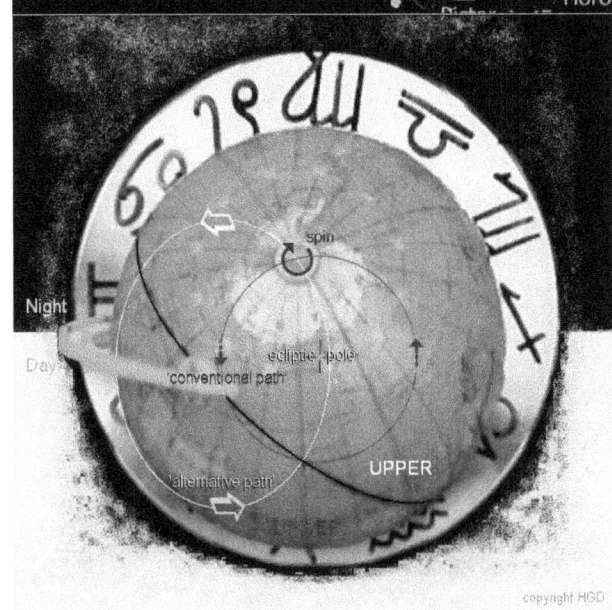

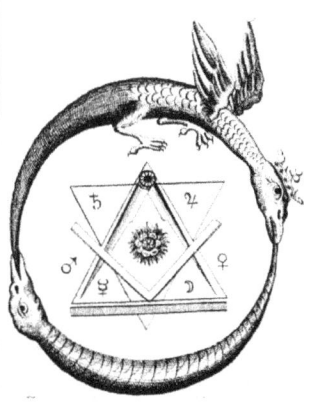

impact direction & collision crater
N.pole
spin
S.pole

gyration
precession
model
TWO LANDS
DIVIDE
38°
Polaris / Meidum
MERIDIAN
52°
NIGHT
rotation
precessional
EQUATOR
spin
Solstice
PLANE of ORBIT
present era
Ecliptic path
Equinox
DAY
cataclysmic
Ecliptic
Giza
POLAR AXIS
precession
AXIS
copyright HGD 2K4

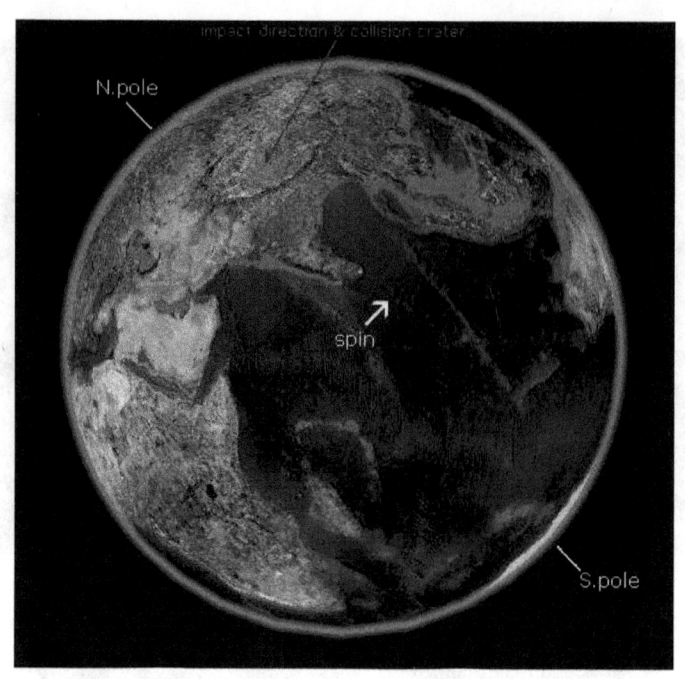

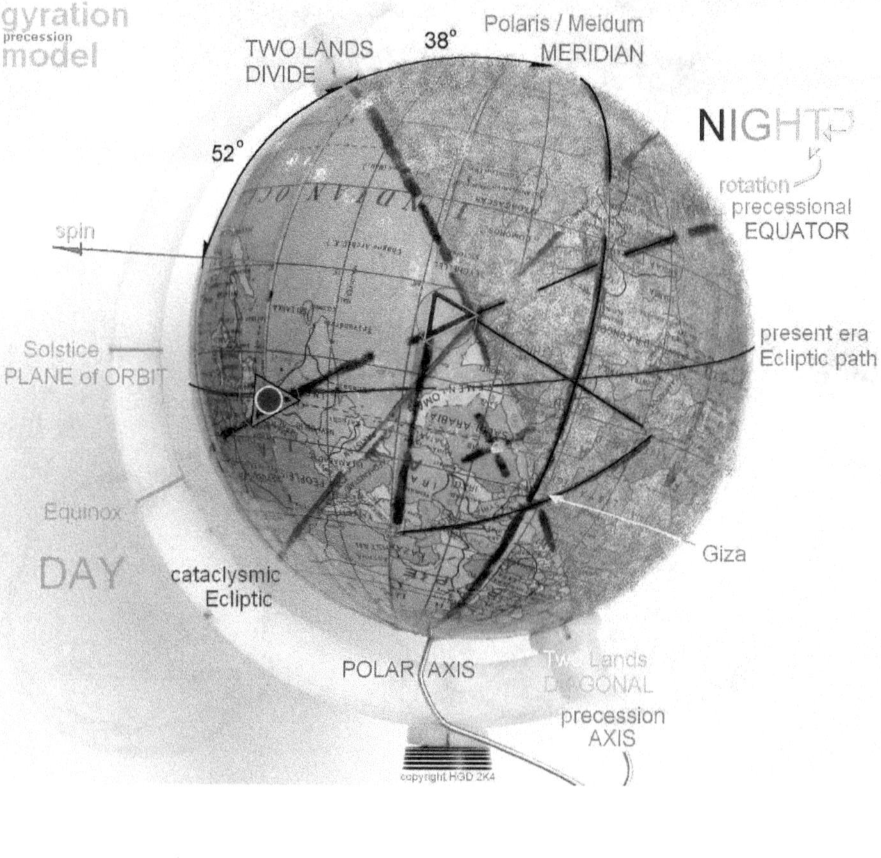

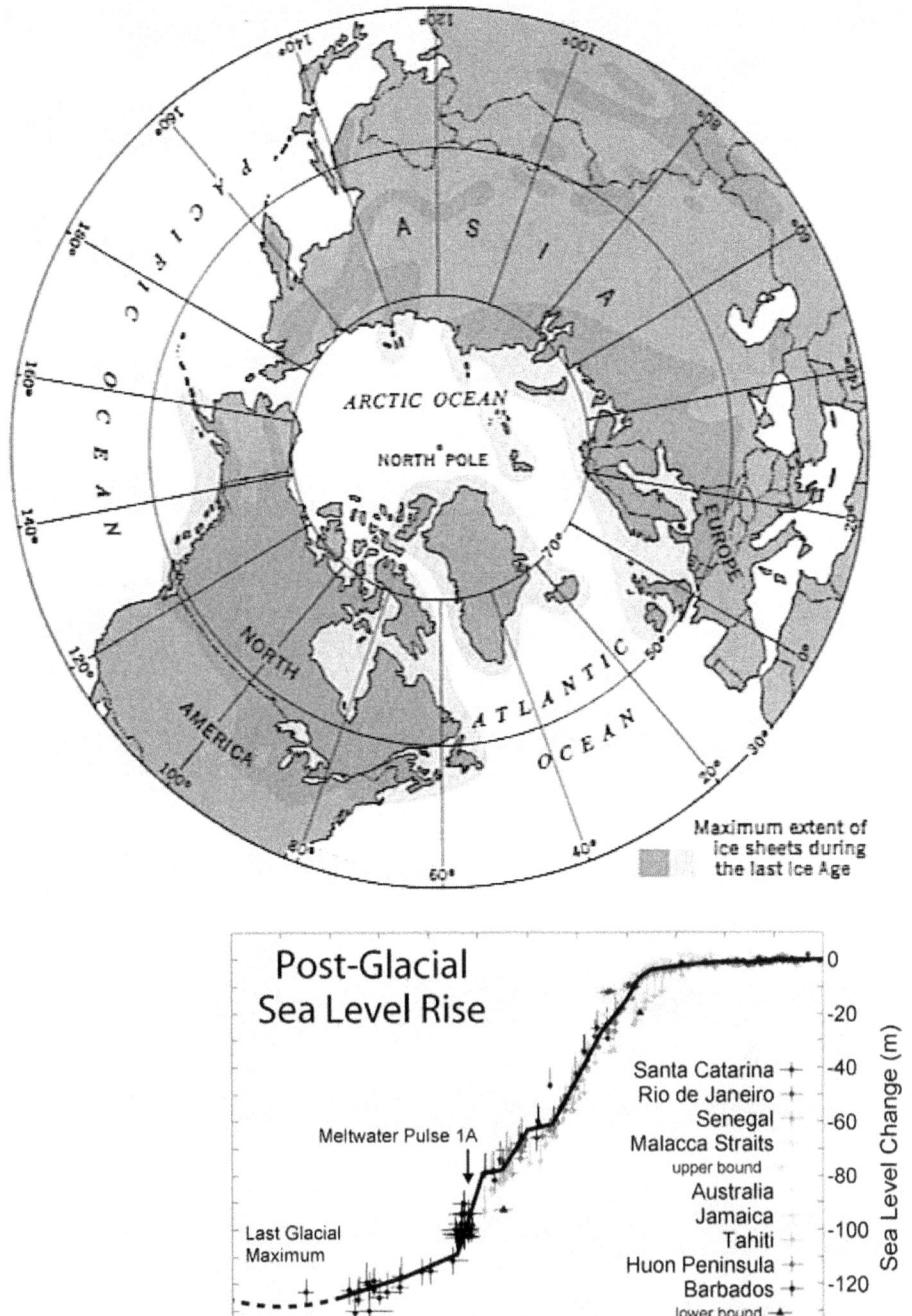

GALAXY ARMS   to POLARIS &
               Meidum Pyramid

SAO 40756   RA 5H 59' 55"
MENKALINAN   RA 5H 59' 30"
Bent Pyramid
Auriga
CASTOR
POLLUX
Red Pyramid
SAO 58636   RA 5H 59' 43"

PLEIADES
ALHENA
Seven Sages
Open Cluster
NGC 2169
SAO 113389   ALDEBARAN
E
BETELGEUX
Zawyet el Aryan
Pyramid
Giza
  E D
Z   ORIONIS
                Declination
                measurements
SC-HIS   0°
Line   Latitude   W
SIRIUS   RIGEL
Heliopolis   Abu Rawash
             Pyramid
             Two Lane
             Diagonal
6 Hour
Right Ascension

copyright HGD

Orion
Pup   CMa   Aur   Cas   Ph.5
New Outer Arm Perseus
Vel   Cep
        Carina-Sagittarius
Cen   Norma   Cygnus
        Crux-Scutum   GC
                                Cyg
Nor
                                Aql
        Sagittarius

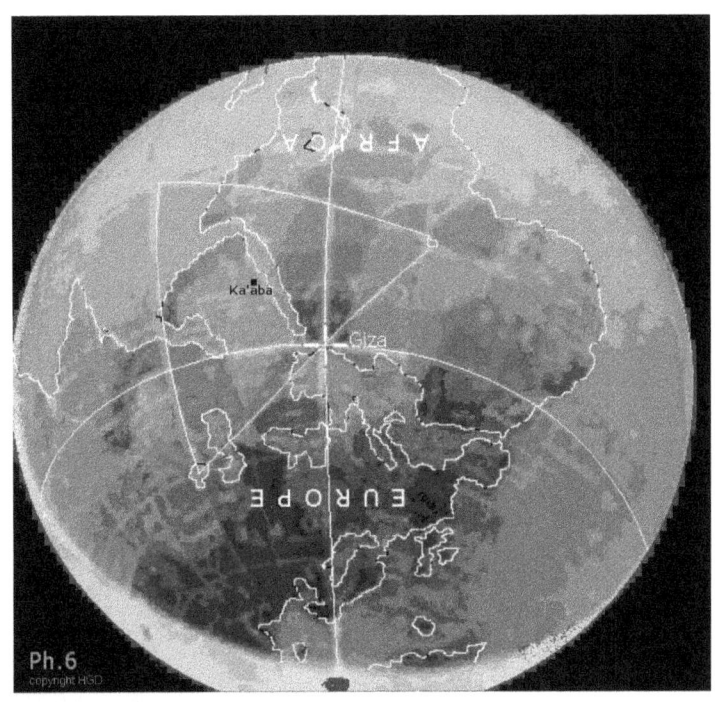

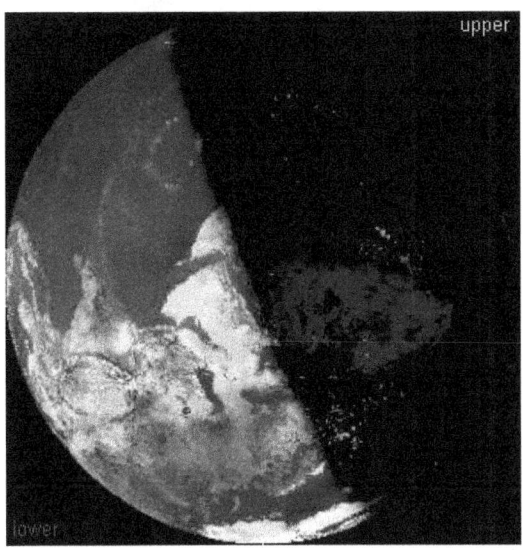

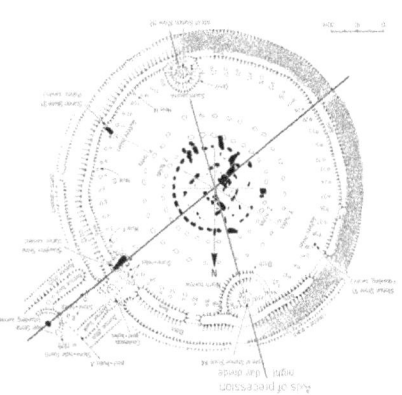

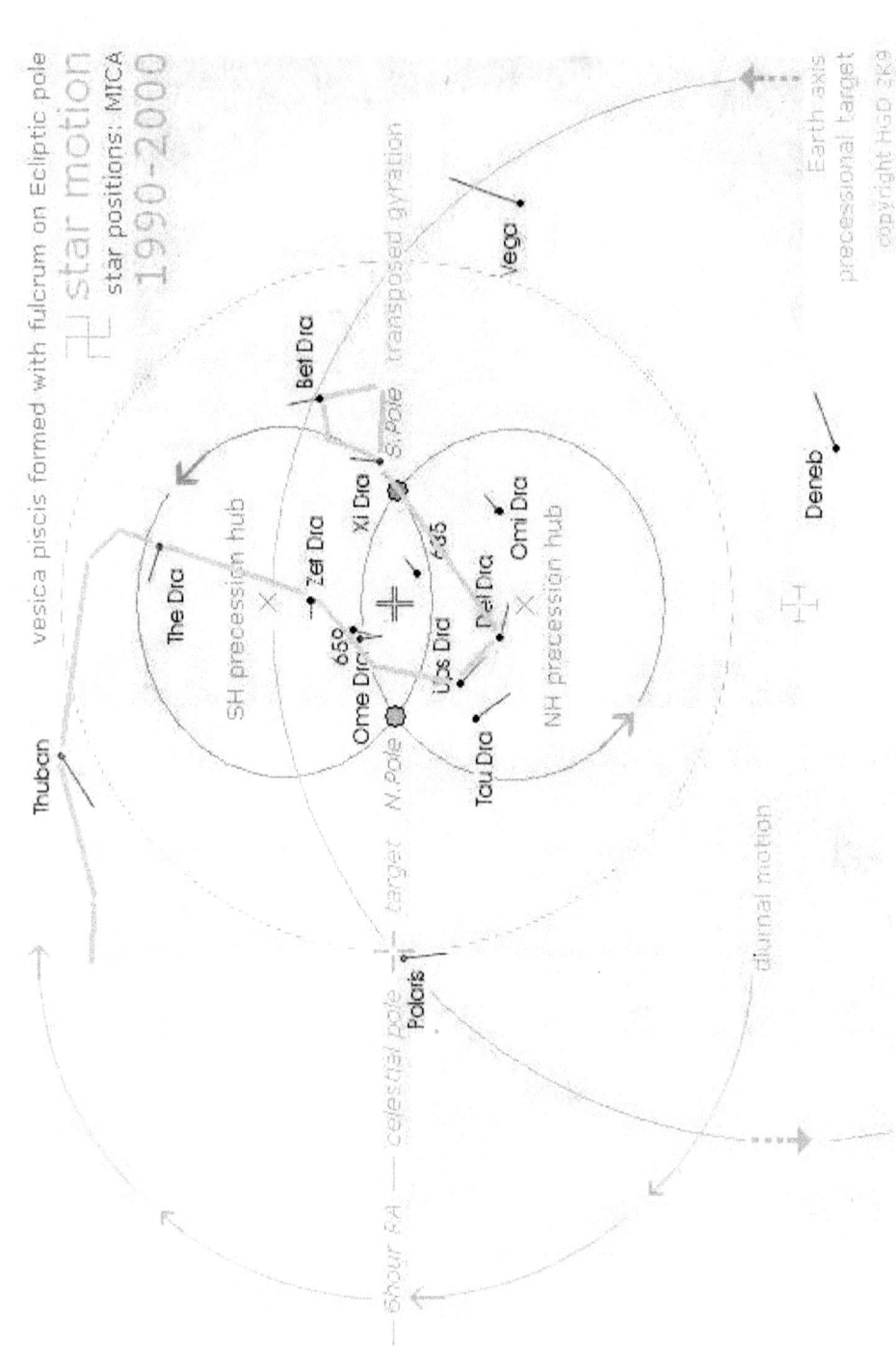

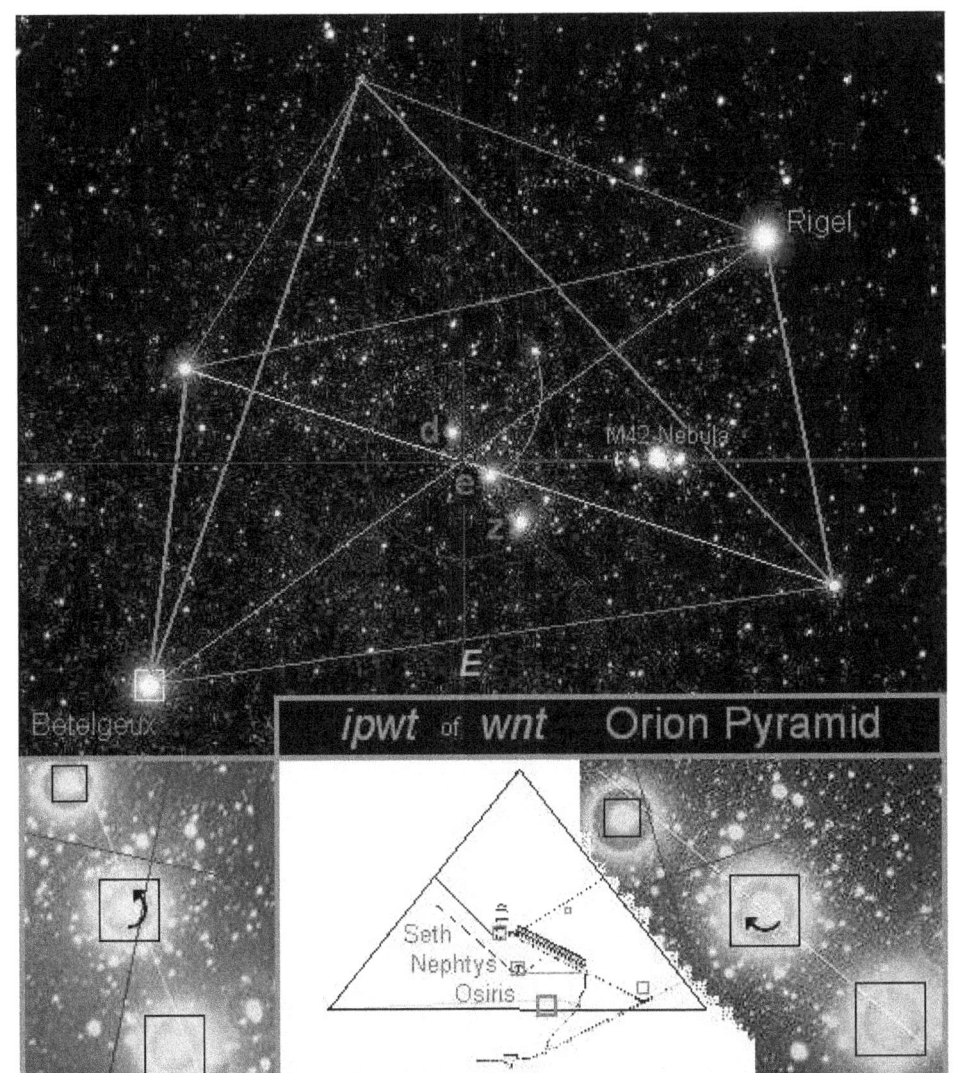

Ph.4

Ph.3

Ph.2

Ph.1

'...this pyramid of the king is Osiris, this construction of his is Osiris.'
{PT.Utt.600}

Chapter 4
CORRELATION

[A] **Orion:** stick man, persona, constellation

'I shall not be turned back at the gates of the Duat. I ascend to the sky with Orion...'

{Coffin Text 236}

In the quest for eternal life, Egyptian kings were enticed by the heavens. Now, thousands of years later, still compelled by survival, we are urged to pursue the meaningful association with stars in seeking the source of rebirth.

Orion is profusely cited in ancient funerary compositions and is among the most notable of constellations that grace our night sky. Situated on one of the outer spiral arms of the Galaxy, where star birth literally takes place, this famous constellation is set in the surrounds that constitute the Duat -an area of the sky referred to in legend but not defined in contemporary astronomy. I will do so in detail and elaborate on the concept as we progress. Orion is uniquely located on the celestial equator and we will see how this is of great relevance. It will also be demonstrated how these stars form part of different geometrical arrangements, yet maintain the same uncorrupted cohesion, particularly in respect of their rising and setting characteristics. Mythology attempts to describe scientific astral events but is composed in abstract. We will delve deeper into that in sections to follow but first, as the topography is integral throughout this work, it is paramount that we acquaint ourselves with the composite: produced here in its most rudimentary depiction, in standard astronomy lines, is the stick-like figure that represents the constellation of Orion and labeled with names of relevant stars.

'Behold he has come as Orion, behold Osiris has come as Orion...
O king, the sky conceives you with Orion, the dawn-light bears
you with Orion... you will regularly ascend with Orion from the
Eastern region of the sky, you will regularly descend with Orion in
the Western region of the sky... your third is Sothis...'

{Pyramid Text 820-2}

In Greek mythology, Orion was the fearsome and arrogant hunter. There are various accounts and many artistic depictions of his form. In Egyptian lore, we'll focus on *Sah*, 'the far strider' and Osiris, who was 'long of leg' and 'lengthy of stride'. From funerary texts we can also deduce that the king was somehow conceived as a reincarnation in Orion. For the benefit of familiarity and easy identification, we transpose the stars over a realistic human form: of the three that constitute the head of Orion, the star Meissa is most prominent. The four stars that outline his body are Betelgeux and Bellatrix -these represent his shoulders, while Saiph and Rigel represent his knees and foot. The three celebrated stars that form his belt are midway between these four. They consist of the three primary stars: Alnitak, Alnilam and Mintaka. In astronomical jargon, the Greek Alphabet (lower case) is used for identification purposes of stars within the same constellation. The brightest star is usually Alpha (α) and others would follow in alphabetical order, as determined by their brightness.

Alnitak	= zeta	(ζ) Orionis,
Alnilam	= epsilon	(ε) Orionis,
Mintaka	= delta	(δ) Orionis.

His sword is suspended from the belt and made up of an open cluster, several stars and one of the finest nebulae visible with the naked eye. The M42 Nebula (Latin for cloud) in Orion's sword is the most conspicuous and some 1600 light years distant from Earth. Nebulae can be formed by stellar birth or the death of a star.

The stars in Orion's Belt are approximately 1400 light-years distant and proper motion is negligible. The quantity we term proper motion, is perpendicular to our sight and any movements, in respect of background stars, are small due to the immense distances and only discernable over very long periods. Sirius, on the other hand, at approximately 8.4 light years distance, is among the closest stars to Earth and exhibits larger proper motion. Identified with the goddess Isis, Sirius is the brightest of all stars observable from Earth and is situated in the constellation of Canis Major, adjacent to Orion.

Bauval demonstrated the Queens Chamber South shaft's alignment with Sirius and that the Kings Chamber South shaft aligned with zeta-Orionis on the astronomical meridian. The three pyramids at Giza and the three stars in Orion's Belt form a match. I want to reiterate that it is not my desire to unduly discredit the work of other researchers, but it should be pointed out that the figure correlation, as presented in *The Orion Mystery*, is skewed. I will expand on that in the sections to follow and also reveal how a wider correlation of stars and pyramids unequivocally form part of a great concept. First, I want to clarify the relation between the Giza plateau and the mythical Rostau through an ingenious approach to the interpretation of texts, which will give greater insight into the concept of ground-sky dualism.

[B] Celestial Rostau

Identifying the Neteru star-gods of the first time.

The gods *(stars)* are born in the East. They are the four children *(stars)* of the sky goddess Nut: Osiris, Isis, Seth and Nephtys. These gods are associated with stars in an area of the sky that hosts the constellation of Orion. This diagram depicts the celestial domain of Rostau and stellar counterparts of the gods of ancient myth. From various inscriptions it is known that the Egyptians associated the star Sirius with the goddess Isis. Further hypothesis identifies the principal belt star with the god Osiris.

Their birth, in effect, is demonstrated to be associated with observance of their appearance above the horizon. Hypothetically, let's assume that this epoch dawned c.12000BC and for the time being, disregard the astronomical technicalities of perceived motion and proper motion. The 'First Time' of Sirius can be interpreted as the time when the bright star of Isis made an appearance above the horizon. Orion would have been at minimum declination. This is a result of the pendulum motion of the horizon against the background of the sky, caused by the Earth's axial precession, which takes thousands of years to complete a cycle. A subsequent rebirth is enacted annually, when Sirius performs a heliacal rising -another term for its first appearance, after a seasonal absence and occurs at dawn, when it can be observed as resting on the horizon. This event could be witnessed from Giza, situated at 30 degrees North latitude. Known as the Sothic Cycle, it occurs every 365 days and forms the basis of the Sothic Calendar. Among thousands of stars, Sirius happens to be the only one that exhibits this exactness of motion. This again demonstrates the astronomical insight of the ancients. The texts describe the rebirth of the star Sirius and dual interpretation that demonstrate the association of gods with stars:

'The sky is pregnant of wine, Nut has given birth to her daughter in the dawn light, I raise myself indeed... my third is Sothis...'

{Pyramid Text 1082-3}

Mythical terminology:
'Your sister (Isis) comes rejoicing for love of you. You (Osiris) have placed her on your phallus and your seed issues in her, she being ready as Sothis (Isis), and Horus Sopd has come forth from you as Horus in Sothis.'

{Pyramid Text 632}

Stellar terminology:
'Your sister *(Sirius)* comes to you rejoicing for love of you. You *(z-Orionis)* have placed her on your phallus and your seed issues into her, she being ready as Sothis *(Sirius),* and Horus *(Saiph?the Sun)* has come forth from you as Horus who is in Sothis.'

{Pyramid Text 632}

'Thoth and Horus then come to help Osiris to the sky; Horus comes, Thoth appears, they raise Osiris from upon his side and make him stand... Raise yourself, o Osiris, Isis has your arm, o Osiris; Nephtys has your hand so *go between them*. The sky is Given to you, and the Fields of Rushes, the Mounds of Horus, and the Mounds of Seth...'

{Pyramid Text 959-61}

This text also provides us with a clue and substantiates the position of Osiris -i.e. between Isis and Nephtys. *But where is Nephtys?* The ancients associated the star Sirius with the goddess Isis. Further association of the star z-Orionis (Alnitak) with the god Osiris is deduced through correlation. We recall that the shaft from the Kings Chamber aligned with its celestial counterpart. The star **z**-Orionis (Osiris) equates then to being between the star Sirius

(Isis) and the star **e**-Orionis (Nephtys). With these clues and vivid interpretation, I postulate the association of Nephtys and Seth with the Orion Belt asterism as follow:

'...*you* will regularly *ascend* with Orion from the Eastern region of the sky, *you* will regularly *descend* with Orion in the Western region of the sky... *your* third is Sothis (Isis)...'

{Pyramid Text 820-2}

If *'you'* and *'your'* could be interpreted as Osiris in this context, and the text tells us that: '...*your third* is Isis...' -then it would be reasonable to deduce that; *your second* to be Nephtys, and; *your first* to be Seth. This is the order in which these stars make their appearance (ascend) in relation to the star **z**-Orionis (Osiris) above the Eastern horizon: Seth (1), Nephtys (2), followed by Osiris (0) and then Isis (3). The reader will recall that the Greek name for the star Sirius is Sothis, which was used in the translation of the Pyramid Texts. Some texts are in the first person term: *'my'*

'The sky is pregnant of wine, Nut has given birth to her daughter in the dawn light, I raise myself indeed... *my third is Sothis*...'

{Pyramid Text 1082-3}

Their setting (descend) below the Western horizon repeats this numerical order in relation to Osiris: Seth *first*, Nephtys *second* and Isis *third*. This defines the remarkable aspect of the constellation of Orion as an ideogram of deeper symbolical meaning -a concept, where numerically, Osiris represents *'zero'*. The difference in declination is minutes of a degree. *see* diag.[P]

There is much debate around the brightness of the stars versus the size of the pyramids and perhaps the order of descent or declination variance can be considered. I will explain in the following sections the cosmic duality of Rostau and demonstrate the complex notion, mentioned at the beginning of this chapter, namely pyramids=stars=gods. What otherwise sounds like magical tales, difficult to fathom, can now, for better comprehension, be depicted schematically. This is done by introducing geometry, which as we go along, becomes the major medium of interpretation and for clarification of the ancient star cult. A line, which I refer to as the 'Sothis line', forms a trinity with the star Sirius, associated with Isis -the mother of Horus, via the star z-Orionis (Osiris -the father of Horus) and connecting to e-Orionis (Nephtys -the consort sister) the middle star in Orion's belt. The angle of this line would vary depending on the epoch due to proper motion of Sirius, but it connects to the fixed intersection of a diagonal axis formed by the four stars, which define the outline figure of Orion -i.e. between his shoulders and knees. In summary, the star Sirius is the goddess Isis, while the three stars in Orion's Belt are the gods Osiris, his sister Nephtys and their brother Seth. Rostau is located in the constellation of Orion and has a counterpart on the ground at Giza.

'I am Osiris, I have come to Rostau in order to know the secret of the Duat... I live on white emmer, filling the Winding Waterway...'

{Coffin Text 241}

'I have passed over the paths of Rostau, whether on water or land... they are at the limit of the sky'

{Coffin Text 1035}

The Dogon, a tribe of Mali, are reportedly in possession of incredible information concerning the binary system of the star Sirius. It has been argued, as a possible explanation, that they could have been informed of this by a French scientist in the 1930's. This African tribe, however, worships Sirius and have deep rooted traditions involving the cycles of Sirius B. Known as Sirius A and B, the latter is a dwarf star visible only by means of powerful telescopes and orbits Sirius A in cycles of 50 years.

Another controversial theory is that the Dogon's tradition evolved from Egypt. Nowadays it's in vogue to surmise the Egyptians stemmed from other African races... whatever the case, the question of how sophisticated knowledge was obtained in the first place still remains. Knowledge more than 5000 years old, yet surpassing that held by modern science was possessed by the ancient Egyptians in the pre-dynastic times, before 3200BC. With systematic progression through the chapters that follow, the reader will be able to verify the truth of that for 'self.

The dwarf star, Sirius B, is the object of another theory on the possible identity of Horus. This is based on the passage which states that Horus is *in* Sothis (the star Sirius). A parallel exists also with Jesus in the womb of Mary. During the early stages of formulating my hypothesis, I proposed that the star Saiph, which marks the heliacal rising of Sirius, correlates with Horus -the divine *sun* and god of Letopolis -possibly associated with the geographic proximity of a Temple. It seems most likely however, that the true association lies in the relationship of the Earth and the Sun –through the Ecliptic -omnipotent influence on our planet. More light will be shed on that in the conclusion chapter.

[C] Terrestrial Rostau

'All the world which lies below has been set in order and filled with contents by the things which are placed above; for the things below have not the power to set in order the world above.'

(*Kore Kosmou*)

The anthropomorphic stars of the gods.

This diagram relates the Egyptian legend of the gods, who were 'born in the sky and inhabited the Earth', as referred to in various ancient texts. It identifies the terrestrial region of Rostau and geographic counter parts of the gods. Pyramids are demonstrated here as being the geographical counter parts of the gods. The duality involves celestial and terrestrial mapping of sky and Earth longitude meridians therefore, when side by side comparisons are made cardinal directions become inverted. This unfortunately creates some confusion, although it is a phenomenon known to astronomers as well. The effect would be the same if one held a road map or atlas up to the sky and tried to orientate it, then placed it on the ground and orientated it. East and West will correlate, but North-South will be inverted –and just in case the reader wondered why this whole book is 'right side up' it's to facilitate side by side comparison. The diagrams are intended to be viewed as though one is looking at a true image of Egypt, in the sky, while standing on Earth. The same as if one was in the sky and looking at Egypt on Earth with the pyramids representing stars. It is not a mirror image but a true image. When applying this to a map it would therefore be 'swung down' and the North-South cardinals would be inverted. In the next section, with topographical maps, I discuss it again and further clarify this orientation issue. The region which encompassed the cities of Heliopolis, Letopolis and the Giza pyramids was a symbolic landscape, with its counterpart in the sky: Orion dwells along the banks of the Milky Way. Bauval demonstrated a resemblance between the layout of the three pyramids at Giza and the three stars in Orion's Belt. He pointed out that the Southern shaft of the Kings Chamber was directed at the star z-Orionis. It can be deduced that the shaft, emanating from the Great Pyramid, was thus aligned with its celestial counterpart. In the previous section it was demonstrated how the stars can be associated with the gods. The Orion correlation theory (OCT) is thus further corroborated and the idea expanded with Rostau having a terrestrial equivalent –a geographical counter parts of the gods. Sothis (Sirius) correlates with the obelisk of Sesostris I, at Heliopolis. It is thought to be the place where the sanctuary of the Phoenix once stood and which housed the sacred Benben during the Pyramid Age. The two obelisks of Alexandria (Cleopatra's Needles), had originally stood in the great Sun Temple of Heliopolis. The diagonal, which I refer to as the 'sothis line', extends from Heliopolis (Isis associated) to Giza, where it passes through the Great Pyramid (Osiris) and continues to the South-West of the Second Pyramid (Nephtys). Is this iconic of the Ecliptic of a certain age perhaps? Furthermore, the Third Pyramid (Seth) may be more accurately referred to as the '*First* Pyramid'.

It was demonstrated in the previous section how this line connects to the intersect convergence of two intersecting diagonal lines that form a cross, by the four stars of the outline figure of Orion, between his shoulders and his knees. Letopolis existed before the Pyramid Age, and is believed to have served as the geodetic marker for other sites in the area. According to Egyptologist Georges Goyon (*Le Secret des Batisseurs des Grandes Pyramides; Kheops*) the Great Pyramid is aligned on a meridian with Letopolis. Horus is associated with Letopolis, which is due West of the Temple of the Phoenix at Heliopolis, the sacred mound and great temple of the sun god, Ra. This configuration constitutes a Pythagorean triangle.

Geodetic terminology:
'Your sister (Obelisk@Heliopolis) comes rejoicing for love of you. You (Great Pyramid) have placed her on your phallus and your seed issues in her, she being ready as Sothis, and Horus Sopd (Temple@Letopolis@Nahaya?) has come forth from you as Horus in Sothis.'

{Pyramid Text 632}

'Thoth and Horus then come to help Osiris to the sky; Horus comes, Thoth appears, they raise Osiris from upon his side and make him stand... Raise yourself, o Osiris, Isis has your arm, o Osiris; Nephtys has your hand so *go between them*. The sky is given to you, and the Fields of Rushes, the Mounds [pyramids] of Horus, and the Mounds [pyramids] of Seth...'

{Pyramid Text 959-61}

The above text also provides us with a clue and substantiates the position of Osiris; i.e. between Isis and Nephtys. Terrestrially that equates to the Great Pyramid (Osiris or his throne) being between Heliopolis (Isis associated) and the Second Pyramid (Nephtys). According to legend, Seth was married to his twin sister Nephtys, but despite this, her loyalties were with Osiris. The name Nephtys means, 'Lady of the House' and refers to the Palace of Osiris, the Great Pyramid. This will be reinforced and demonstrated in the next section. Betelgeuse and Rigel are the two principal stars and most conspicuous of the four that comprise the outline figure of Orion. However, it is not inconceivable that architectural features mark the 'geographic positions' of the stars Saiph and Bellatrix as well. An archaeological inspection could determine whether it is the case. *see* maps [x].

The Southern shaft of the Queen's Chamber aligns with Sirius, but does not pierce the pyramid throughout; instead it is *stopped within the core* of the structure by a portcullis door. This is a deliberate design feature, perhaps with a connection to Sirius being on the Western bank of the celestial Nile and terrestrially Heliopolis (associated with Isis/Sirius) being 'across the river', on the Eastern side of the Nile River. The shaft is also iconic to the sothis line - connecting Isis with her consort Nepthys. (Sirius *does not correlate* with Letopolis -the probability allocated in *Secret Chamber*, Fig.17) Sirius is in fact associated with Heliopolis, possibly a particular temple or obelisk that once would have occupied a prominent site. This corresponds with the texts and the actual correlation, which I demonstrated in the diagrams. The inscription on a stela in Heliopolis states: 'My beauty shall be remembered in His House, My name is the Benben and my name is the lake...' Isis has also been referred to as the lady of the lake (we will see how the distant Lake Aral is incorporated into a correlation that anchors a terrestrial projection of the ever intriguing Duat). The Inventory Stela text -found by Auguste Mariette during the mid 1800's, while excavating the small chapel called "The House of Isis", next to the Great Pyramid refers to Isis as the *'mistress of the pyramid' -was it the pyramid of Osiris?* Her terrestrial association is with Heliopolis, which was the seat of a powerful priesthood, whose *initiated* members were the *custodians* of a *sanctuary of knowledge*, the Great Temple of Ra, the *Sun* God. The ravages of time, plunder and urban encroachment have left the ancient city of Heliopolis buried under a suburb of Cairo.

In summary, Heliopolis represents the goddess Isis in broad, while the three Giza pyramids represent the god Osiris, his sister Nephtys and their brother Seth respectively. Letopolis is possibly associated with Horus. Are the three Giza pyramids the 'Mounds' of Osiris, Nephtys and Seth? They should actually be referred to as the Osiris Pyramid (G1), the Nephtys Pyramid (G2) and Seth Pyramid (G3)! The stellar Horus, the son of Osiris and Isis, was believed to be the first man-god to rule Egypt as Pharaoh. Khem, also known as Assim, later called Letopolis**,** was the site of a temple which outdated the pyramids and was closely connected with the falcon god of the sky, Horus.

[D] Two Lands division

'Geb commanded the nine gods to gather... He judged between Horus and Seth; he ended their quarrel. He made Seth king of Upper Egypt, upto the place where he was born, which is Su... and made Horus king of Lower Egypt, upto the place where Osiris drowned... which is the *'Division-of-the-Two Lands'*. Thus Horus stood over one region and Seth over one region... They made peace at Ayan. Then it seemed wrong to Geb that the portion of Horus was like that of Seth. So Geb gave to Horus his inheritance, for he is the son of his first born... Then Horus stood over the Two Lands... He is the uniter of the Two Lands... who arose as King of Upper and Lower Egypt...'

(**Shabaks Stone** Miriam Lichtheim translation; *Ancient Egyptian Literature*)

Literal interpretation of the mythical verdict of the god Geb, on dividing the Earth into two.

This section, dealing with the two 'Egypts', is fundamentally important in comprehending the motive of the overall schema. The diagram echoes textual description and illustrates the division of Upper Egypt and Lower Egypt cosmically. The history of Egypt begins with the union of the 'Two Earths', which is a variant hieroglyphic interpretation of 'Two Lands'. According to historic sources, the event of unifying Egypt was attributed to a legendary 'Scorpion King'. The land in question was not Egypt as we knew it, but a region with a cosmic duality and which specifically contained the House of Sokar. It is harmonious with a universal mapping scheme and pivot of the sublime Duat.

Celestially, a diagonal line between the star Rigel and the star Betelgeux (i.e. between Orion's knee and shoulder), separates the star **d**-Orionis from the other two in Orion's Belt. Seth (**d**-Orionis) is thus severed from the Sothis line and so too, from Nephtys and

Osiris. The reader will recall that although Nephtys was married to Seth, her loyalties were said to be with Osiris. We see here how Nephtys together with Osiris become separated from Seth, her husband, by a line that diagonally intersects the celestial equator at 52 degrees. It thus divides celestial topography into the two hemispherical domains. I will call this line the Two-Lands-diagonal. From Betelgeux, this line cuts across the Milky Way, past the star Alhena and transits the star Castor in the constellation of Gemini and continues in an arc around the celestial globe.

It is clear to see why it is said that Seth (**d**-Orionis) is identified from an early age with the Hyades in Taurus, as this constellation is within his allocated (upper) sector. A valid question, of course, would be the origin of Zodiacal signs and whether present day signs were known to the ancient Egyptians. The lower part contains the throne of Osiris (**z**-Orionis), as well as Sirius in Canis Major and is ruled by Horus.

'He is Horus who arose as king of Upper and Lower Egypt, who united the Two Lands in the Nome of the Wall...'

(Shabaka Stone, British Museum)

Was the God - King Horus present to witness this event?
Was the scribe of the Shabaka stone relating a fictitious tale, based on real geographic features?
Was Osiris merely a component of a star cult, depicted as Orion with terrestrial duality? Was it an historical event of the First Time?

Egyptologists date the unification of the Two Lands at c.3100BC, when Pharaoh Menes joined Upper and Lower Egypt. According to ancient tradition, the first Kings of Egypt were the gods themselves, but Egyptologists regard the gods as mythical Kings only. These findings will entice a rethink of such statements. When matched with the right topography, the texts provide crucial information that can yield a tangible interpretation. In the epic

battle, between Horus and Seth over territory, an eye and testicles were sacrificed between the two parties. Considering that the topographical anatomy of Osiris was compromised, a concordance is also evident in the geographical physique of Orion. *see*:
map [X] (a) Two Lands division
      (b) geographical Osiris/ Orion figure

Earlier, we have seen how the stars assumed the role of gods in a grand play, with the setting of heaven as the backdrop. Reproduced in a terrestrial duality, the Two-Lands diagonal is between the Abu Ruwash Pyramid, North-West of Giza and the Zawayat el Aryan Pyramid, South-East of Giza. This isolates the Third Pyramid (Seth) from the other two (Osiris & Nephtys) at Giza. Nephtys (Second Pyramid) her name meaning the 'Lady of the House' and the Palace of Osiris (Great Pyramid) where her loyalties were, can again be geometrically interpreted with her position in relation to Seth (Third Pyramid) and the division line. The Third Pyramid becomes separated from the Great Pyramid and the Second Pyramid by a line that intersects Earth's polar meridian at 38 degrees. This line traverses the Globe and divides it into two equal halves. '...the portion of Horus was like that of Seth...' The division is determined by the perpendicular relation that exists between the Sun and the Earth. Remarkably, at a specific time, one half is illuminated and the other that is in darkness, correlate with this division. The 'division of the Two-Lands' is a Global phenomenon, with the hub at Giza. The deity Anubis can be associated with this balance and transition of darkness into light. The cycle of precession can be monitored from the pivot point at Giza and a reference that anchors us in time to a specific era. From Zawayat el Aryan, the line passes Saqqara and Memphis, continuing to the Nile and beyond. To the South of this diagonal is Upper Egypt, with Saqqara and Dahshur extending past Meidum and it is the territory awarded to Seth. Lower Egypt, North of this diagonal, encompassing Memphis, Heliopolis,

Letopolis and the Nile Delta area, with the principality Busiris, was the area over which Horus ruled. Busiris is the contemporary Greek name but originally: Per-Usire (named after Osiris, who was also referred to as 'Lord of the Djedu').

Let's dwell for a moment on terminology and word choice for geographic interpretation. 'Upper' meaning up-river, toward the source, or from where the Nile flows and 'Lower' meaning down-river, and the direction in which the Nile flows into the Mediterranean Sea (from South to North). Rather confusing but 'upper' is a technically more correct expression with regard to anatomy and crown issues, also, it is worth observing that the celestial sphere concords with the 'upper' part (above zero degree latitude declination) and the 'lower' half (below zero degrees declination). *see* diag.[F]

The Zawyat el Aryan Pyramid *is not* the star Bellatrix and the Abu Ruwash Pyramid *is not* the star Saiph in the correlation, as allocated in *The Orion Mystery* and cause for distortion. The Zawayat el Aryan Pyramid, in fact, represents the star Betelgeuse (Orion's shoulder) and the Abu Ruwash Pyramid, is representative of the star Rigel (Orion's knee). The cause for Orion's Belt being 'out of kilter' in relation to a celestial meridian is precession related. I will demonstrate this in greater context in the sections to follow.

The lower part of the allegorical Orion figure, is not proportionate to the upper part, which poses a problem to the seemingly obsessive accuracy of the ancient planners. Terrestrially, a positional discrepancy involving the distance between the pyramids and the topography of corresponding stars in Orion is evident but perhaps explainable: the ancient Egyptians knew the constellation of Orion as *Sah*, the 'Far Strider'. It is related to geodetic projection from a specific focal point. The Globe was mapped with Giza at the fulcrum and viewed from an extra terrestrial peripheral –most likely from the Sun. This is elaborated on in the Conclusion chapter. Another connection is with Seth's accusation of Osiris before the gods and wherein mention is made to a transition of Osiris and 'long legs': becoming 'long of leg' can also be as a result of a 'shrunk' upper body -i.e. a celestial projection from a specific point. The upper torso is contracted and the portion below the belt elongated (a similar effect can be observed in ones own shadow cast on the ground, during early morning or late afternoon, with the Sun from behind). Observed from Northern, or Southern extremes, Orion's diurnal arc 'slides' higher or lower in relation to the horizon -variables of its min. & max. culmination at meridian transit, which occurs over long periods and is a consequence of Earth's wobble.

'It was he (Osiris) who attacked me (Seth)... when there *came into being* this his name of Orion, *long of leg and lengthy of stride*...'

{Pyramid Text 959}

Although set in the Northern hemisphere, the pyramids represent half of the celestial sphere -reflecting Earth's Southern hemisphere and a pre requisite was compliance with an observable scale. The (-)Fourth(+) Dynasty correlations of relevance, are from uppermost: the Meidum Pyramid, followed by the Bent Pyramid and the Red Pyramid at Dahshur, then the Zawayat el Aryan Pyramid. Forming the hub is the Giza 'Belt Pyramids' and to which the proportion relates. From there follows the Abu Ruwash Pyramid -effectively situated in Lower Egypt, then the Heliopolis obelisk, lowest.

Could it also be that these two archaeological sites are much older than they have been credited? Were the 'incomplete' pyramids abandoned, destructed for roads to lead to Rome or were they destroyed with powerful weapons in a battle? Was it a symbolic enactment of the dispute between Horus and Seth over the throne of Osiris and does a geometrical division of the Two Lands corroborate a unified plan?

'Thoth and Horus then come to help Osiris to the sky; Horus comes, Thoth appears, they raise Osiris from upon his side and make him stand... Raise yourself, o Osiris, Isis has your arm, o Osiris; Nephtys has your hand so go between them. *The sky is Given to you, and* the Fields of Rushes, *the mounds [pyramids] of Horus, and the mounds [pyramids] of Seth...*'

{Pyramid Text 959-61}

The Abusir Pyramids *do not correlate* with Orion's head, as allocated in *The Orion Mystery*. The pyramids and Sun Temples near Abusir, in fact, are along Orion's raised arm and represent other celestial counterparts. It is not inconceivable that other, as yet undiscovered, architectural features are located in the desert South-West of Zawayat el Aryan, a position that geographically represents Orion's head. Also due West of Zawayat el Aryan, is his other shoulder. To the North-East of Abu Rawash, in the vicinity of Nahaya, Orion's knee could be located. An archaeological inspection could determine it.

Chapter 5
UNIFIED SCHEME

Hub & circle: Rostau Giza divide

'At Giza we are confronted by a set of monuments which bear every sign of ointelligent design, yet we are ignorant of the principles upon which these designs were based.'

(**R. Cook,** *The Pyramids of Giza*)

In his work *Sacred Science,* R.A. Schwaller de Lubicz describes ancient Egypt as the true repository of 'sacred science', philosophy and astronomy. The Great Pyramid is one of the wonders of the ancient world and considered to be a mathematical principle in stone -an enigma still evading catch up by modern science and leaving people throughout the ages to ponder on how, why, who, when? The base dimension of the GP encapsulates time, rather than distance. This time relates to Earth's orbit around the Sun. The latitude setting of G1 thus relates a solar year: the path traced by the focus of the Sun, Solstice to Solstice or Equinox to Equinox. Could these for stations represent the four horses of apocalypse? The indisputable message of the pyramids is a four dimensional mathematical expression –a message across space and time that implores us to look at our planet. Earth's precession causes variance of geography and polar orientation in relation to the Galaxy. The pyramid builders captured a Zodiacal fix by correlating Earth and sky at a specific time during its long cycle. This 'moment' is captured by the demarcation, which unites, or divides light and dark –comprising two unequal sectors in Egypt but notably two equal hemispheres that constitute the Globe and is observable from space only...

In the last section we have seen how this division has dual connotation and the conclusion chapter is immersed in this. The 'vanished builders' of the pyramids had intricate knowledge of the multiple motions of the Earth and its shape. When the Brits arrived on the scene somewhat later and with primitive instruments, a very capable Petrie none-the-less performed a stirling act in surveying what they found there –already weathered and antiquated. The feature, to the West of the Second Pyramid, dubbed 'workmen's barracks' by Sir Flinders, incorporates what appears to be a mechanism comprising 72 calibrations, by which variance in the shadow cast by G2 could possibly be employed to monitor divergence in Earth's axis – coupled with precession. This factor may have played a role in the detail regarding final placement of Khafre's pyramid. In the Pyramid Age, Egyptians evidently possessed advanced astronomical knowledge and I propose this as evidence of rapid devolution and a topic of investigation: in the third millennium BC, they measured and gridded their land with spherical *four-dimensional geometry*, based on astronomy -esoteric *magic* or sacred geometry? –that required capabilities of which, only *some* were much later attributed to the Greek philosopher-mathematicians such as Thales, Pythagoras (6th century BC), Eudoxis, Plato and Democratis among a number of great tongue-twisters. Alternatively, we have to come to accept that the feats at Giza are misattributed.

The architects (and not necessarily priests) assigned to the project would have been required to prepare an overall design layout, which entailed not only interior and exterior detail of the pyramids themselves, their causeways and related structures such as the Sphinx but all Temple complexes that occupy the Giza plateau. The genius and wizardry of the ancient master builders, now with the source identified, becomes clear, in logical simplicity. The breakthrough on 'how' the Giza plateau was set out, followed my discovery of the geometric diagonal that determines the Two-Lands divide. Rostau-Giza is at the hub and it is important to realise the celestial duality of the geometry incorporated -on both, micro and macro level. The Two-Lands axis is at a diagonal angle: 38 degrees in relation to the North-South longitude Meridian and 52 degrees in relation to East-West latitude. The Sphinx lies parallel to the equator and faces due East. The centre of the Giza plateau hub is located along the Sphinx latitude, at a point near (under) the North-West corner of the Second Pyramid, where the diagonal axis intersects it. This point is accentuated by sothis line, which extends at 45 degrees from the North-East corner of the Great Pyramid and intersecting the diagonal axis, thus forming the hub centre. These angles, intriguingly, are incorporated within the design specifications of the Great Pyramid, namely the 52 degree angle of slope of the side faces and the two Southern star shafts, which emanate from the so called King's and Queen's Chambers at 45 degrees and 38 degrees.

Shaft:	Gantenbrink:	Petrie:
Kings Chamber south	45°00'00"	44°30'00"
Queens Chamber south	39°30'00"	38°28'00"

(source of shaft angles; *The Orion Mystery*)

[E] Survey grid & co ordinates

Motivation and method of setting the pyramids at Giza.

Before commencing with the gigantic undertaking of construction, the engineers responsible for the project at Giza would have been required to perform another task: a survey -a thorough horizontal survey could be achieved by means of plane geometry relationships, calculated and projected on a true North-South and East-West oriented rectangular grid, with successive traverse lines. The circumpolar stars of the time could have provided a means for orientation to true North. It would appear that they used both linear and angular measurements from two primary coordinates. The diagonal axis is a geometrical relation, determined by two pyramid sites North-West and South-East respectively of Giza. Not equidistant either, the two coordinates are situated on the same diagonal. Derived from a celestial counterpart this diagonal also represents the Two-Earth's divide, which is a geodetic line that circumscribes the World. The section -approximately 13km - between the Abu Ruwash Pyramid and the Zawyat Al Aryan Pyramid designates Earth's precession axis. By means of triangulation, applying principles of geometry and trigonometry, all the angles could be measured and in a chain of triangles, plot the entire plateau. The raised bedrock evidently posed no problem to the genius of the engineers. The structures were set exactly where they were required and with great precision. The squares of the base of the three Giza pyramids face the four cardinal directions, each set on its own meridian. Azimuth measurements could have played a role. *Was the survey done from overhead or, by means of a Global Positioning System?* Once achieved, by whichever means, vertical surveying and plotting of the required heights and slope-angles could be addressed by yet more ingenious methods prior to the advent of the dumpy level.

'What we may be looking at here are the fingerprints of highly sophisticated and perhaps even technological people capable of awe-inspiring architectural and engineering feats at a time when no civilisation of any kind is supposed to have existed anywhere on Earth'.

(*Keeper of Genesis,* **R. Bauval & G. Hancock**)

It is clear that the builders of the Giza necropolis were not concerned about geological constraints. They put the three pyramids along a North-East to South-West line that originates in Heliopolis. The 45 degree diagonal bisect of the GP's square is determined by this line. The Second Pyramid was offset to the South of this line and the Third Pyramid to the South-East because they wanted to do so and by no coincidence whatsoever. Using ratios of the Great Pyramid, the two co-ordinates, which link with Zawyat Al Aryan and Abu Rawash can be determined. The NW coordinate is also the centre of a circle that unites G1, G2 & G3 by one corner from each, tangent to the curve. The builders of the great pyramids achieved this remarkable unified geometrical configuration more than 4500 years ago. Proposed theoretical method, formulated in mathematical jargon, by means of which, the Giza structures can be created *from a single point*:

Begin by orientating a page with South at the top and place an axis **XX** (East __ West).

Next, place a 90* intersecting axis **YY** (North | South).
Then bisect @45* (NE / SW) for a diagonal G1-G2-G3.

To determine the NW coordinate, measure **a+b** (GP: time based dimension ratios) along axis **XX** (in W __ direction).

At the sum of **a+b**, along axis **XX**, place a secondary 90* intersecting axis **yy** (N | S) in other words, parallel to axis **YY**.

From this intersect (NW c/o), measure a 38*\52* diagonal axis **YX** (SE\NW) to intersect axis **YY**, thereby determining the SE coordinate. The single starting point G1, together with the two coordinates, thus produces a Pythagorean triangle.

The sum total of **a+b** produces the radius and center of the circle that scribes a curve, tangent to the base corners of G1, G2&G3.

a=the intersection of **YX** and the 45* G1-G2-G3 diagonal. This intersect produces the Sphinx **xx** parallel to **XX**. This intersection is also the center of another circle, being the hub of Rostau-Giza. The curve connects the NE corner of G1, via one of its 'satellites' with the head of the Sphinx and valley temple of G3.

Perhaps a pseudo math guy ☺ would venture to analyze this and allocate values to **a** and **b**? While the acute knowledge, specialized instrumentation and equipment required continues to baffle minds, the issue of manpower, technical ability and method fuels perpetual argument and speculation. Whether any architectural features are present at the coordinates can be verified by an on-site inspection. All this ingenuity was possible in an epoch (the Bronze Age) when the wheel was not invented. Then it can be safely assumed that neither had the development of sophisticated instrumentation for magnification. With a little imagination however, detail not quite clear to the unaided eye, appear nevertheless to be included in the master's plan... The three great pyramids, their causeways, the small subsidiary pyramid South of the Second Pyramid, the three small satellite pyramids lined up alongside the Eastern face of the Great Pyramid, the other three satellite pyramids lying near the South-Western edge of the site, the Sphinx, temples and other monuments bear the markings of a huge astronomical diagram -an immense model of the sky. Giza, indeed comprises a unified concept but seemingly the whole of Egypt is an image of Heaven.

Prophecy of Thoth:

'Do you know, Asclepius,
that
Egypt is made in the image of Heaven,
or so to speak
more exactly,
in Egypt all the operations
of
the powers which rule and work in Heaven
have been brought down to Earth below?
Nay, it should be said
that
the whole Cosmos dwells
in this our land and its Temples…'

(**Thoth** to his disciple –*The Lament*)

[F] Wider plan

Validation for a grand unified plan of the sacred temples in Egypt.

The Hermetic Texts comprise an ancient body that was compiled at the dawn of the Christian era. It is believed these writings are based on the work of the Egyptian god of wisdom, Thoth. They are explicit in terrestrial and celestial correlation. Some alternative researchers' have suspected that Giza incorporated a wider plan, but it remained to be proven. I can make the statement that Giza and the entire Memphite necropolis is a map of the heavens, because I can substantiate it. I will detail how Giza combines with other sites in a grand unified concept –derived in its entirety from a celestial master plan. *see* diag.[G][P][Q] Distant structures, in the greater Memphis area and beyond, such as Meidum far to the South would have required geodetic compensation for curvature over topography some 3km wide and over 80km long –defying any rope stretching exercises. Areas under consideration here is the Memphis Necropolis, with Dahshur in the South, Abu Ruwash to the North-West of Giza, Letopolis further North and a Heliopolis situated North-East of Giza. The enormous distances and scale constraints mean that not all sites are always simultaneously present in overlays.

The meridian in this diagram is the core element that links the three Giza pyramids and five other pyramids in a North-South correlation. It has been common belief that the primary 4th Dynasty pyramids number 7, however, with the inclusion of the Meidum Pyramid there are 8 pyramids, classified as Old Kingdom pyramids, that all form part of a cohesive wider plan. Egyptian deities were often associated with 'natural features'. According to one version of the Hermopolitan cosmogony, claimed to have evolved earlier than any other cosmogony, an Ogdoad of Eight gods created the world. This Ogdoad were called the souls of Thoth and possibly conceived as 'hatching out' on to the primeval mound, after the receding floodwaters of the Nile. The texts state that 'out of the lotus created by the Eight, came forth Ra, who created all things, divine and human.' If this refers to the 4th Dynasty pyramids it would mean they were already there before the last Deluge, some 13000 years ago!

The (-)4th(+) Dynasty pyramids are distinguished by entrance passages that align with the polar axis and clearly form part of a unified plan. Incorporating Heliopolis and Letopolis, in a greater geometrical correlation, it covers a strip of desert over 80km long. Uppermost of these, the Meidum Pyramid, unfortunately does not appear on this diagram due to scale restriction. It is an integral component however -of the prime meridian, where it is representative of Polaris, the current pole star, in the constellation of Ursa Minor. *see* charts [P][Q]

The structure is accurately aligned to the four cardinal points and serves the purpose of an anchor, with celestial connotations. Sometimes referred to as a satellite pyramid, a small subsidiary pyramid is present. The Nile River generally concords with a band of open clusters and in broad terms, are within the Milky Way. The Milky Way runs roughly South-North. Of relevance is the inter-relationship of the pyramids with a particular meridian. The 8 pyramids that constitute this unified plan are set out according this meridian and adhere to cardinal orientation. The pyramids represent stars on a scale adapted to facilitate construction within practical geographical boundaries (the sky does not fit on Earth).

The uppermost of the remaining seven then, is the Bent Pyramid, the only Egyptian pyramid of this form (rhomboidal), and situated at Dahshur. Its hieroglyphic name translates as *'the Southern Shining Pyramid'* and it has a subsidiary pyramid. Also at Dahshur is the Red Pyramid, the hieroglyphic name meaning: *'the Shining Pyramid'*. These two are along the same meridian, although offset in relation to one another, as is the case with their stellar counterparts. A common factor is evident, namely the slope angle of 43,2 degrees links them –like some kind of iconographic pointer.

Considering that their stellar counterparts are positioned along the same meridian, it offers a feasible explanation. These two important monuments, incidentally, are surrounded by a military base and had been out of bounds to the public until late 1996. They have a geometrical, parallel diagonal relationship with the Great Pyramid and Second Pyramid at Giza. A correlating relationship is also evident in their counterparts in the sky. *Are these pyramids at Dahshur of greater importance than authorities admit or Egyptologists realise? Do they conceal information that is of utmost importance to us?*

At Zawayat Al Aryan, a secondary 3rd Dynasty pyramid known as the Layer Pyramid, is not individually counted as part of the seven in the Memphis area, but it also clearly represents a stellar counterpart along Orion's raised arm (star SAO 113389). To the North-West of the Layered Pyramid, its original name unknown, it is the principal 4th Dynasty pyramid at Zawayat Al Aryan, commonly known as the Unfinished Pyramid, is off-set to the cardinal directions. This may indicate a change in course or geodetic compensation for curvature of the Earth. All that remains of this pyramid, comparable in size to the Second Pyramid at Giza, is an enormous trench. (The site at Zawyat Al Aryan is also situated next to a military base).

Next in this order are the three Giza pyramids (G1, G2 and G3). The upper one is the Third Pyramid, its hieroglyphic name translating as *'the Divine Pyramid'* (three queen subsidiary pyramids are present). The pyramid in the middle being the Second Pyramid, the hieroglyph creating some confusion, as it translates as *'the Great Pyramid'* (one subsidiary). The lower one, of course, is *the* Great Pyramid (three queen subsidiaries) the hieroglyph name being; *'the Pyramid which is the place of Sunrise and Sunset'*. The last of the seven pyramids visible within the map/diagram is situated at Abu Ruwash and in hieroglyphs bears the name; *'the Pyramid which is the Sehudu-star'*. It is described as the unfinished remains of a granite casing and a subsidiary pyramid is present. In this diagram we have a visual depiction of the 'sothis triangle' formed between Heliopolis, the Giza pyramids and Letopolis. Static angles of 45 degrees, 52 degrees and 38 degrees are projected in relation to the terrestrial North-South meridian and the East-West latitude line. This is in accordance with the topographical map and Giza survey plan coordinates. The unified plan is superimposed on the starry background of the Duat. (The stars Aldebaran and e-Taurus no.311 *do not correlate* with the Dahshur pyramids as claimed in: *The Orion Mystery, Keeper of Genesis, Heaven's Mirror and Signs in the Sky*) This mismatch has been the cause of Orion being 'out of kilter' in relation to a true meridian and the cause of much debate among many 'experts'. The wrong stars were matched with pyramids. I reveal accurately matched correlations. The pyramids at Dahshur, in fact, correlate with stars in the constellation Auriga; the star Menkalinan which is represented by *the Southern Shining Pyramid* (the Bent Pyramid) and the star SAO 58636, which is represented by *the Shining Pyramid* (the Red Pyramid). The hieroglyphs that refer to these pyramids thus reveal indisputable stellar association. The Red Pyramid and the Bent Pyramid at Dahshur are representative of the stars SAO 58636 and Menkalinan respectively. The subsidiary pyramid next to the Bent Pyramid correlates with the star SAO 40756. This constitutes a matching 'subsidiary star' of the star Menkalinan. This is the correct correlation with a terrestrial longitude and meridian offset imitated in the celestial sphere.

Pyramid placing is stellar in nature: correlating with stars. Pyramid orientation is solar: tracking the Sun. The implementation of a grand scheme of pyramid construction is now indisputable and graphically demonstrated. This concludes a single, unified plan of the 4th Dynasty pyramids, which was devised from the outset of the enterprise. An apparent similarity, however 'approximate and subjective', cannot be denied or ascribed to chance by even the most obstinate. I rest my case.

125

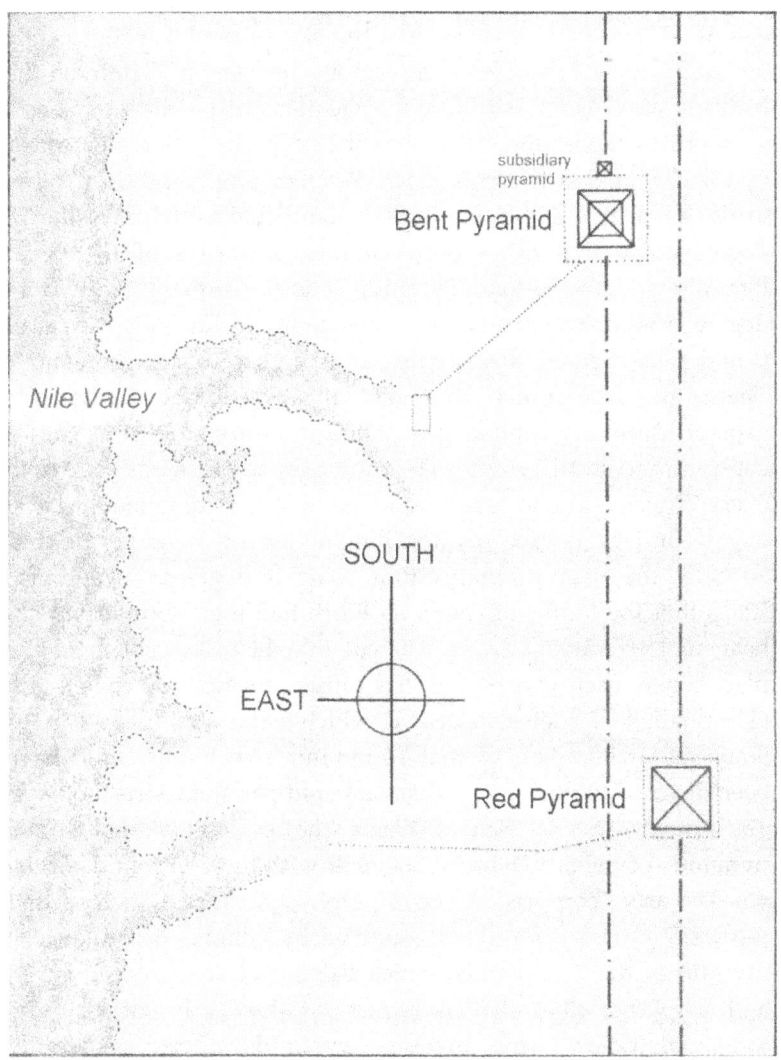

FIG. XI. Dahshur Pyramids –offset

The geometrical anatomy of Osiris-Orion persona.

According to legend, Osiris was killed by his brother Seth, at the age of 28. He then departed into the sky to establish the cosmic kingdom of the *First Time Duat*, among the *stars* of Orion, on the banks of the celestial Nile. Can the age of Osiris be interpreted as a geometrical expression - the value of 28 degrees -the angle formed by the diagonal between the stars Bellatrix and Saiph, in relation to the 45 degree sothis line? More significant perhaps, is the 28 degree angle that exists between the causeways of the Great Pyramid and the Second Pyramid. It is the sum of the two 14 degree cross quarters, adjacent to the equinox sunrise. *see* diag.[E] Could Giza be the timekeeping device that tracks precession? There are also other numerals that could be interpreted geometrically and contained in the Osirian myth, such as the 72 conspirators (and 17th day). The equinoxes advance by 1 degree in every 72 years, due to precession. The two lands diagonal has a 38 degree and 52 degree relationship in respect of longitude and latitude –the mean difference thus being 14 degrees. Legend also states that the tombs of Osiris on Earth had their counterparts in heaven. The body of Osiris was cut into 14 pieces and over the place where each was buried, Isis caused a sanctuary to be built. (The phallus was never recovered, which leaves 13 pieces).

Some researchers believe that 14 pyramids or tombs could have been devoted to the various dismembered parts of Osiris' body. In *The Orion Mystery*, Bauval likens the possibility that the 6 pyramids of the 5th Dynasty, together with the 7 pyramids of the 4th Dynasty, comprising the Memphis Necropolis, serve that purpose. I wish to propose another hypothesis based on the division of the Two Lands, which I demonstrated in section [D] and map[x](a), that the cutting up of the 'body' of Osiris is terrestrial Orion. This involves pyramids, more specifically connected to the 4th Dynasty and immediately around Giza. We also read in the texts that 'the mounds (pyramids) of Horus and the mounds of Seth' are given to Osiris'. Based on interpretation of the texts, I propose the following: the pyramid at Zawayat Al Aryan (large incomplete), the three Giza pyramids and their seven small subsidiaries, the Abu Ruwash Pyramid, together with its subsidiary gives a total of thirteen, which comprises the terrestrial 'body' of Orion. (Body in this case perhaps meaning torso and the exclusion of 'head' and 'arms', making it rather complex, but since we are dealing with mythology thousands of years distant, nothing is clear-cut, straight forward logic). This interpretation identifies Osiris with Orion in a greater context, and encompasses all of Rostau in the sky as well as geographically. Again we have textual evidence that Osiris is Orion: '..*when there came into being this his name of Orion...*'

'It was he (Osiris) who attacked me (Seth)... *when there came into being this his name of Orion*, long of leg and lengthy of stride... Thoth and Horus then come to help Osiris to the sky; Horus comes, Thoth appears, they raise Osiris from upon his side and make him stand... Raise yourself, o Osiris, Isis has your arm, o Osiris; Nephtys has your hand so go between them. *The sky is Given to you, and* the Fields of Rushes, *the Mounds of Horus, and the Mounds of Seth...*'

{Pyramid Text 959-61}

'Behold he has come as Orion, behold *Osiris has come as Orion...* O king, the sky conceives you with Orion, the dawn-light bears you with Orion... you will regularly ascend with Orion from the Eastern region of the sky, you will regularly descend with Orion in the Western region of the sky... your third is Sothis...'

{Pyramid Text 820-2}

[G] Sacred geometry

Cosmic master plan and the source of sacred geometry.

This diagram identifies the cosmic source of the master plan, which is always visible despite the effects of precession, the pole star of particular epoch or meridional transit of other stars. Unbeknown to us, it has always been visible in the night sky! Scale unfortunately precludes the star Polaris, in the constellation of Ursa Minor, to fit in the picture. It is part of the master plan however, as was demonstrated in the previous section. *see* diag.[P]&[Q] Polaris incidentally is the pole star of our era. The relative position between Orion and other constellations remains proportionate due to 'fixed stars'; their relevant positions remaining the same year after year. These constellations are clearly identified in a section to follow, but for now it is the geometric relations that are of relevance. Diagonal lines between Betelgeuse and Rigel and between Bellatrix and Saiph, form a cross axis and the centre point of a circle around the Belt stars: Alnitak, Alnilam and Mintaka (**z**, **e**, **d** Orionis). As with the case of the Great Pyramid and the Giza circle, **z**-Orionis is tangent to this circle.

Numerous technicalities, such as lack for curvature compensation can affect measurements and map projections. The motion of precession has an influence. The proper motion of Sirius can affect the angle that connects it to the belt stars (the relation of this angle changes to the meridian and latitude). The Orion cross is unaffected –the Sothis line connects to the intersection formed by the cross lines. The First Time and the co-ordinates of Sirius could possibly be determined with precision from this configuration. The terrestrial angles involving Giza, however, would be a constant fixed in time so to speak. *Now* we can ask; when? The meridian and latitude (declination) lines can be used for cardinal alignment of any pyramid or temple in any epoch, once a point of reference along the cycle of precession is established.

The *'Seven Sages'* were the only divine beings who knew how the temples and sacred places were to be created and it was they who initiated construction at the 'Great Primeval Mound'. The Sages are said to have specified the plans and designs that were to be used for all future temples. This esoteric knowledge and wisdom of the highest order was deemed too secret for profane eyes, only accessible to a few chosen initiates. Open star clusters such as the Pleiades, a classical reflection Nebula which is the easiest to spot with the naked-eye, is also known as *the seven sisters* or M45 and can contain hundreds of thousands, even millions of stars.

Why does the Pleiades feature prominently in orientation of temples around the Globe? Is it speculatively too radical to conceive a star cluster as initiating sacred geometry? Then who were these beings, these gods, with incredible knowledge of astronomy and the human psyche – thousands of years ago when the technological evolution of mankind was still supposed to be in its infancy? From where did they come?

Adventure update

Three months had passed since my arrival in the Cape. I was still reading *Fingerprints of the Gods* and enjoying Graham Hancock's thoroughness and accounts of personal experiences. It is well told and thought provoking but provides no new evidence on Egypt. I was aware that there is abundant other literature on the subject, but circumstances did not allow me to digest all of it at that time.

Robert Bauval claimed 'new and stunning discoveries' in a forthcoming book and that another, to be co-authored with Hancock, was 'pre-sold to four major publishers'. *I was* sitting with stunning discoveries and fervently attempting to formulate the graphics descriptively for others to comprehend. The frustration of compiling a manuscript was taking its toll. For those that can relate, by necessity, I also had to contend with advancing my computer skills beyond mastering the start button... Other times I woke up in the early hours between midnight and dawn, restless, in a duel with time and feeling helpless to communicate. The abandoned project in Lesotho seemed so distant and reading extracts of my journal even seemed unreal. Occasional news would trickle through -the most significant was that the vehicle had been repaired and subsequently wrecked in a collision... Harassment by attorneys and being blacklisted added to my adversity. It was political instability in the first place that impacted on my livelihood -tourism is not encouraged by threat of a civil war and the situation in Lesotho took long to stabilise. My find is priceless and could alleviate my dire economical predicament but how do I tell that to the Bank? I had to focus on the task of writing come hell or high water. For diversion I enjoyed a daily walk at dawn along the Camps Bay shore for some exercise, fresh air and appraisal of perspective. The curvature of the Earth is most discernable across the span of Ocean and testimony of our inhabitation of a finite sphere. First and last light reveal time, motion and cyclical interchange: merging prologue and epilogue.

The relevance of emotional diversions in academic research may be questionable, however, motive for existence is expressed through philosophy. The human emotion factor is integral to consciousness and in distinguishing higher dimensional existence from basic instinct. Life is a multiplicity of possibilities in varying intensities, manipulated through the capabilities of the human body, driven by the force seated in the brain. Reward is through physical sensory experience. The quest is eternal consciousness, challenged by striking a moral balance between reproductively driven primordial needs, evolution and a return to the source. The fusion of purpose and motive is manipulated and molded -cast in a time solid, destined by fate. Our memories comprise the solid, therefore our consciousness should strive for honorable fate. In the deck comprising emotion, 'love' surely is the wild card -*the Joker*... Can the Moon's gravity influence emotion?

Full Moon occurring twice during one month, is a rare event that only happens once in two years, or so. This was the reason for the occasion at Clifton Beach -a magnificent cove at the foot of the steep western slope from Lion's Head, which terminates in a dazzling white beach. Huge granite boulders, surf-washed by endless motion to rounded shapes, emerge from the turquoise blue of the Atlantic Ocean and form the flanks of the four beaches that comprise Clifton. Opulent accommodation clings to the slope that overlooks the bay. A warm summer Sun and a group of friends made for an enjoyable afternoon. The unhurried sunset, lingering twilight, then hundreds of candles in the sand illuminated the clusters of revelers and set the mood for the pending darkness and rising of the 'blue Moon'. The 'festive season' brought some joyous and cherished moments of shared emotions, meaningful existence, belonging and the wonderful intoxication of love! Another memorable journey was away from the city, to the hinterland and magnificent setting of Wellington with vineyards, horses and a picturesque mountain range.

In September 2001, before writing the manuscript, I had presented my findings to reportedly one of the biggest publishers in the Southern hemisphere. It had been established that the topic has an international audience and my publishing hopes seemed to be realised through a verbal commitment: undertaking of representation and promise of producing an early publication. For the process to commence, the work had to be formulated. Publication of these incredible discoveries -surely, the greatest archaeological discovery of all time -is bound to unleash heated debate among skeptical authorities and those in search of the truth and enlightenment. I was convinced that this knowledge could contribute to the posterity of the human race and set about compiling it enthusiastically, in spite of my limitations. Pioneering, it has all the elements of jealously guarded secrets, fame and fortune –posing a threat of rewriting history, I found myself in an unusual situation that required confidentiality until the work was ready to be published. Some researchers have dedicated a lifetime to searching for answers that still elude them. The key to unlock the secret message of the pyramids lies in astronomy and the medium to decipher the code of the gods is mathematics. Exposure in archaeological and scientific journals will ultimately bring acclaim but informing the general public, who should be the keepers, will be a long process, besides, a capitalistic mentality is still at the order of this age and my endeavours require funding. There is huge potential for exploitation through various means -in its entirety, or comprising several volumes, ideally audio visual. All sections interact, yet some can stand independently. The diagrams are unrivalled and the real power of the work. They demonstrate and clarify ancient, mystical lore in unprecedented context and would be particularly suitable for the electronic media. Money 'makes the world go round', right? Well, then I had rights to protect.

'…we are again seeking messages from an ancient and exotic civilization, this time hidden from us not only in time, but in space… Extraterrestrial intelligence will be elegant, complex, internally consistent and utterly alien. Extraterrestrials would, of course, wish to make a message sent to us as comprehensible as possible… We believe there is a common language that all technical civilizations, no matter how different, must have. That common language is science and mathematics.'

(Professor **Carl Sagan** – *Cosmos)*

Chapter 6
GEOMETRICAL ASTRONOMY

Pyramids = stars

During Johannes Kepler's quest to solve the mysteries of the universe he realised that there were only five solids that would be tangent to a circumscribed sphere. The structure of the solar system, he felt, had been explained through Greek geometrical philosophy (his publication: *Cosmographic Mystery*).

'The achievement he rated highest is now considered a curiosity, a relic of his ancient heritage and an example of the aberrations which occurred during the transition from medieval to modern science... To us, his configuration of nesting geometrical solids is more fitting for a garden sculpture than an astronomy book. It has the appearance of crank science and absolutely no physical foundation for his architecture has come to light -nor does any scientist anticipate that one will... He felt that the world was essentially mathematical: by studying geometry, we study the world. This is an ancient attitude, not a modern one.'

(Professor **Charles A. Whitney**, *The discovery of our Galaxy* -1971)

Perhaps an ancient attitude, or dabbling into a little pseudo history, is just the key required, so let's return to the basics of pyramid research and compare how various arrangements of lines, which have common connecting points (based on 'fixed' stars), can take on geometrical shapes such as a triangle, square, star, pentagon or combinations thereof, like a polyhedron –a pyramid, which consists of four isosceles triangles that converge to a point and are set on a square base.

Five geometric depictions of a pyramid/star:

[1]   Triangular side view, or elevation of a pyramid.
[2]   Polyhedron top view, or plan of a pyramid.
[3]   Two inverted triangles forming a six pointed star.
[4]   Pentagon forming a pentagram, or five pointed star.
[1&4] Combined three-dimensional pyramid & star.

Multiple components of these forms are also present in fractal geometry and even integrate cymatics but venturing there is beyond the intended purpose of this work. Of relevance here, is alertness to the fact that symbolism is expressed through geometric form. Some of the depictions are hieroglyphic versions of a pyramid or specific star and in some cases even represent 'the soul of a departed King'. When viewed from an angle, as opposed to perpendicular sight, an apparent distortion of the visual appearance of an object occurs. This is a consequence of perspective viewing and does not detract from what it stands for. It should be borne in mind that the 'sky pyramids' in the diagrams are viewed in *perspective*, albeit illusory. In effect then, we could say it's a study of something that does not exist… an obelisk also represents a pyramid -materially, the bulk of the body surrounding the pillar does not exist physically, other than its manifestation in concept. The focus of interest therefore is not so much the medium but the notion it represents –the message.

'Something subtle almost subliminal- which I am now convinced is of immense relevance to us as a species on this planet, an event whose time has come, to understand it, to see it to fathom its meaning, a type of intellectual archaeology was required, a gigantic historical puzzle needed to be pieced together, and I set myself the daunting task of undertaking this…'

(**Robert Bauval**, *Secret Chamber*)

[H]
GEOMETRICAL STARS

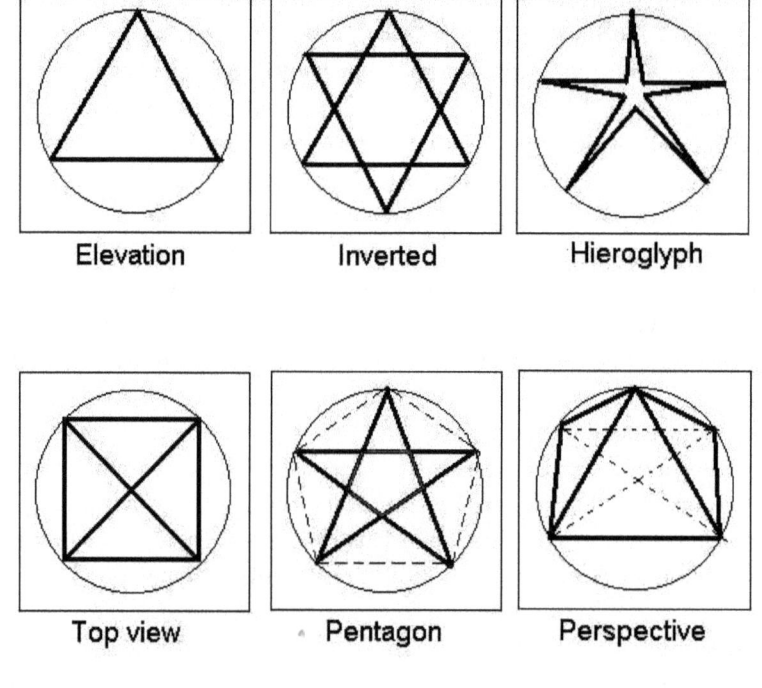

FIG. XII Pyramids=Geometrical Stars

[1] The Duat

Celestial map of the Duat, within actual celestial topography.

The Duat is denoted by a hieroglyph comprising an encircled five pointed star. The Duat 'after world' is reputedly located in a region of the 'deepest, most central' part of celestial topography and accessed via Rostau, where Orion is located. In this diagram, for reasons which will become apparent, I identify a specific area of the sky as the Duat: encompassing the constellations of Orion, Canis Major, Canis Minor, Gemini, Auriga and Taurus, with the Hyades and Pleiades star clusters, is where the gods of the First Time established their cosmic kingdom -the land of the souls.

In the last section we saw how various geometrical shapes, based on common fixed points produce different geometry. In this instance the triangle represents the elevation of a pyramid in a geometrical projection onto a vertical plane. It resembles the Great Pyramid, complete with missing capstone, marked by the 'Twins' - the two prominent stars, Pollux and Castor, in the constellation of Gemini. They form an open angle at the apex of the triangle. The two corners at the base of the triangle are defined by the star Sirius and the Pleiades star cluster. It is possible that a specific star, with a particular characteristic, was selected among the cluster. Another noteworthy observation is that the meaning of the word 'tepi' translates as: the beginning/base of triangle and the hieroglyph for Sirius/Isis is a triangle. Hieroglyphic triangles also refer to the 'land on one side of the Nile' -meaning the hemisphere East or West of the longitude that passes through Dahshur and Meidum and which demarcates the polar axis. The 'land on both sides' is the entire Globe. The word 'tepi' also translates as 'tooth' and when seen in silhouette against a horizon-dwelling Sun, the pyramids at Giza appear as teeth. In the next section we'll see how the celestial triangle takes on a three dimensional form. This area of the sky is host to at least eleven of the brightest stars.

Data for *relevant* stars among top thirty brightest listed:

No	Name	App. Magn	Spectral Type	Distance (pc)	Notes
-	-				-
1.	Sirius	-1,47	A1V	2,7	double
6.	Capella	0,08	G8iii	14	double
7.	Rigel	0,12	B8ia	250	
8.	Procyon	0,38	F5iv-v	3,5	double
12	Betelgeux	0,80	M2ia-iab	200	variable
13.	Aldebaran	0,85	K5iii	21	
17.	Pollux	1,14	K0iii	11	
23.	Castor	1,59	A1 v.	14	double
26	Bellatrix	1,64	B2iii	144	
27.	Elnath	1,65	B7iii	92	
29.	Alnilam	1,70	B0ia	490	

(*Source: Night Skies*, Dr. **Peter Mack**)

By knowing the luminosity of a star, the distance can be found. Stellar spectra are classified into 10 main groups, each represented by an alphabetical letter. The sequence from hot to cool is: O,B,A,F,G,K,M,R,N,S and expressed in a **mnemonic**:

O Be **A** **F**ine **G**irl **K**iss **M**e **R**ight **N**ow **S**weetheart

Each class is divided into 10 **sub classes** of **0 to 9** -placed after the letter. **5 luminosity classes** are denoted by Roman numerals **i. a/b. ii. ii. iii. iv. v.**

Our Sun is a **G2v.** classified star and is expected to have a main sequence lifetime of about 10^{10} years. Regarded as a 'typical middle age star', our Sun has been burning nuclear fuel in its core for over $4,5 \times 10^9$ years.

Mnemonics is the classical art of memory printing basic archetypal images onto memory (*detail study;* Frances Yates, *The Art of memory*). A typical example of this application was demonstrated in the above classification of stars. Doctor Giordano, Bruno

Nolano, professor in philosophy and highly proficient in mnemonics, had hopes that Europe would adopt the ancient Egyptian religion; a magical religion discovered in Hermetic texts, as the true religion of the world. Did Bruno see the ancient texts as exuding a mnemonic message?

'...Those wise men (of Egypt), then, in order to obtain certain benefits and gifts from gods, by means of profound magic, made use of certain natural things in which the divinity was latent, and through which the divinity was able and willing to communicate itself for certain effects.'

(**G. Bruno**, *Spaccio della Bestia Trionfante*-1584)

Bruno, through metaphysical speculation, imagined the Universe to be infinite. He visualised the cosmos as being inhabited by numerous other worlds, referring to ancient hieroglyphs as the language of the gods (Giordano Bruno, *On the Infinite Universe and the World*). Borne in mind, this was during the Middle Ages Renaissance, some 300 years before hieroglyphs were deciphered. In a classic example of an establishment that cannot be tolerated as self-conceived civilizers of the world, Bruno was arrested by the Papal inquisition in 1592 and put into a dungeon in Rome. After a lengthy bogus trial at the Vatican, he was taken to Campo de' Fiori in February 1600, a wedge stuffed into his mouth, tied to a pole and burnt alive.

"In Bruno we have the perfect example of how a powerful intuition can know what scientific minds have trouble perceiving..."

(**Robert Bauval**)

[J] Duat perspective

Stars are separated by mind blowing distances and to render perception of this, let's digest some astronomical data for an entrée. Light travels 7 times around the Earth in 1 second. For the light of a star at one end to travel across the diameter of the Galaxy to the other side would take hundred thousand (100 000) years, yet this is minute in the scale of the Universe... One of the most distant objects that the eye can see is a faint smudge of light, in the constellation of Andromeda, called M31 or NGC 224, which is an *external galaxy*- very much like our own, but larger. The light we can see now, left there 2 200 000 years ago, yet Andromeda is a sister galaxy to our own and one of our *nearest neighbours!*

The apparent brightness of stars does not necessarily relate to distance. The sky, from our Earthly peripheral and for purposes of passive observation, might just as well be a flat surface. For ancient man there were not many clues to indicate otherwise and without the aid of modern science, it would be an eternal debate. In the last section, the realm of the Duat was identified by means of two-dimensional geometry. This diagram still comprises the same celestial topography, although the scale is drastically reduced to show converging lines. We now transit to three-dimensional geometry, where the triangle incorporates a perspective view. It was demonstrated earlier in this chapter, how various geometrical shapes can be derived from common fixed points –bearing in mind that distances between the stars are not proportionate to the actual form. Therefore, perspective viewing is an illusion, convincingly portrayed on a flat (two dimensional) surface. This configuration shows a technically correct rendition, as perceived by a viewer on a horizontal eye-line, with two distance points, each consisting of two converging parallel lines that merge into respective vanishing points to create a three-dimensional phenomenon, which I call 'the Duat pyramid'. The projection is consistent with the methodology whereby an isometric view of the Great Pyramid could be derived from elevation and over head plan. It could be argued that although strange, it may be a coincidence, however, we shall see how this particular region of the sky is unique in the overall scope of our Galaxy, with which ancient man(?), bizarrely, seemed well acquainted.

The inscription on the New Kingdom stela, situated between the paws of the Sphinx, states that the location of the Sphinx is beside the House of Sokar. If we dare to project the demarcation of 'modern day' constellations and terminology onto ancient literature, a thought springs to mind: could it refer to the constellation of Leo, the celestial counterpart of the Sphinx being situated beside the Duat pyramid, the House of Sokar?

Orion perspective

Isometric inspiration in the stars.

This configuration, still within the Duat region, shows the rendition that delineates the perspective of the Orion constellation. It has a geographical duality at Rostau, Giza -representing the blue print for the Great Pyramid, still with some secrets to reveal and which we will analyze later.

'I have passed over the paths of Rostau, whether on water or land...they are at the limit of the sky. As for him who knows the spell for going down into them, he himself is a god in the suite of Thoth, he will go down to any sky he wishes to go down to...'

{Coffin Text 1035}

'...we have stumbled upon a message of primordial antiquity that was composed not just for the Pyramid Age, and the Horus Kings of ancient Egypt, but for *all seekers after the truth- from any culture, in any epoch- who might be equipped to put texts and monuments together and to view the skies of the former times.*'

(**R. Bauval & G. Hancock,** *Keeper of Genesis*)

[K] **Mysterious symbolism**

'...thinking with the heart and feeling with the mind'

(**Joseph Ritman** - founder of *Bibliotheca Philosophica –Amsterdam*)

Some revelations here tread the 'fringe' of receptiveness and may be reminiscent of 'crank science' but it's a lure to evoke expansion of rationale. Political and religious squeamish should therefore brace themselves in entering this frank zone -consider it a 'Suisse' journey, where neutrality crosses paths with The Bank and bestowed in unreserved equality... While we are in the region, the Pontifical Swiss Guard maintains the security of the State of the Vatican City and the safety of the Pope, who sports some interesting symbolic attire and paraphernalia but we'll skip that. The reader may ask what this holy seat has to do with ancient Egypt. Well, equally, besides complementing the impressive Baroque architecture and keeping time, one may ask what a 5th Dynasty obelisk from Heliopolis, at the center of the elliptical piazza of St Peters Square, has to do with Christianity. In representing God's domain, this intermediary of dubious ring-kissing practice enforced brutal untruths in the past. Today with a population of well under 1000 citizens and a non commercial economy, it's just a wealthy enterprise.

Freaky as it may seem, this diagram is intended to have a symbolic impact on the subliminal, without elaboration of printed words. Those not familiar with the sky may be surprised by the actual scale of Zodiacal forms. Likewise, legendary figures and the magnitude of events portrayed in myths. In retrospect and upon completion of this work, the reader may well realise that it comprises a cryptogram to the riddle in its entirety. *The Penguin pocket English Dictionary* defines a pentagram as a 5-pointed star used as a magical symbol. This also incorporates the symbolism of Islam and lest we forget, the three dominant world religions have their mutual origin in ancient Egypt. Star cult practices continued into the modern world and incorporate various designs and configurations. Rituals and ceremonies are performed rigorously but most often, with the original context lost. This work may revive deeper insight to some obscure habits. Subsequent to my 'spontaneous exposure' to the mysterious triangle of the Duat, I have come across other configurations, outside of Egyptology, that convincingly support a mutual esoteric tradition –intrinsic knowledge of a momentous event with dire consequences, regarding the existence and evolution of humankind on planet Earth. The concept is embezzled in various enigmata -paintings, engravings, architecture and even whole city layouts (e.g. Washington DC) –and from early times, right up to the present. The Eiffel Tower, in effect, also represents a pyramid. Another, the largest on our planet, cloaked in patriotic pride, is the George Washington Monument -a giant stone obelisk with an owl perched atop, which in the dark of night is somewhat reminiscent of a KKK hood, comprising 13 tiers and keeping vigil like the eye on a Green Back… yes, it is very alternative but relevant, so skip a chapter if necessary, or dare to proceed directly to the conclusion but eventually it will have to be faced, albeit in a New Age…☺ a little hypothesis is much less harmful than some of the blatant BS, that Egyptology and history has amply concocted as gospel. Not to forget gospel itself and conspiring politics -the cornerstone of 21st century western civilization in amalgamated classics: the 'Know Nothing Party', Skull & 322 Bones, the woo-hoo cronies of Banking and Oil in clandestine Bohemian Wood gatherings, wheelin' an' dealin' star wars weapon systems to ward off the Gray Alien threat from Orion… Siriusly, will you *now* take me to your leader? It has been demonstrated how alternative arrangements of lines, with common connecting points, can take on the shape of a geometrical star. Those with the faculties and inspiration will derive numerous more mathematical and transcendental formulae -perhaps even a Zionist UFO gunship, complete with NWO emblems... yes, it can be another book!

Giza is represented as three star/pyramids, constituted by geometrical relationships. This diagram shows the constellation of Orion as an allegorical star/pyramid and the combined constellations that comprise the Duat as a star/pyramid. Symbolism is a powerful tool in conveying information and the point I am trying to make is: to the right intelligence, the knowledge of an entire concept could be encrypted in one image - an ideogram that renders piles of written text superfluous. The provision: one need to be initiated/ educated with the base knowledge from several other disciplines –an understanding of universal nature and a willingness to investigate and gain insight, comprende? ok, then:

'Betake yourself to the Waterway, fare upstream... traverse Abydos. The celestial portal to the Horizon is open to you... may you remove yourself to the sky, for the roads of the celestial expanses which lead up to Horus are cleaned for you... for you have traversed the Winding Waterway which is in the North of the sky. The Duat has grasped your hand... *where Orion is...*'

{Pyramid Text 798-803}

...and now for the chorus, all together in gospel choir tone:

'I shall not be turned back at the (pearly?) gates of the Duat. I ascend to the sky with Orion...'

{Coffin Text 236}

Orion & the netherworld

The Duat can be represented by various geometrical depictions. In this case a six-pointed star formed by two triangles, the one inverted with the bottom point formed by the star Rigel, such as found in the symbolism of Judaism... well, there you have it -a Jewish Duat! Thus, religion *can be reconciled* into one big happy family and I am pretty confident that pilgrims of the bells & chimes from Eastern philosophy circles need not be left out in the Himalyan cold by bickering over trivial differences. This is not a theological work however, I'll leave that to others, more capable... Speaking of no difference, actual points of reference are the same stars in the sky. Follow the literal interpretation of this text:

'...the Duat has grasped your hand *at the place* where Orion is...'

{Pyramid Text 803}

Open cluster NGC 2169, is located at the centre of the Duat, where Orion's raised hand is. The dual element: 'as above, so below' applies here also. The Global projected correlation is located in the holy city of Mecca –the navel of the World (*see* Ph.6). Believed to be of heavenly origin and associated with Biblical Jacob, the black stone in Saudi Arabia does indeed have a celestial counterpart – the Qa'aba is held up in Orion's hand, at the navel of the Duat. Is Jacob's ladder a component –the stairway to heaven?

'...may *a stairway* to the Duat be set up for you to the place where Orion is...'

{Pyramid Text 1716-17}

For Christianity's take, Osiris bears a unique location on the intersection (cross, if your orientation so prefers) of the celestial equator and the celestial meridian: *the place* where Orion is -the celestial equator is an extension of Earth's equator into space and the Ecliptic is Earth's orbital plane. The observable Ecliptic cuts through this topography, where the pivot of the precession cycle can be monitored in the triangle of the Duat. With its antepole situated among the giants in Easter Island, Earth is transposed against this configuration in the sky for a union with heaven.

Not to sideline Greek mythology, where Orion and Scorpio were placed in opposite sectors of the sky, which happens to be astronomically true: the constellation of Scorpio and the constellation of Orion, we know today, occupy opposite sides of the heavens. We also recall that the legendary unification of the Two-Lands was first attempted by a ruler, referred to as the Scorpion King –was it an event? Could the text be interpreted as: 'the Duat has grasped Orion's hand...' with geometrical connotations? The gateway of the Duat -the celestial portal, where "souls pass into the nether world" as per the rebirth cult, is where the navel of the Globe (World axis) is located. That concept and its significance will be expounded as we progress.

Chapter 7
ESOTERIC GEOMETRY

[L] Celestial pyramids

'Newton... was the last of the magicians... he looked at the whole universe as a secret that could be read by applying pure thought to certain evidence... a sort of philosopher's treasure hunt to the esoteric brotherhood. He believed that certain clues or evidence were to be found in the heavens... By pure thought, by concentration of mind... would be revealed to the initiate...'

(J.M. Keyness, *The Royal Society-1947*)

I identified the Duat as a specific by using a geometrical arrangement. It adopted a three-dimensional form, in the shape of a pyramid. Based on the mounting evidence, with Rostau and its connection with Orion demonstrated in celestial and terrestrial dualism, I will now take this idea further. This diagram shows two sky pyramids. The larger one represents the Duat and the smaller one represents Rostau, which constitutes the constellation of Orion and the celestial home of the gods, which I will refer to as the Orion pyramid. Of course, both geometrical patterns of connected dots that appear to look like pyramids may be random coincidence and were never part of any mythology or astronomy of any past civilization or doctrine. Well then I lay claim to it and explain it as having been revealed to me by pure thought and concentration of mind! And so too, any aspect, celestial or terrestrial, connected to it, I claim to be the inventor of... but do reserve comment until a study of this work is completed. The constellations, and these 'connected-by-dot forms', are not restricted to static or upright positions as would be relevant to the Earth's horizon, depending on ones location. Regardless, the sky progresses *as a whole* from East to West. This is a result of the Earth's diurnal spin, which is also the mechanism responsible for the perceived effect of the Sun and the Moon to rise and set. The orientation in tilt of Earth's axis towards, or away from the Sun, while on its orbiting path over the course of a year, at breakneck speed, furthermore has an effect on the arcs of rising and setting celestial bodies.

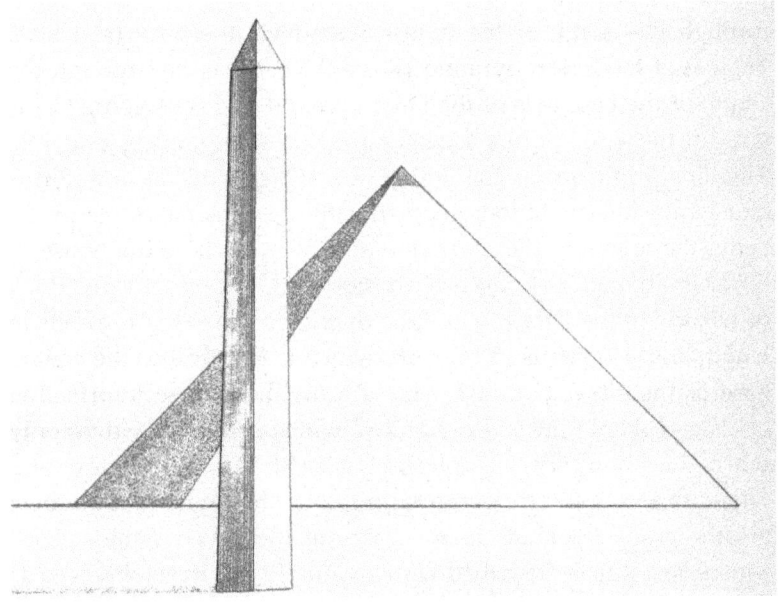

FIG. XIII. Pyramid & Obelisk

[M] Pi (π) in the sky

'The main difficulty which Egyptologists face is the re-creation of a state of mind of human society 5000 years ago... Whereas in the last 5000 years man's spiritual world-picture and his moral laws have changed out of all recognition, the laws of physics have remained unaltered. The knowledge that these same laws were operative and had to be obeyed 5000 years ago in exactly the same way as today provides a reliable link between the pyramid builders and ourselves.'

(Dr. **Kurt Mendelsohn**, *The Riddle of the Pyramids*)

The 'hidden circle of the Duat,' in the body of Nut.

This diagram depicts the base of the sky pyramid. A line passing through the centre of the base axis and via the apex (star SAO 112406) of the Orion pyramid (Rostau), then passing through the centre of the base axis of the Duat pyramid and continuing to the apex of the same, forms a geometrical capstone to capstone link. This line originates as the Sothis line, which extends from Sirius and is my interpretation, geometrically demonstrated, of Rostau being the access to the Duat -the after world where the house of Sokar is situated. The seventh division *Shat Ent Am Tuat* (the Book of what is in the Duat) refers to a district in the sky: 440 cubits in length and 440 cubits in breadth, which is identical to the square base of the Great Pyramid! This affirms the precise information contained within ancient scriptures, which becomes evident only when we know how to interpret it in the correct context and where to locate the topography to which they refer. Shown here are the cross diagonals to the bases of the sky pyramids. Each square base can be inscribed with an individual circle (observed as an ellipse). The four base corners of the Orion pyramid are defined by the four stars that constitute the outline figure of Orion: Betelgeux, Bellatrix, Saiph and Rigel.

The four base corners of the Duat pyramid are defined by the stars: Sirius, Procyon, Capella and the Pleiades cluster. This square is within a circle. Egyptian funerary texts speak of 'the hidden Circle in the Duat... in the body of Nut';

'Whosoever shall make an exact copy of these forms...and shall know it, shall be a spirit and well equipped both in heaven and Earth, unfailingly, and regularly and eternally... it shall act as a magical protector for him both in heaven and upon Earth.'

(**Shat Ent Am Tuat** - eleventh & twelfth divisions, E.A. Wallis Budge translation; *The Egyptian Heaven and Hell*)

It has been said that the Great Pyramid is a model of half of the Earth. Another proportionate measure, which is dealt with extensively in the conclusion chapter, is found along the Two-Lands division: cutting the Globe into two hemispherical portions. This also has an element of duality in the celestial sphere: cutting it in half between hours 5-6 & hours 11-12. *see* diag.[Q]
This diagram demonstrates multi-dimensional esoteric geometry and discloses the cryptic key to an archaic riddle. Documents referred to as the 'Old Charges of Freemasonry' and dating from the fourteenth century refer to 'the sacred science of geometry'.

'...seven liberal sciences be as it were all one science that is to say Geometry. For thus may a man prove that all sciences in the world be Geometry... all is Geometry.'

(**Fred Pick & G.Norman Knight,** *The Pocket History of Freemasonry*)

[N] Duat obelisk

'...the purpose of the ancient master-builders was sublime, and that they did indeed find a way to initiate those who would come after- thousands of years in the future- by making use of the universal language of the stars. They found a way to send a message across the ages in a code so simple and so self explanatory that it might rightly be described as an anti-cipher'.

(Keeper of Genesis, **R. Bauval & G. Hancock)**

The missing capstone and the celestial Obelisk of the Duat.

A pyramid can also be represented by an obelisk, which is a four-sided upright monolithic pillar that terminates in a pyramidion at the vertex. The pillar is the central core of a larger imaginary pyramid structure. If the four sides of the apex were to be extended by imaginary lines down to ground level, they would connect to an imaginary square ground plan which makes up the base of the imaginary pyramid. This diagram reflects the cosmic inspiration for the capstone. An allegorical shaft and chamber system adds another interesting dimension. The 'missing capstone' of the Duat pyramid (the Great Pyramid blue print) is marked by the stars Pollux and Castor, the two bright stars in the constellation of Gemini, also known as the Twins. Whether the Great Pyramid ever had a capstone or not is debatable. The symbolism of a missing capstone is far more intriguing and captivating than if there was one present. Perhaps this was exactly the intention of the builders. The path of the precessional Sun is iconographically expressed in a wandering capstone -the monolithic base symbolically supports the Sun and is representative of the world axis. In the following chapter, my findings are transposed onto astronomical charts, where they are shown in relation to the Ecliptic and the constellations.

'For I am Sokar of Rostau, I am bound for the place where dwells Sokar…'

{Pyramid Text 445}

It was said of the Memphis Apis bull that he dwelt in the 'soul of Ptah'. He was connected with Osiris in pre-dynastic times, where he acquired the title; 'Bull of Ament' (the Underworld). The reader will recall that the House of Sokar is situated in the 5th hour division of the Duat. Sokar was also identified with Ptah, god of the Memphite Necropolis and the after-world Duat. Imhotep, the son of Ptah, is credited with the Step Pyramid near Saqqara. There is also a Temple to Ptah in Memphis.

In this diagram of the Duat the allegorical King's Chamber correlates to Memphis. The Kings Chamber is represented by the star Alhena and the Queens Chamber is represented by the open star cluster NGC 2169. Does the trinity of stars that represent Orion's head indicate the third chamber? Osiris within this imaginary Duat pyramid is the equivalent of Khufu's pyramid terrestrially (*see* Fig.IV diagonal configuration) Interestingly, the 5th hour right ascension meridian is locked between the horns of Taurus, the bull.

Are we the subjects of a cosmic joke, or are we the recipients of a wonderful gift of knowledge from the gods?

Chapter 8
SKY CHARTS & ANECDOTES

[O] Planetary paths

'The king's sister is Sothis, the king's offspring is the Morning Star'

{Pyramid Text 357,935}

From Earth the plane of the Ecliptic can be observed as the apparent path of the major planets, traced out against background stars. It is a result of their orbital motion around the Sun. The diagram shows typical motions when they occur within the Duat region. The Ecliptic path passes through the Duat pyramid, along the vicinity of the Grand Gallery. The path of the Sun can be plotted on the Earth and the celestial globe, with duality. Venus and Mercury, being inner planets and closer to the Sun than the Earth, are only visible for short intervals before sunrise or after sunset. Both exhibit retrograde motion -i.e. appear to rise and then fall back again: In the case of Mercury, that is after about 20 days. Venus for example, would appear to 'ascend' and then 'descend' after about 105 days. Plotting strategic transits of Venus reveals an irregular pentacle. Observed over a period of 8 years, Venus is an evening or, a morning object for 4 years respectively (and for 1 in every 8 shines brightest, when closest to Earth). At times the retrograde motion of planets can occur very close to the vicinity of the Kings Chamber and Queens Chamber and these events would not have passed unnoticed by observers in distant epochs either. Mars, an outer planet, has a large retrograde motion. When this occurs in the Duat triangle, Mars appears to ascend, reaching a stationary point, then descend to another stationary point, before continuing to ascend again. This migration is a slow and can be observed over months. The paths of the two largest planets, Jupiter and Saturn, along with that of the Moon and the Sun all follow the Ecliptic (where Orion's raised hand is). The migration of the Moon is easily noticeable, moving Eastwards by the amount of its diameter in 1 hour. Venus, also known as 'the evening star' or 'the morning star' is the brightest object (planet) in the sky after the Sun and Moon and like Sirius, the brightest star, is also associated with rebirth. Comets can also make their appearance in the same region and no doubt would have been observed with great interest by ancient astronomers.

Comet Encke
Talmudic sages believe that a comet crossing Orion can signify destruction on Earth. The projected path of comet Encke during the year 2020AD is particularly interesting. It will traverse the Pleiades star cluster and Orion, passing 'over' the stars Meissa and z-Orionis (Alnitak), then, proceeds along Orion's sword (the isle of fire?) in evocative fashion. The reader will recall that the star z-Orionis is dually representative of the Great Pyramid and Osiris, or his throne. We have also seen how Osiris is associated in greater context with the constellation of Orion. At one time (eg.1974AD) comet Encke transited the star Alhena -the Kings Chamber of the Duat pyramid and in 10AD its passage was between the stars Pollux and Castor -the capstone of the Duat pyramid.

In Ancient Egyptian art, the Phoenix was usually depicted as a grey Heron. The apex stone, or pyramidion, on top of a pyramid is also known as a Benben Stone and said to be symbolic of the Phoenix. The Phoenix brought the life-giving essence, the magic *hike (heka)* from beyond the limits of the world, the Isle of Fire… the place of everlasting light, where the gods were born in the Duat. The magical fire-bird and chief messenger that had alighted on the primeval mound of creation and set in motion time and a new cosmic age -filling the world with that which it had not known. The sothis line extending from Sun-associated Heliopolis, perhaps delineates the ecliptic of a particular epoch. The icon of the Great Pyramid's missing apex is connected to the intersection of the South-Western corner at the base of the Second Pyramid – the junction of the two lands diagonal and the sothis line.

'This is the sealed thing which is in darkness, with fire about it, which contains the efflux of Osiris, and it was put in Rostau. It has been hidden there since it fell from him, and it is what came down from him onto the desert sand...'
{Coffin Text 1080}

The Phoenix is said (narration by Heliopolitan priests to Herodotus, *Histories ii*) to come from *Arabia*, carrying the parent bird encased in myrrh. In order to do this, it is said it first forms a ball as big as it can carry, then, hollowing out the ball, it inserts its dead parent, subsequently covering the aperture with fresh myrrh after which the ball is exactly the same weight as it was at first. The Phoenix bears the ball to Egypt and deposits it in the Temple of the Sun. This is being cyclical, perhaps it may be in iconic reference to the precessional capstone/Sun returning to its apex. *Did these events form part of the dot-connecting stellar cult? Do they have a bearing on the internal layout and features of the Great Pyramid?*

[P] **Celestial dome**

'This is the Land...the burial of Osiris in the House of Sokar...Isis and Nephthys without delay, for Osiris has drowned in his water... Horus speaks to Isis and Nephthys: "Hurry, seize him ..." Isis and Nephthys speak to Osiris: "We come, we take you..." They brought him to. He entered the hidden portals in the glory of the lords of eternity. Thus Osiris came into the Earth at the Royal Fortress, the North of the land to which he had come. And his son Horus as king of Upper Egypt, arose as king of Lower Egypt in the embrace of his father Osiris...'

(**Shabaka Stone**, British Museum, Miriam Lichtheim translation; *Ancient Egyptian literature*)

Some scholars of Egyptology consider the text of the Shabaka Stone as merely a dramatic play of no historical value, yet others place great value on its content, believing it to be based on ancient sources from the pyramid age. This oblong black basalt stone, with rounded leading edges, bears a small font hieroglyphic inscription. What cannot be overlooked is the 11 point star at the centre of the edifice. It is crudely chiselled and despite whatever other purpose it served, makes a bold statement that brings to light an overbearing emphasis on the Sun and in the process almost obliterates, but certainly pales the text into an insignificant backdrop. The scribe of this text indicates that he was commissioned by his King to renew a work of the ancestors, which had become antiquated. Based upon the Shabaka Stone, we have seen the division of the Two-Lands demonstrated. This was supported by stellar identification of the gods, based upon the much older Pyramid Texts and leads us to a new hypothesis. We'll see the Memphite theology geographically applied in the conclusion chapter, where the motion of the Earth is interpreted.

'The paths are in confusion... it is those who know them who will find their path; they are high on the flint walls which are in Rostau, which is both on water and on land...'

{Coffin Text 1072}

'...behold Osiris has come as Orion... you will regularly *descend* with Orion in the *western* region of the sky...'

{Pyramid Text 820-2}

This star chart shows the Western horizon during the early morning hours, at the onset of winter, prior to dawn and with the Sunrise to follow. The stars in Orion's Belt are almost parallel to the horizon, with the Duat pyramid setting upright.

Does Osiris (z-orionis, the celestial counterpart of the Great Pyramid) 'enter into the Earth' with the constellation of Orion going below the horizon? Was Osiris physically buried in the Great Pyramid?

'...I suggest that it's as scientific or at least quasi-scientific documents that the Pyramid Texts need to be read, not as mumbo-jumbo. I'm already satisfied that they respond to precessional astronomy. There may be other keys too: mathematics, geometry - particularly geometry... Symbolism... What's needed is a multi disciplinary approach to understanding the Pyramid Texts... and to understanding the pyramids themselves. Astronomers, mathematicians, geologists, engineers, architects, even philosophers to deal with the symbolism -*everybody who can bring a fresh eye and fresh skills to bear on these very important problems should be encouraged to do so.*'

(**Robert Bauval** in communication with Graham Hancock, *Fingerprints Of The Gods*)

Westcar Papyrus interpreted with observational astronomy:

This document (Papyrus Westcar -item No.303, Antiquities Museum, Berlin -complete transcript in Appendix), which was discovered in 1824, lacks the first part of narrative and bears some damage. The fourth tale describes a terrestrial event with a cosmic link. The setting is the 4th Dynasty and Prince Hardedef informs his father of a real magician, the Djedi, who is alive and well in King Khufu's own time. King Khufu had been searching for (the number of) the secret chambers of (the sanctuary of) Thoth. On instructions from the King, Hardedef collects the Djedi and his books from up-river. The Djedi magician informs the King that although he does not know (the number of) the secret chambers, he knows the place where (in a flint box *or limestone sanctuary?*) the Temple of Re, Lord of Sakbu in Heliopolis is.

When commanded by the King that it be brought to him, the Djedi pronounces that someone else is ordained for the task, namely the *eldest* son of the three children who are in the womb of Ruddjedet (the wife of a priest of Re). The eldest, he says, will be high priest in Heliopolis, but only after King Khufu is succeeded first by his son and grandson. She is due to give birth on the 15th day of the first winter month and King Khufu announces his intention of going to see for himself the Temple of Re, Lord of Sakbu, but that the sand banks of the river are dry, therefore posing a problem. According to the narrative, the Djedi magician performed a miraculous act *during* the time of Khufu -by 'making water over the dry sand banks', in order for the King to cross and see the temple of Re, Lord of Sakbu, for himself. For performing this act, the Djedi was assigned to the palace by Khufu, as a reward.

King Userkaf is said to have founded the 5th Dynasty and built a pyramid at Saqqara. Kings Sahure, Neuserre and Neferirkere erected their pyramids at Abusir. The first texts discovered were those in the pyramid of Unas, last ruler of the 5th Dynasty, located south of Zozer's Stepped Pyramid and near Saqqara. A popular theory of interpretation of this manuscript is that the Djedi prophecy relates to the 5th Dynasty rulers, in which case it would be the temples and pyramids near Abusir. This would imply pyramids at a time *after* the rule of Khufu's grandson, Menkaura, and therefore after his death. The son of Ruddjedet, who is said to have been ordained for the task, could not have brought anything to Khufu after his death. I therefore propose the following as the most plausible interpretation:

In observable celestial terms, the 'three triplets' are in fact Orion's belt ('in the womb' of Ruddjedet). The eldest being **z**-Orionis (highest above the horizon), followed by **e**-Orionis (a bit lower) and then **d**-Orionis (lowest). The difference in altitude between the three stars, above the horizon, is in minutes of a degree.

Terrestrially, the three triplets are in fact the Giza pyramids -the oldest being the Great Pyramid, which is Khufu's supposed own pyramid! In other words, the Great Pyramid, which is the counterpart of its stellar equivalent, the 'eldest descendant' in Orion's Belt, can provide King Khufu with that which he has been searching for: (the number of) the secret chambers of the sanctuary of Thoth. The tale is modelled on an event that preceded Khufu.

[Q] Celestial globe

'...land of ancestors lies in the middle of the Earth; and the middle of the human body is the sanctuary of the heart, and the heart is the headquarters of the soul, and that is the reason why men of this land... are more intelligent...'

(**Isis to Horus**, *Kore Kosmou*)

This astronomy chart is a spherical projection and should be viewed in concave perspective, as if the observer is *inside* the celestial sphere. It shows the Duat triangle, where it is anchored between the stars Pollux, Castor, Sirius and the Pleiades cluster. The constellation of Ursa Minor, with the star Polaris, can be seen here, which was not possible in other overlays. The 6th hour Longitude Meridian links Orion to Ursa Minor via the constellation of Auriga. Orion is situated on the celestial equator, which is an extension of Earth's equator into space. The 12 constellations that constitute the Zodiac are contained in a belt -9 degrees inclined to Earth's orbital plane. The celestial sphere, which is imaginary (as a sphere), forms the backdrop and when correlating stars and pyramids ought to be viewed with Earth in the foreground, with the fulcrum on Giza and super imposed over the background stars. The four colures of the celestial globe coincide daily in alignment with the terrestrial cardinal points.

'When the lines about the Earth are considered from the mathematical precisions, it will be found that the center is nigh unto where the Great Pyramid... still is located...'

(**Edgar Cayce** Reading 281-42)

'At the correct time accurate imaginary lines can be drawn from the opening of the Great Pyramid to the second star in the Great Dipper, called Polaris or the North Star...'

(**Edgar Cayce** Reading 5748-)

Edgar Cayce (1877-1945), an American psychic who performed readings while in an altered state of mind, predicted that a secret chamber containing records would be found in the GP at the close of the 21st Century. It is believed that there exists an immense universal source of information, which could be logged onto; the so called 'Akhashic Records' -a type of cosmic library, or super spiritual computer, which contained all the information and thoughts of the world throughout history. Is it also the carrier of messages, which long ago had been aimed at primed initiates, in genes that hold the remote memory of our genesis? or, is it indeed that we are one with the Universe and beginning to discover the dimension of time and awakening to Universal consciousness? According to the Cayce readings, humankind will make the greatest archaeological discovery of all time involving the pyramids of Giza.

'For here those that were trained in the Temple Sacrifice as well as in the Temple Beautiful were about the sealing of the Record Chambers. For these were to be kept as had been given by the priests in Atlantis or Poseidia when these records of the race, of the developments, of the laws pertaining to One were put in their chambers and to be opened only when there was the returning of those into materiality, or to Earth's experience, when the change was imminent in the Earth; which change we see, begins in 1958 and ends with the changes wrought in upheavals and the shifting of the poles, as begins then in the reign in 1998..'

(**Edgar Cayce** Reading 378-16)

'I have passed over the paths of Rostau, whether on water or land... they are *at the limit of the sky*. As for him who knows the spell for going down into them, he himself is a god in the suite of Thoth, he will go down to any sky he wishes to go down to...'

{Coffin Text 1035}

Chapter 9
THE SECRETS OF ORION

Orion pyramid

'O Horus, the King is Osiris, this Pyramid of the King is Osiris, this construction of his is Osiris; ...'
{Pyramid Text 600}

'Behold he has come as Orion, behold Osiris has come as Orion... your third is Sothis...'
{Pyramid Text 820-2}

In 1872 the two mysterious narrow channels, which emanate from the 'Queens' chamber, were discovered. The Southern shaft from the Queen's Chamber is obstructed by a portcullis door with two metallic fittings attached to it and still with about 17 metres to the outside face of the pyramid. The Northern shaft makes a sharp bend to the west, after rising relatively straight. The deviation is a deliberate design feature. *Where does it lead to?* The shaft and chamber system of the Great Pyramid of Giza is encrypted in the constellation of Orion...

The reader should take note that this diagram is no longer that of the Duat pyramid, but the constellation of Orion. We are now entering the Orion pyramid –the body of Osiris! Once again we have a situation where the North and South cardinals of the celestial Meridian are inverted, when comparing the orientation of a sky and ground pyramid. Celestial North of the Orion pyramid and South of the Great Pyramid, is the same shaft emanating from the King's Chamber in both pyramids. The East elevation corresponds in geographic and cosmic duality. Is the isle of fire that is referred to in texts, the path along the Great Nebula in

Orion, the gaseous emission nebula -the place of star birth? The two star shafts of the King's Chamber have a common point of origin, situated below the chamber. In similar fashion, the two angles of the shafts from the Queen's Chamber also culminate at a point below the chamber. When viewed in this manner the shafts are fixed on static points - other stars. What are they telling us? Could these be geometrical celestial bearings? Al Ma'mun, who broke into the Great Pyramid during the 9th century, was a patron of science with a particular interest in astronomy. He was inspired by the rumour of secret chambers, supposedly containing astronomical charts of great learning. The charts may indeed be contained within the *blue print* of the Great Pyramid!

'This is the *word* which is in darkness. As for any spirit who knows it, he will live among the living. *Fire is about it,* which contains the *efflux* of Osiris. As for any man who shall know it, he will never perish there, since he knows what shall be in Rostau. *Rostau is hidden since he fell there,* for he is one who has come down from upon the desert, and he possesses *writing material...* Rostau is for Osiris. As for any man who is there, he will see Osiris every day, his breath will be in his nose, and he will never die...'

{Coffin Text 1087}

'This is the sealed thing which is in darkness, with fire about it, which contains the efflux of Osiris, and it was put in Rostau. It has been hidden there since it fell from him, and it is what came down from him onto the desert sand...'

{Coffin Text 1080}

The 'sealed thing, which is in darkness with fire about it and which contains the efflux of Osiris,' is situated above the ascending corridor where it transforms into the Grand Gallery. Do the granite plugs conceal something that correlates with the gaseous emission nebula in Orion's sword?

Secret chambers

The cosmic blue print of Rostau, sanctuary of Thoth.

'Ye holy books written by my perishable hands, they have been anointed with the drug of imperishability by Him who is master over all, remain ye undecaying through all ages, and undiscovered by all men who shall go to and fro on the plains of this land, *until the time* when the heavens grow old, *shall beget men worthy of you.*'

(Prophecy of **Thoth**: Hermetic writing- *Kore Kosmou*)

Throughout the centuries, there has been the suspicion that the Great Pyramid held further secrets; that somewhere inside was a hidden chamber and that one day this chamber would be found. In an ancient papyrus Ipuwer, an Egyptian Sage, describes the dreadful scenes and events of a political upheaval that appear to have occurred during the reign of Amenemet I (*c.*1990BC).

'Behold, the district councils of the land are expelled... a man smites his brother and the same mother. The districts of Egypt are devastated... we know not what has happened to the land... civil war pays no tax...woe is me for the misery of this time. Remember ...it is said he is the shepherd of all men. There is no evil in his heart...where is he today? Does he sleep perchance..? *that which the pyramid has concealed has become empty* and the palace is destroyed'

(*Admonition of* **Ipuwer**, *Leiden Museum Papyrus* No.344)

"I am more than ever convinced of the possibility of the existence of a passage and probably a chamber containing possibly the records of the ancient founders..."

(**John Dixon** in letter to Piazzi Smyth, 1871)

Westcar Papyrus Circa 1650 BC
(Prof. Adolf Erman translation) published in 1890 and later comparative interpretation by Egyptologists:
Gardiner -vs- Green.

ipwt -versus- pdwt of *wnt -versus- wnw*

King Khufu has been searching for *ipwt* (the number of) of *wnt* (the secret chambers) of Thoth, as he desires the same for his own 'tomb'. The magician Djedi informs King Khufu that he, Djedi, knows not the [arithmic constituent-closed structure] but knows the place where, however, and declares that he's not ordained to bring it to Khufu but the eldest in the womb of Ruddjedet.

ipwt - pdwt ; **secret chambers** - *archive - plan - lines*
wnt - wnw ; **sanctuary** - *chamber - room*

Whichever hair splitting version is fancied, the sanctuary of Thoth, which is defined by a constituent of geometrical lines in the sky, contains the secret chamber *zeta*-Orionis -the starry counterpart of the Great Pyramid and the star god Osiris -in the belt of Orion.

'...again it may be a purely mythical building. But that it was a building consecrated to Thoth, and that the *ipwt* were its secret chambers...I hope to be able to prove, or at least to make exceedingly probable... And indeed, what ambition could have fired Cheops (Khufu) more than to possess in his own pyramid a replica of the mysterious chambers in the hoary sanctuary of the god of Wisdom?... **I conclude, therefore, that the word *ipwt* means "secret chambers", and that Cheops was seeking for details concerning the secret chambers of the primeval sanctuary of Thoth**...'

(**Alan H. Gardiner**, *Journal of Egyptian Archaeology, 1925*)

In Masonic tradition the Freemasons predict that some day a man will locate this buried vault and that he will be an initiate "after the order of Enoch".

(**Joseph Jochmans** – *Time Capsule*)

In 1988 a Japanese scientific team, led by Professor Sakuji Yoshimura, detected the existence of a cavity off the Queen's Chamber passage, some 3 metres under the floor. They also detected a tunnel outside and to the south of the pyramid, which appeared to run underneath the monument. A method whereby electromagnetic waves are transmitted and the echo analysed by microcomputer can detect a vacuum. Why the Egyptian authorities halted the project before any further exploration could be done, is also a mystery.

The anomaly under the Queen's Chamber passage correlates with the star Alnitak (z-Orionis), which is associated with the god Osiris -the celestial counterpart of the Great Pyramid and has remained a sealed secret, undiscovered for thousands of years. Can these chambers be referred to as: the Seth Chamber (King's Chamber), Nephtys Chamber (Queen's Chamber) and the *primary* Osiris Chamber? -the diagram identifies this as ***ipwt***. It is embedded in the rock at the base of the pyramid, below the Queen's Chamber. Access may be via an internal N-S passage (similar to that of the KC and QC) or, a concealed grand entrance from the Mortuary Temple in the East face of the GP, is very realistic and practical, as it leads off the causeway. It now beckons to be entered and for the hidden secrets of the Great Pyramid, to be unconditionally revealed to all… for the first time!

Adversity & update

I caution to think, the reader who managed to get this far would agree, that it is a complex and conventional logic defying connection with a remote past. To have advanced to reading this line was in itself an arduous journey and in the conclusion chapter we'll embark on an astronomical one, so buckle up!

To conclude that this has been an unequalled interpretation of ancient Egypt and its mysterious monuments would not be an overstatement. To say that it has raised even more questions would be correct and to believe that these are valid questions, demanding answers, would not be unfair. I cannot provide all those answers unequivocally. The seed has been planted and it needs to be nourished. The knowledge and expertise to pursue the quest is out there and can be procured in the specialists of various disciplines. In the epilogue of his book *Riddles of the Sphinx*, Paul Jordan commented: "there is precious little of worth to be learned from unscholarly speculation… the sheerly fanciful speculators, with their pyramid builders from Atlantis, their 'encoded' astronomical messages from remote antiquity to the very times we live in, their secret chambers… their 'ancient wisdom' by the bucketful, are to be sure an irritant to the Egyptologists…"

It can be duly pointed out that the remarkable discoveries presented in my work were achieved in a short space of time, with little resources, crude equipment and research not focused on Egyptology as a conventional academic discipline. Agreed, it was not within the framework of strict scholarly methods and yes, not without informed speculation, conjecture or proposition -a pyramidiot approach? Then again, *who* defines scholarly? We are, after all, investigating a time period of some 5000 years ago and to which even the expert Egyptologists have not come forward with plausible explanations! Perhaps rekindling ancient geometrical philosophy is what made success possible. This is an unusual and multi-facetted subject -a tough call for an individual in trying circumstances and hopefully the average reader will be forgiving of my shortcomings. Initially I seldom had access to the internet and research resources were not always available in a library. Unable to purchase, I had to be content with browsing in a bookstore, which is hardly sufficient for an investigation of this nature and only got to thoroughly read several books years after my own first edition. To determine the locations of pyramids, the only means at my disposal was a 1:150000 scale topographical map from an Atlas. The apparent minor discrepancy between the photographic-imposed master plan and geographical map projections could be due to numerous technical reasons but most likely due to lack of curvature compensation -projection of curvature onto flat overlays. I could not risk approaching astronomy, Egyptology or mathematical faculties for endorsement at a premature stage as the nature of my work and 'proper credentials' would in any case be a handicap. Scientific breakthroughs are assumed to be forthcoming from within the establishment only. Being considered for publication in credible scientific journals, as an independent researcher in a field labelled as 'pseudo-science', would be naïve but who are the authorities in astro-archaeology, or archaeo-astronomy? Another challenge was to avoid repetition of much discussed, researched and documented detail, yet provide enough, minimal and relevant background to substantiate the context of my discoveries. This book needs to be studied and not read but how does one qualify the level of entry? Few would have the required acumen to jump in at the deep end, so what will stimulate one to laboriously follow the progressive case to its conclusion? Unfortunately I could also not give a first hand, in depth account of the appearance, conditions and 'feel' of the physical geography, or of the monuments themselves but only as I saw Egypt in the heavens. Remarkably, I had never been there and had to rely on accounts, information and data compiled by others, so building a picture. Research was done mostly through metaphysical reasoning and instinct –the thrill of communication with a sophisticated intelligence, of unknown origin, across time… I was restricted by not being a seasoned author but my primary objective was to reveal my findings, not compete for a literary prize. To write about monuments that I have not experienced first hand, seems idiotic. Then again, I have not been to space either ☺ -space cake, spaced out and astral travel being somewhat different to writing authoritatively about stars… The pyramids have been written about for many years and will be for many to come. Quotes and passages, sometimes indirectly relevant, from various sources were intentionally used throughout the work to verbalise my own sentiments, in appropriated context. The very passages in ancient texts were inspirational and indeed a medium to make the right connections. I hope researchers will appreciate that the triumph is collective and inclusive of the earliest researchers and thinkers. The invitation, challenge and objective should be to find solutions -to fulfill a quest for knowledge and the truth!

It had been 8 months since my arrival in the Cape and I was beginning to experience a serious case of publishing woes. I had valid reasons for feeling anxiety and experiencing frustration: after some intermittent co-operation, the big local publisher that I had first approached, contrary to earlier discussions, was suddenly not prepared to deviate from their 'standard contract'. According to guidelines set out by The Writers Guild, on royalty percentages of secondary rights, I would be greatly exploited. The uniqueness of my discovery lends itself to being of great value to other media, outside of book publishing. The exclusion of American territory, as a future security and initially agreed to in negotiations, was later reversed. I was strongly advised by an attorney to have a publication deadline included in the contract but there was a lack of willingness to commit to a publishing date. The payment of an advance by local publishers is a non issue –they want everything but offer nothing in return –and we failed to reach a consensus. Instead of being resourceful, inventive and assisting in creating a book to suit this unique discovery, *they* forfeited a golden business opportunity! Optimistic that other deals... *ahem*... would be plentiful, I pursued representation elsewhere. Publishers abroad are almost exclusively accessible through a literary agent only, which is also non-existent locally. I had approached tens of dozens literary agents and although a few had expressed some interest, nothing came of it. Apart from expressions of skepticism, agents mostly deal with existing clients and in certain genres only. This kind of publication is deemed 'too specialised' by a hesitant industry and left me with the frustration of not being able to divulge my findings. Self-publishing, which offers many benefits such as full control, ownership and speed was an option but I did not have the means to fund it. Prospects of starting a family, publishing setbacks, emotional ordeals and bruised hearts became an arduous plight. The anniversary of my arrival in Cape Town had passed among serious conflict and pressure that disappointingly led to relationship disintegration. I had really wished for a happy ending and my emotional state was shot - being on the brink of processing the book but distress prevented any joy -I could not even begin to explain it, even less fathom it and feared that I had lost my dignity, my spirit a casualty and enveloped by depression. Out of desperation to escape relentless conflict, I had threatened to return to Lesotho, although it was not what I really desired. There was nobody to talk to and I felt alone and afraid -was it 'the cosmos at work' or was my sanity abandoning me?

The average individual just gets a glazed look when discussing this topic and 'authorities' in a field that is still in the process of being defined are rare. Although it is understandable that academics are hesitant to comment on sensational claims, I had some consolation and a feeling of relief in being able to reveal my findings to an academic at last: Anthony Fairall, Professor of astronomy and the Director of the Planetarium in Cape Town, was reviewing my thesis. This is only one component of a riddle that incorporates a multitude of disciplines. However, an apparent similarity cannot be denied or ascribed to fortuity -my case is sufficiently substantiated and with broader academic co-operation, resources and data, further progress can be made. Several attempts, at the time, to get in touch with Graham Hancock, directly and through his publisher in Johannesburg, Robert Bauval and Erich von Daniken all came to naught. I sent e-mails regarding my claims and findings to the National Geographic Society, Carte Blanche M-Net Television and an array of other media –to no avail. I appealed to the American Research Center in Egypt, the American Institute of Archaeology, the Council of British Archaeology, the International Association of Egyptologists and even to NASA -need I say, I was not overwhelmed by any response... one would have thought that the quest was to resolve the riddle of the pyramids -perhaps attitudes will change with an eventual effort to study my work.

Documenting this knowledge was paramount and required following a meticulous and systematic process. I had to rely on my own strategies and adapt accordingly. My situation was one of isolation over long periods and despair with severely limited means, essentially through lack of capital. Amid the ongoing feud, that was to leave a void for a long time to come, I had stopped writing. Eventually the self-publishing route led me to Durban and although processed under duress, it presented a welcome distraction. The limited first edition was in print in South Africa within 2 years after reading *Secret Chamber* in the Maluti Mountains and I am respectful of the outcome, albeit with sacrifice and shortcomings. The associated experience provided an invaluable education and the next objective was international exposure by establishing a website. Optimistically, I sent *hundreds* of emails regarding my findings around the world. Egyptologists are obviously not always right and refusal to recognize new ideas or approaches is an attitude that does not benefit the development of science. Their allusion of pyramids being tombs only and the wrangling politics around the issue is not in the interest of humanity and needs to be remedied. Why did it take a decade to open a door? Doors such as these are beckoning to be discovered, yet in the process humour our ignorant incompetence. I am not advocating negligent destruction of any kind, however, mankind does have the technological potential to do an investigation and in the process do a thorough restoration of the most important time device ever constructed on this planet.

Perhaps a means can be devised to slide back the massive granite 'plugs' in the ascending corridor to reveal their secret. If temples can be moved to accommodate a dam, as was the case in the Valley of the Kings, then surely pyramids can be explored in the interest of Earth's inhabitants! The exact purposes of the elaborate interior systems of the great pyramids are still unclear. I firmly believe that with a concerted effort, it can be resolved. A normal archaeological dig would start at the foundations of a site, resorting to paint brushes and consequentially forming a picture of how the original or, final product, was achieved on available evidence. Perhaps an 'unconventional' approach is required: considering all possibilities, then through a process of elimination, do an investigation. The mind needs to be free to perceive, as radical it may seem, we can only conceive what we can visualise. While living among the Basotho, the Duat triangle with its 'missing capstone' was my revelation. I had stumbled upon a solution, the nagging question was: to *what -why*? This necessitated reverse unravelling of origin and myth. There seemed to be a central theme and I attempted to make the connection by matching bits and pieces of texts, which led to the discovery of a greater correlation, followed by Rostau and the pyramid blueprints. This catapulted me onto a wild roller coaster ride aboard the Maat & Heka Express in a headlong experience with existence and purpose. The journey led to Cape Town, not Cairo and subsequently continued to the Natal North coast, where terrestrial projection of the triangle would be conclusive in the breakthrough on the purpose of the pyramids. The only remote commonality is longitude, otherwise these locations are very distant from Egypt - in fact, in opposing hemispheres, although roughly equidistant from the equator. While doing further refinements in Gauteng, new discoveries still came unabated, all of which was exciting but also distracting as the task was getting bigger and I did not have the faculty to process it. Other connections exist in sites and monuments elsewhere but hasty research would lack the thoroughness that it deserves. Conclusions need to be drawn with exactness, certainty and truth. Theories have to be argued and tested before they can be accepted –but can *somebody* please do so? Comprehension lies in unraveling the 'story' into coherence. Evidence may be beneath an ocean, swallowed by the Earth, or on Mars and perhaps even in remnants of an exploded planet.

Who are we and where do we come from? Is modern religion modelled on an ancient star cult? If the books of Thoth could reveal 'accurate knowledge of the truth' and facts about the origin or destiny of mankind, and if those books are concealed in a sanctuary, should we not get to them before being annihilated and obliterated?

Chapter 10
THE CONCLUSION

Earth gyration

It is difficult to believe that our civilization was capable of landing men on the Moon, robots on Mars and sending probes beyond our Solar System, when evidently we are ignorant of the characteristics of our own home. Defying verbal expression, Earth motion is generally likened to a gyroscopic device, with Luni-Solar gravitation regarded as the basis of precession. Regardless of whether this may be the actual cause, let's first acquaint ourselves with some observable intricacies. Climate change and the adverse associated consequences, is not satisfactorily understood by our society and begs for pioneering science to engage cross-disciplinary philosophy in investigation of origins. Current models do not explain the trigger of ice ages and strange as it may seem, contemporary science has no concrete knowledge of how ice ages wax and wane –so it is conveniently avoided.

I advocate gyration as the primary driver that integrates all motion into the collective mechanism that constitutes the root cause. My conclusion is: due to Earth's variable axial tilt, the Sun will advance very near to the latitude of the Arctic and Antarctic and unleash a catastrophe of unimaginable proportions...

Antediluvian history echoes a universal warning of violent destruction. It forewarns of a looming apocalypse: devastating global flooding followed by an ice age. Word-wide, mythologies and architectural devices, that diligently track the Sun, bleat this out. Many sites, some with 'boat graves', lay claim to being 'the navel of the World' but how many points of rotation can there be, or, are they commonly related to one axis, through spherical geometry of the highest order?

According to Mayan folklore there had been four previous cycles that ended in cataclysms on the Earth: *"there was water for 52 years* [degrees?] *and the sky collapsed"* as a result of *"great movement of the Earth"*. Legend in the South American Andes region refers to *"overturning of the World, space, time"*. Ancient Sumerian texts also convey that the gods chose a man, whom to give knowledge to on how to withstand the Great Deluge. The Book of Jubilees refers to secrets of Enoch/Thoth of *"what was and what will be"*. It is indeed an event, again destined, for our not-so-distant future -a consequence of the motion of the Earth, alas precession.

In eventually getting to address the 'why?' component, a verifiable break-through has been made with regards to the existence of meticulous ancient knowledge, that relate to this phenomenon: retardation, or precession of the equinoxes, this cycle takes some 26000 years to complete one circuit and is also referred to as a Great Year. It is a deliberate and precise axial motion, rather than the commonly referred to 'wobble', such as that of a spinning top that is about to topple and which suggests an out of control action. Then again, not knowing its instigator -it may have been a massive comet hit that introduced this wobble -be it whatever, we are sitting with, or rather atop, the problem... Any rotational movement must have an axis, albeit imaginary. We shall discover how this cycle regulates vitally important climatic conditions and resultant eco systems on planet Earth. It is a wheel within a wheel gyroscopic-like effect with two independent actions: the one that the Earth spins around on its daily, 24-hour-cycle and the very slow rotation of precession. The Earth, in fact has two axes -the primary concept has been obscured from science. The respective motions of two cycles act in opposition but interact with the orbit of the Earth around the Sun and the consequence is: regions that occupy dark, icy confines on our Globe become exposed to the Sun and vice versa, with devastating effects. The motion of precession, in fact, regulates the orientation of the polar spin axis and causes greater or lesser inclination. This occurs very gradually while the diurnal (day-night spin) action continues unabatedly. The perpendicular relation between the two spheres, determined by the orbit of the Earth around the Sun, is a constant. It is the alteration that the Earth (as a whole) undergoes, *within* this constant (due to varying axial tilt), which concerns us most. The North Pole alignment in the present era is with the star Polaris, however, by the time of attaining max. inclination, Earth would have rolled with its poles to 38 degrees North and South of the plane of the Ecliptic -we are living on an unstable planet! This is the code of the gods, which now raises the questions: who and when? If it is known by any Earthling, it is being kept secret.

"Extraterrestrials would, of course wish to make a message sent to us as comprehensible as possible…"

(**Carl Sagan** – *Cosmos*)

Imagine the Globe as a 'glass sphere' and its contents could be reshuffled (an organized reshuffle, not chaotic crustal shift) without affecting the position of the sphere. The orbit of this sphere around the Sun is a constant regardless of the arrangement of the sphere's contents. The Earth undergoes a rotational tilt or tumble, which does not affect its definitive relationship with the Sun -the orbital plane remains unaltered. The tilt is a consequence of the motion of precession and instigates an alteration in *the apparent path* traced by the Sun around the Globe. Over eons the extent of shift is significant and alters climatic conditions in relation to the oceans and continents, in other words, the contents of the sphere. The definitive Sun-Earth relationship remains fixed at all times and is the only true directional point of reference, expressed in a holy alignment of Virgo-Sun-Earth-Pisces. The Ecliptic lies almost 24 degrees north and south of Earth's equator, or more accurately, the equator lies almost 24 degrees North and South of the Ecliptic, during our present age. Obliquity, in astronomers jargon, quantifies the tilt of the polar axis in relation to the vertical, referred to as the pole of the Ecliptic. Astronomers believe that Earth's poles traces a circle of 47 degrees in diameter on the celestial sphere around a vertical middle point, or so-called still point, referred to as the pole of the Ecliptic. It is popularly pointed out that ideas, which challenged 'accepted astronomy' during the Middle Ages often resulted in persecution, however, the scourge persists even today -'you will fall in with what is dictated or' -no money, no life... Introducing new ideas, especially when it contains the taboo components of pyramids and extra-terrestrial intelligence, is challenging. Complication arises when we view the Globe in a 'downside up' position but it is of important relevance. If the reader finds it irritating, turn the book 'upside down' but the truth cannot be contorted to suit habit.

Alternative approach

Un-conventional for its perspective but essential to comprehend the principle in context, it is necessary to understand ancient Egypt. The pyramids are mysterious monuments that have eluded meaningful explanation for long enough. Their 'message' is interpretable through geometry and in conjunction with astronomy, geology and last but not least, mythology -if the reader desires answers, these are pre requisites and if it is of importance, will initiate him/her self into the elementals as we progress.
Our whole Galaxy revolves, together with us and our Sun. However, for observation purposes, we'll regard the Sun as a stationary body and observe Earth's, motion at periodic intervals. The absolute relationship between the Sun and the Earth is defined by Earth's orbit: it is a constant, perpendicular relationship held by the two bodies, regardless of an elliptical orbit -perpendicular to its plane of orbit, Earth is divided by day and night (similar to the Moon, when it is in half phase). Where the two sectors merge, a demarcation line can be drawn -being a

sphere, one half is always illuminated by the Sun. In accordance with ancient interpretation, Antarctica is oriented at the top position -the Nile flows from 'upper' (South) to 'lower' Egypt (North). This observation is from a remote distance; a peripheral in space, such as viewed for the first time by modern mankind with the circling of the Moon by the 1968 Apollo crew.

The Old Empire pyramids combine purposefully in a device that monitors Earth's progression through the Zodiacal Age. The motion of this cycle is not sufficiently comprehended by our civilization but one which mankind cannot ignore... Undeniable evidence implicates the originators of the true pyramids with the probability of resembling an advanced posse, or alternatively, we have devolved! Suppose we could stop all motion and analyze the geodetic composition: Earth's polar spin axis, is demarcated by a meridian that follows the length of the African Continent, along the Nile River. The geography, that hieroglyphs refer to as 'the land on both sides of the Nile' is reconciled by this meridian. It is delineated by the Meidum Pyramid, the Bent Pyramid & the Red Pyramid at Dahshur, extending up to, and beyond Abusir. With Giza at the hub, Upper and Lower Egypt is divided by a diagonal intersect. Demarcated by the Zawyet el Aryan Pyramid and the Abu Ruwash Pyramid, I shall call this the 'Two-Lands division'. By means of this icon, the pyramid builders thus geometrically capture the Sun-Earth perpendicular relationship geographically and *at a specific time*. Notably, by extension, it also divides the Earth. The associated symbolism of recent archaeological findings is noteworthy: it has been determined that the lower casing of the structure at Abu Ruwash was of red granite and the upper part of white limestone, in accordance with the two Egyptian Crowns. These two pyramids are approximately 13km apart and not equidistant from Giza. From the hub, a ratio 5:7 interestingly brings up the digit $0{,}7143 \times 100 = 71{,}43$. Of primary significance, this diagonal also represents the axis of precession.

This diagonal geodetically encircles the World: roughly described, it follows the Adriatic coast of Italy, traverses Greece [Temple of Apollo?] crossing the Mediterranean Sea, where it links with Giza. From there it proceeds along the Red Sea [two toned Moses Fish - parting?], clipping the horn of Africa [Axum obelisk / Lalibela rock hewn churches?] and transits the Indian Ocean, in the vicinity of the Seychelles Islands -continuing to Auckland Island, between the New Zealand coast and Antarctica. From there to French Polynesia in the vicinity of Tahiti and continues across the Pacific Ocean to the Gulf of California and Mexico. Then diagonally across the United States of America, in the vicinity of Denver and beyond, before crossing the North Atlantic Ocean en-route to Ireland, followed by Stonehenge, Paris [Arc de Triomphe?] before completing the circuit at Rostau Giza, the hub of the diagonal axis. This command of intricate geodesy is the legacy of a civilization long before our own and they accorded great importance to it for the benefit of future generations. The purpose of the pyramids is to monitor the status of precession and to convey information regarding the characteristics of our home, planet Earth.

There also exists an important element of duality in the stars. In Genesis Chapter 1:14 we read that "...stars serve as beacons for *fixed time*, years and days." Further on, in Chapter 13:10 we are informed that Egypt is the garden of God. The geometrical configuration is reflected in celestial topography; incorporating stars of Orion and other constellations, the meridian defined by Polaris, Menkalinan and star SAO 58636 correlates with Earth's polar axis; the celestial divide is demarcated by a diagonal that links Rigel, Betelgeux and Castor. Although we are aware of its various motions, other than its present status, the orientation and synchronization of our planet in time-unison with the Galaxy, is unknown to Earthlings (strange but true). Incredibly however, there exists an *ancient* source that unveils revolutionary comprehension of this motion-time commencement: the layout of pyramids, in unison with their counter parts mapped out in the sky, provides a time-fix for aligning our planet in relation to our Sun, the Zodiac and most remarkably, the Galaxy (by ingeniously overlaying Earth against Heaven). From the location of our Solar System, viewed in flat plan, there are 12 'spokes' that divide the Galaxy. Earth is situated on the Orion arm (at the Auriga intersect), which reaches to the Galactic Centre and across, where it links with Sagittarius, on the opposite side. Viewed from Earth, it is observable in cross section –take the lead:

'...*the Duat has grasped your hand at the place where Orion is...*'
{Pyramid Text.803}

Fundamentals of a time machine

Use a Globe model, set on its standard mounting of approximately 24 degrees and which displays the Ecliptic. Rotate it to align Earth's orbital plane on the horizontal. Arrange 12 calibrations to represent the Zodiac around the globe (a translucent bucket is useful) and for a backdrop, employ a spherical projected star chart with the fulcrum on the 6 Hour RA Meridian -between Orion and Gemini, where it intersects the Galactic equator at right angle. To overcome scale restriction, extend this meridian and mark Polaris where the North Pole targets it.

The two equinoxes correspond with Pisces and Virgo –the latter aligns with the intersection formed by the international dateline and the equator (with Earth set on its spin axis, the mounting will be in alignment with Sagittarius and Gemini). This, together with the horizontal Ecliptic, determines the present era and Sun-Earth perpendicular relationship: the North Pole is inclined toward Gemini and the NH solstice correlates with Bangladesh.

Now, remove the globe from its mounting and circumscribe a line (rubber bands create a straight edge): 52deg. N & S of latitude\ 38deg.E & W of longitude -from the latitude & longitude intersect at Giza -roughly along the Red Sea, this is the Two-Lands division. The two points, midway between where this diagonal cuts the equator, provides the coordinates for the axis of precession: 41deg.W long. x 53deg.N lat. and 138deg.E long. x 57deg.S lat. (these readings may vary, depending on accuracy). Configure the other lines: mark the polar meridian, along the Nile River, draw the triangle with its base between Lake Chad and the Aral Sea - where the longitude of the Aral meets the Equator is its apex.

Replace the globe in its mounting *but importantly*, use the precession axis holes and align the mounting with Pisces and Virgo. Orientate the N.Pole with Polaris, so too bringing the Ecliptic onto a horizontal plane -the globe thus again concords with the present era but is now set on its precession axis. Finally, slowly rotate the globe against Earth's spin direction, causing the focal point of the Sun to shift from Bangladesh Eastward, at right angle to the axis of precession, thereby tracing its precessional equator over one revolution and -voila! 26000 years elapsed...

Earth's precession equator lies at around 24-26 degrees North and South of the Ecliptic. This is also where the oblate mass is. Modern age astronomers have calculated that one degree of rotation takes **71,6** years - a complete circuit thus takes 25776 years. Genesis **1:14** offers a possible mathematical interpretation; 1 divided by 14 equals 0,07143 x1000 =**71,43** x 360 =**25715** This is merely an interesting observation, bearing in mind that the principal objective of this work was an attempt to create simplified order, to understand the concept, and not minuscule mathematics.

Analysis of time & motion

"...and there was darkness and there was light".

Spinning on its polar axis, Earth completes a revolution in 24hours, which in turn comprise smaller units of time. (This spin generates equatorial oblateness). The basis of time is measured in Earth's equator, which is calibrated in geodetic units with intersecting longitude meridians that converge at the poles (a spherical object, its measure is expressed in nautical arithmetic constituents, hence the Pi component). Our cardinal reference is the Sun, not East... Precessional time is tracked by the longitude segments of the Globe passing through the 'static' focal point of the Sun. *This focus (eye) represents the 'detached capstone'* - commencing from and returning to the apex of the triangle in one revolution. For demonstrative purposes, suppose precession takes 25920 years to complete a 360 deg. revolution at a rate of 72years per 1degree of arc. Then 360 divided by 24 longitude hours, equates to 15 degrees. 25920 years divided by 24 longitude hours translates as 1080 years over every 15deg. longitude unit (note: rounding is introduced for simplification).

Earth is suspended on the intersection formed by Virgo & Pisces + Gemini & Sagittarius (the solstice & equinox fixes). Representing 'houses' of the Zodiac, they are comparable to the 3&9 + 6&12 locations on an analogue clock, with Earth at the hub. These references, together with the division correlation and the present era fixes make it possible to plot Earth's gyration cycle. Precession causes a divergence involving longitude and change in orientation of Earths axis. The effect is observable from Earth in the equinox sunrise advancing through the constellations of the Zodiac and change of polar stars. Compounding matters however and in contrast to popular belief, the axis of precession is inclined and *not* perpendicular to the Ecliptic orbital plane, thus exhibiting an obliquity factor, similar to Earth's polar spin axis but intersecting it. This is the governing principal of obliquity: Earth's spin axis is slowly twined around and from the center of the Earth outward, two cones form as the poles trace circles on the celestial sphere. Entwining effect may explain the symbolism in mythologies. *see* FIG.VIII [also refer Enoch 76:4] These circles, with radii of 38 degrees, are virtually tangent and *not* concentric to the pole of the Ecliptic. This is radically different to the current understanding of precession, which presents an astronomical problem: the still point in heaven is not where it was thought to be..!

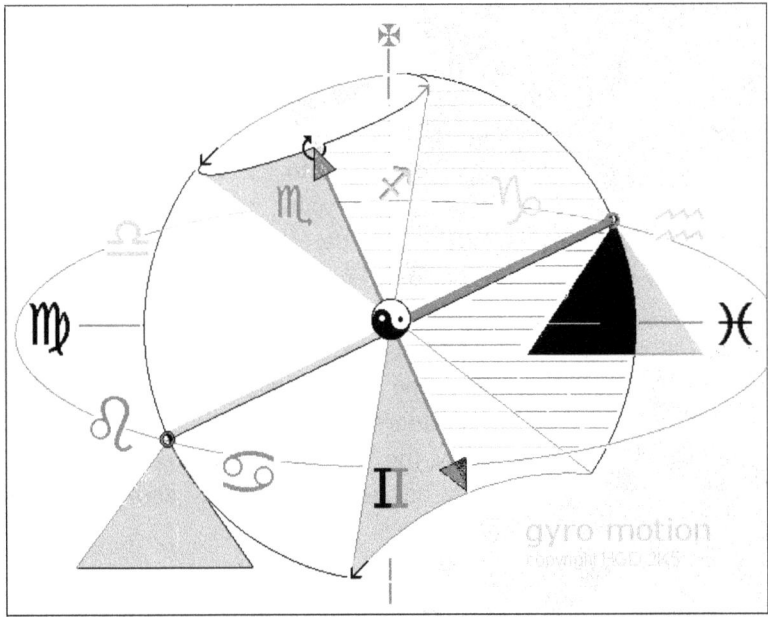

FIG. XIV gyro motion

Observing the spectacle from a static, extra terrestrial peripheral - from the perspective of the Sun, 'housed in the Twins' -provides a purer interpretation of the phenomenon. Earth performs a gyrating dance to two different rhythms, simultaneously maintaining a fixed orbital plane around the Sun. When the Sun is over the Equator, day and night in the two respective halves are of equal duration -an ideal reference. This occurs twice during one orbit around the Sun (a solar year). Half of Earth is continuously illuminated by the Sun, while the other half is in darkness (the two portions face opposite directions into space). The polar axis constantly spins the Globe through the division between day and night. Experiencing the event on Earth is that of sunrise-midday-sunset-midnight back to sunrise, so completing one revolution.

More relevant to this study, is the day-night reversal, which occurs as a consequence of Earth's retrograde revolution -alas precession: Significantly, at a specific moment, the 'Two-Lands division' is in unison with the perpendicular cut of the day|night divide. Precession ushers in a change every half revolution (180 degrees-13000 years apart) when a reversal takes place and the geography that was in darkness then revolves into the illumination of the Sun. For half of the cycle, Earth's polar spin axis is relatively upright, albeit varying but during the other half, one quarter in particular, is subject to dreadful divergence... The two respective peaks occur at the two equinoxes –i.e. the two instances when both poles, along Earth's spin axis, converge vertically with the light|dark division. By mapping Earth and sky, with a correlating meridian, the pyramid builders captured a fix in time. The geometrical configuration of the pyramids, modeled on the sky, provides references harmonious with our Galaxy and enables us to plot any epoch, past or future.

Deviation of Sun's path

Despite the irregularity of an elliptical trajectory, Earth's orbital plane around the Sun is consistent. This constitutes the Ecliptic. It is important to differentiate between 'the path of the Sun' and the Ecliptic as they are not necessarily one and the same. One orbit around the Sun delineates the progression of the Sun around the circumference of the Globe. This constitutes its path. Variation in the angle of Earth's polar spin axis will influence the observable path traced by the Sun on the Globe.

Precessional revolution shifts the Sun's focal point Eastward *and*, due to its inclined action, subsequently causes it to gradually fluctuate between the N & S hemisphere (the axis of precession has an obliquity factor of around 24/26 degrees). This variable combines with the orbital plane of the Earth to generate various paths for the Sun. Deviation is apparent in relation to the continents and oceans, with ensuing climatic implications -the magnitude determined by the extent of tilt.

Earth's orbital motion around the Sun, in conjunction with the obliquity of its axis, brings about the seasons and is the factor, which governs the N & S latitude limits of the Sun. These boundaries -solstice to solstice (a tropical year) -are determined by the degree of inclination in Earth's polar axis. The Sun's *present* reach is contained between the latitudes of the outmoded tropics: Capricorn & Cancer -thus the Ecliptic accords with the *present era* path of the Sun. The Ecliptic of our age could be referred to as the Ecliptic of Pisces, however, currently in transition to the Ecliptic (Age) of Aquarius, with associated variation in the path of the Sun.

Precession phases

'...without roots in science, the interpretation of myths is a risky business'.

(Rand & Rose Flem-Ath, *When The Sky Fell*)

Ancient history can indeed corroborate science. Mythology comprises a body of knowledge, preserved in symbolism and abstract. The primary motivation behind the enormous efforts of the pyramids –the 'words of Thoth in stone –was not for the enterrment of the King but knowledge... of the 'gates' and what is in the 'the Duat'. The ancients did not create an intricate doctrine based on the whereabouts of the Sun at night -they weren't daft, they monitored the the course of the dung beetle as it pushed the Sun along... The progression of the Scarab through 'the hours' in the after world, which constitutes the 13000 year long night of a Great Year, represents the pace of precesssion.

Seth was king of Upper Egypt
Horus occupied Osiris' throne in Lower Egypt
Horus stood over one region and Seth over one region...
the portion of Horus was like that of Seth
which is

the 'Division-of-the-Two Lands'

Then Geb retracted his decision and gave Seth's portion to Horus
Horus stood over the Two Lands as the uniter
of Upper and Lower Egypt

The trial of Horus and Seth lasted 80 years [1 degree of arc in 72 years equals 25920 + 80 = 26000]. The 'cross', 'death and resurrection' are components of prophecies that express an event.

Consolidating the legend

We have seen how the diagonal between the Abu Ruwash Pyramid, via Giza and Zawyet el Aryan, divides Egypt but essentially the Earth, *equally*. The two domains house the seats of power: Osiris' (G1 /Alnitak) and Seth's (G3 /Mintaka) respectively. This configuration has a heavenly counterpart that corresponds accordingly: Rigel via the Orion Belt stars to Betelgeux and beyond divides the celestial topography into two sectors also. The geography, divided by light and dark, 'exchange places' after a half precessional revolution and face opposite directions. The 1/2 Earth previously illuminated, is in darknesss and vice-versa.

During the golden era (Sun on apex of triangle = stable equinox - i.e. upright polar axis) Osiris ruled over all Egypt. Then Earth precessed by 1/4 rotation and Seth executed a dynastic coup, forcing Osiris from the limelight. Osiris' geographical anatomical figure, represented by pyramids (ref. anthropomorpic gods article), entered the perpendicular night divide, where he established and afterworld kingdom in the Duat, where the figure mapped out in stars represents his spirit form (as below..). Seth then reigned terra firma, as his domain gyrated through the illumination of the Sun over the following 13000 years –the time during which axial tilt causes destruction and chaos.

Seth said he was merely *defending himself*. The two territories 'compete' perpetually as Earth revolves precessionally, exposing one to the Sun, while the other faces the starry Duat. Seth claimed that *Osiris attacked him* when becoming 'lengthy of stride'. The geometrical anatomy of Orion presents an elongated perspective but also, the two intersecting axes (legs) of the Earth, at the pivotal hub of Giza, mimick a 'walking action' as Earth gyrates.

Horus, the Falcon god of the sky, was cloned to avenge his father and went in pursuit of his uncle. After an epic time, the eye (Sun) was restored to the domain of Osiris: the other portion is exposed to the Sun -'that which belonged to Seth is then given to Horus', the uniter, by the Earth god Geb -i.e. the domain of Seth, previously favoured by the Sun, returns to the dark side, while Osiris' emerges, shining, resurrected from death...

Arbitration resulted in a power share, equally dividing the geography. The two sectors house the seats of power -the two crowns of Upper Egypt and Lower Egypt, ruled by Osiris and Seth. The White Crown of Upper Egypt and the Red Crown of Lower Egypt represent *the entire Globe*, therefore it should be aligned accordingly: with its crown(s) at the top...

'Two Earths', one portion in darkness, the other illuminated. Earth's **red crown** *(Australia) and* **white crown** *(Antarctica)* slowly encircle the Ecliptic pole, each occupying the celestial crown during two opposing eras. Antarctica remains the principality of Earth's spin axis, however, altered orientation instigated by precession, cause the two continents *(red Australia & white Antarctica)* to exchange places -either side of the light|dark divide -every half (180 deg) turn. Earth's axis performs a pendulum motion and the triangle (tooth/thorn) with its base line (tepi), see-saws in relation to the balance of the Ecliptic, so emulating the scales of Ma'at. The Sphinx faces sunrise and the base line, [tepi], is locked onto the Ecliptic of that age, its back to the equinox sunset [double headed Lion figure?]. Earth's retrograde revolution enacts the division and (Re)unification, symbolized by the double crown -interfacing celestial topography, anthropomorphically -the transit from one era to another, *Zep Tepi ~ the first time...*

The Narmer Palette glyphs suggest sanctification of a 'great door' –associated with taking possession of territory, or is it an inauguration of the other portion on the flipside..? Sher Mor, a member on Graham Hancock's forum, has drawn a thought provoking parallel between the brothers Cain & Abel and Osiris & Seth that neatly reconciles the legends. By reading and participating in the forum I have gained much insight in a variety of topics. Historians are going to have much to reconsider.

'...The beginning of the Horn of the West, the gate of the Western Horizon. This is the knowledge of the power... the knowledge... of the Gates'

(beginning of **Amduat**)

Let's take a look at the terrestrial (Duat) triangle -projected over the landmass of the Middle East and Africa. Its baseline (*tepi*) extends between the Aral Sea and Lake Chad [Pleiades association?] It is significant to note that the goddess Isis, whose celestial association is with the star Sirius, is also referred to as 'the lady of the lake'. Aral Moya is situated at 45.deg. North latitude and 60.deg. East of Greenwich Mean. Are these two lakes natural phenomena –could they be *Nommos* created? The apex of this triangle is situated in the Indian Ocean, off the Horn of Africa, in the vicinity of the Seychelles. It is 'severed' by the precessional equator, which the migratory Sun circumscribes around the World -a 'wandering capstone,' which is symbolic of the Sun. We have seen the heavenly component, complete with 'missing' vertex, in the geometry of the stars. When these two triangles are transposed –one could say: 'like a hand in a glove' -in other words viewed as though the Globe is transparent, they have a commonality and the combined effect represents the 'world tree' or 'tree of life'.

The 'Two-Lands division' (precession axis) also circumscribes the Globe and intersects the precession equator at 90 degrees. We thus have two intersecting circles that form a cross at two equidistant points, situated over the equator, on opposite sides of the Globe and 13000 years apart -one is over the Indian Ocean and the other over the Pacific Ocean. These points form the markers that connect the two stations, which represent the Equinoxes of precession. The geographical triangle occupies the two stations respectively during a precessional revolution. The connotation of 'Maat' and the pendulum balance of Earth can be registered on a calibration comprising the constellations in the Firmament:

From its relative upright position, Earth's axis gyrates precessionally, so shifting from alignment with Gemini- Galactic Centre– Sagittarius. The North Pole traverses Taurus, followed by Aries as it dips toward the celestial equator in Pisces, where max. inclination is attained. Then, via Aquarius and Capricorn, the polar axis again begins to assume the upright position as it again comes in alignment with the Galactic Center and with Antarctica tilted toward Gemini. Minimum inclination is attained soon thereafter. The unstable half of precession thus follows after every stable half of 13000 years –this corroborates accepted world history of the last Ice Age experiencing a climax circa 15000BC.

Unstable phase:
We are fast approaching an era during the cycle of precession when the Sun's perpendicular focus on the Globe will advance to its Northern-most latitude. The occurrence of this precessional solstice, if we may refer to it as such, corresponds with: 135.deg.E longitude and 30.deg.N latitude (off the coast of Japan). The geographic and celestial meridians will correlate at that specific time. *see* as above, so below images. The terrestrial triangle (and Giza) will then occupy its upper-most position in relation to the Ecliptic, signifying **the division of the Two-Lands**.

The triangle, with its base parallel to the Ecliptic plane straddles the vertical day-night division between Virgo-Pisces [Horus in Sothis?Sun transit Sirius]. The Ecliptic of that age connects two ante poles: the one situated in Saudi Arabia, at Mecca, the navel of the World and the other in Easter Island, on the fringe of Polynesia. Departing from this point, as Earth rotates precessionally, over the following 6500 years and 90 degrees of arc later, the *peak* of the *critical quarter* is reached -with the precessional Equinox on the equator, in the Pacific Ocean at 135. deg. West parallel. During this age the polar axis is at its extreme tilt, exposing the latitudes of Antarctica and the Arctic to the Sun in a spell of disaster.

Stable phase:
This ideal equatorial conjunction with the Ecliptic plane occurs after a further 90.deg. of precessional rotation -i.e. 180 degrees/ 13000 years after the commencement of the unstable phase. The golden age of the First Time is heralded in, when Giza again emerges from the dark. The perpendicular focus is then on 45 degrees West longitude and 35 degrees South latitude -the Southern Hemisphere precession Solstice, off the coast of Uruguay/Brazil. The geographical triangle again straddles the perpendicular day/night division [light/dark divide of the Virgo-Pisces opposition] but reversed: 'that which belonged to Seth is then given to Horus' –that signifies **the unification of the Two-Lands.** i.e. the half portion that was in darkness is then illuminated by the Sun. The geographical Duat triangle also occupies its lowest parallel position in relation to the ecliptic plane. The Ecliptic of this age connects the Andean Lost civilization sites of Peru and Bolivia in South America with those located in Japan and Cambodia, on the opposite side of the Globe, which explains their role in tracking the Sun. Other symbolism noteworthy here: at the stable *peak* -when the polar axis is at minimum inclination most upright, the focus of the migrating Sun returns to the apex of the projected triangle. This occurs 90 deg. rotation/ 6500 years from the commencement of the stable phase. At this time -the Indian Ocean Equinox of precession -Antarctica, the white crown of the 'Upper Earth', is closest to alignment with the pole of the Ecliptic (not to be confused with the celestial pole).

Recollections from Sumeria, according to Secharia Sitchin, determine the great deluge to have occurred during the Age of Leo. We have transited from there to the Age of Pisces and are currently on the brink (2012) of entering the Age of Aquarius –i.e. halfway (13000 years) away from and toward returning to the age of Leo. Thus, despite being debunked by scholars and often snubbed even by alternative historians, his interpretation in this regard seems pretty accurate. Astronomers determined these Ages by the constellation in which the equinox Sunrise takes place. It advances through the twelve 'Houses of the Zodiac', with each allocated 30 degrees of arc it can be regarded as remaining for some 2160 years in one constellation before entering the next. This phenomenon is a subsequence of precession. The Eastward migrating focus of the Sun is presently in the vicinity of the Bay of Bengal -over Bangladesh, on the latitude of the Tropic of Cancer, hence the Ecliptic departure of our current age. Gradually worsening climatic conditions will usher in the next catastrophic period, which commences with ground zero hour within two and a half millennia, when the Sun-Earth perpendicular correlates with Japan. Early indications are evident in the evolution of weather pattern and climate -alas, global warming (but not man-made). Seen from another perspective of reference; we have entered the unstable half of the precessional cycle and are presently en-route to being subjected to the catastrophic phase -if the critical age occupies one quarter of the cycle, we have entered into the third quarter -**bluntly put, the end is near!**

Of course, there are a myriad of other natural disasters and calamities that occur. Most apparent of all is the desire in prevailing human behavior to orchestrate our own demise a.s.a.p. In the least likelihood of that failing however, we have been warned and *you* are the parent of future generations...

The last *peak* was experienced 17820 years ago and the next will be 8100 years from present time. This is determined by counting longitude lines crossing the Sun's focus during precessional rotation, measured from our current age. The time to act was yesterday -we can expect that unstable climatic and geological conditions will prevail *long* before the critical peak. There is archaeological evidence in the features of the Scablands in North America, of such massive and repetitive flooding having occurred some 12000 years ago -ref: Earth Shocks, National Geographic Channel; Roy Breckenridge (Idaho Geological Survey); Brett Waitt (United States Geological Survey).

Professor Charles Hapgood's theory, which perceived displacement of Earth's crust (ECD) presented a good hypothesis. However, besides minor tectonic movement, Earths mantle does not 'slip'. Crustal brake up would certainly be random and not exhibit a cyclical and repetitive pattern. There are similarities, resultant in tilting of Earth's axis but effectively, Earth displaces 'as a whole'. Contemporary science is oblivious of this and my 'mission impossible' is in challenging the white coats, with their many pens in the top pocket and calculator in the side pocket, to overcome the threat of myopia.

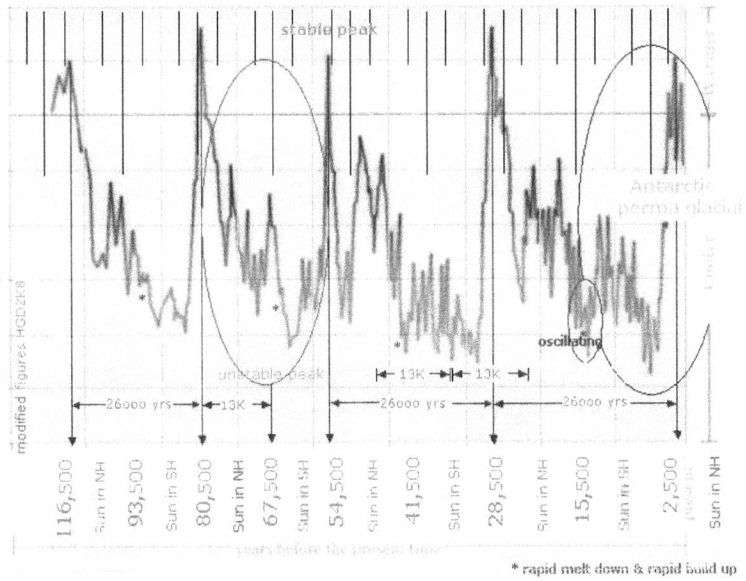

FIG. XV temperature graph

Climate change

'...upon these men (apocalyptists) was laid the privilege and duty of revealing the divine secrets to others... upon the basis of this knowledge... knowing when the end of the world would come...'

(*The Book of Enoch, translated by* **R.H. Charles**, *introduction by* **W.O.E. Oesterly**)

Ice Age cometh...

There are many inconsistencies in Earth history, with numerous cataclysms, for which cause is unaccounted. This knowledge is therefore imperative for those that hope to survive the critical phase: I define an ice age as a period of glacial meltdown *and concurrent* build up, oscillating six monthly between the Northern and Southern hemispheres. This rapid freeze-thaw fluctuation occurs during one quarter of the precession cycle and coincides with max. glaciation, which is generated by radical Earth tilt. This factor is responsible for muddled core data, therefore erroneous interpretation. Polar tilt is the only mechanism that reconciles such great extent of ice -Earth gyration being the primary element, which then interacts with spin and orbital motion. Maximum inclination occurred 17820 years ago (due in 8100 years). Similarly, the two principal annual seasons, where related conditions prevail for long either side of the peaks of mid summer and mid winter, however glacials and intermediate periods constitute millennia and not millions of years, as popularly believed.

The effect of precession is to shift the calendar around, over many years, as the longitude (of the solstice/equinox) processes around the Ecliptic. I argue however, that the Zodiacal Age does not progress around the vertical 'z' axis but integrates an *inclined action*, of approximately 26 degrees. Precession thus not only advances time and seasons but also rolls Earth (with its crust uncompromised and intact), toward, or away from the ecliptic orbital plane. Through this circular pendulum motion, the polar spin axis undergoes a change in orientation -ranging between 104 & 32 degrees. Of interest to Mayan enthusiasts, is the midway transition, when Earth's spin axis aligns longitudinally (as at present) with its South Pole toward the Galactic Center. Our planet, in fact, *rotates about two points simultaneously*... There are no physical axles, yet revolution occur around two separate hubs: rapid spin, and gyration. The latter regulates the poles to revolve in circles, with radii of 38degrees, subjecting Earth's polar axis to obliquity variance from 14deg. to 58deg. Earth's spin produces equatorial bulge -be this raised area water or land, in cubits, feet or meters, it matters not –it merely constitutes undulating topography. What matters, is *the angle* at which Earth spins.

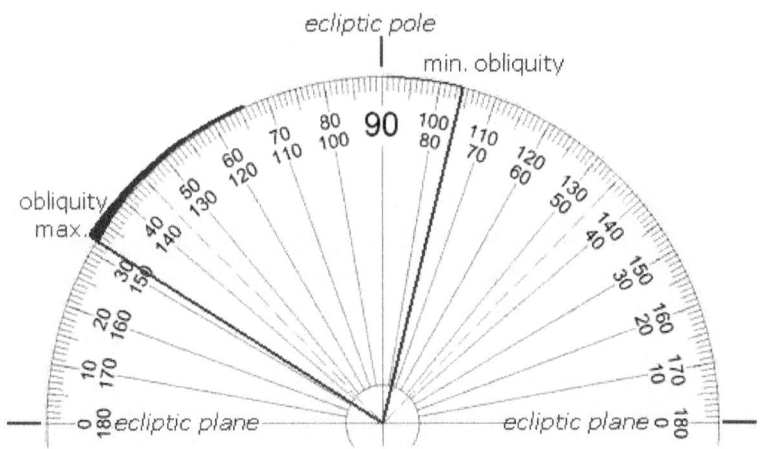

FIG. XVI protractor

Motion and variance is observed in changing star positions. The US Navy logs the coordinates of stars in a Multiyear Interactive Computer Almanac (MICA). Two dimensional star charts produce parallax deficiencies of either the celestial pole, or the ecliptic pole however -the actual aligned 'target' of the axis only becomes apparent through observing diurnal spin. Angle variation is determinable by polar-stellar alignment but there is no need to employ deep space quasars to monitor this. Change is observable in 'the cut' of Earth's dark side as it gyrates slowly around its precession hub, with each pole tracing a circle of 76 degrees diameter, over 26000 years.

The spin angle, in conjunction with the plane of orbit, governs the distribution of Sunlight over the Globe. Should its eccentric orbital path range somewhat closer, or further, from the Sun, it matters not... even if Earth's equatorial and polar circumference (thus too, diameter) measures differ, it's marginal -Earth revolves and the Sun shines. The critical quarter (some 6500 years) during Earth's wobble, when maximum tilt is attained, is of consequence: orbiting the Sun in this orientation, activates amassed ice to thaw in one hemisphere, while re-forming anti-podally. This constitutes a rapid melt down *and* rapid build up of apocalyptic proportion, every six months, continuing year after year, for decades and centuries... following the next two millennia, this phase is entered as the Sun's perpendicular focus migrates some 15 degrees closer to polar latitudes, driving an escalating and relentless catastrophe.

For the full duration of every precession cycle, the zone between the tropics (as defined in the present era) remains temperate, although with evolving climate and eco system variables. The bulk of this zone comprises vast ocean, thus, while North America, Scandinavia, Britain, the Northern parts of Europe and Asia experience an icy grip, suitable habitat is restricted to the central Americas, Southern Europe and the golden arc: Africa, Arabia, Southern Asia and Australasia. Coastal and low lying areas will be severely compromised by flooding however.

Mainstream belief, mistakenly, is that the Earth experienced one ice age during the past 400K years. *Actually there have been four ice ages during the past 100K years...* Science is unwitting of the cyclical regularity that takes place. Historical sea levels concord with the model, which is also corroborated by the temperature chart. Maximum glaciation was attained 93500 years before the present era, repeated 67500 yrs BP then the penultimate ice age 41500 yrs ago and followed by subsequent events:

26.500BC / 28500 yrs BP = penultimate stable peak (two perma-polar ice caps)
20.000BC / 22000 " = global flooding commences, oscillating to glacial max.
13.500BC / 15500 " = last ice age peak, oscillating melt down continues
07.000BC / 09000 " = end of ice age (Sun in SH), sea levels stabilize
00.500BC / 02500 " = stable peak (two perma-polar ice caps return)
      0 ~ present era = precessional focus of Sun in NH
04.500DC / 02500 yrs to next global flood, ice age pending...
10.000DC / 08000   - " -   ice age peak, glacial maximum

Fabled mystery

Brimming with the names of royalty, the territorial claims staked out on the continent of Antarctica is noteworthy. Supposedly a World heritage site, but who effectively holds control? Speculating upon this being the location of Atlantis of legend, conspiring motivation is boundless -not least of all, a summer home, lying reserved under the ice for the elite. *Are there royal-blood descendants with claims to this homeland, which is larger than North America? Or, is there a band of self proclaimed elect among us, with greedy desires for this prime real estate -orchestrating their own salvation and leaving, the rest of humankind, the workers, who toiled for paper money in creating Global infrastructure, to meet their fate of doom? Numbers originally required but now overpopulated, will the meek be blessed by inheriting the chaotic Earth when the top echelon flee? Is the manifestation of illuminati in tracking the Sun? Are we savage primitives, oblivious of the truth and sadly missing experiencing one life and freedom? Are UFO sightings our returning time traveling forebears, who escaped the last upheaval? Is a 13000 years evolutionary gap too great for us to relate?*

There's no shortage in permutations of tactics by those with motive to retain dominion over naive subjects through keeping them ignorant... The Southern Hemisphere is unique, with having a landmass on the pole. When the Sun's focus reaches its Southern precessional Solstice, near Uruguay, the reigning Ecliptic of the epoch takes the path of the Sun very near to the Antarctic Circle! After initial upheaval of shedding its icy cloak, such as occurred between 9000BP & 7000BP, prime conditions emerged for habitation of the South continent -commencing with hot summers and dark winters, that culminate in a golden period between 6500BP & 4300BP. Periodically, Antarctica presents a great new continent, albeit temporary, for around 2 millennia, or so. While in the rest of the radically reduced habitable World, where the viability of agriculture will be determined by many altered factors, combined in ocean currents, wind, precipitation and temperature,

Antarctica, due to favourable orientation of Earths axis, prospers in an era of temperate semi-permanent twilight, like an endless summer. *Could this virgin paradise, with abundant resources be the Atlantis of legend -will we be around still to go and exploit it?*
With the passage of time, the polar axis gradually assumes an upright position again while the focus of the Sun migrates along its precessional equator to the intersect of the prime parallel - defined by the Nile, Giza, Dashur, Meidum, Great Zimbabwe and the Antarctic Pole. With the dawning of this epoch, the equatorial plane of Earth's spin rotation comes closest to converging with the horizontal plane of the Ecliptic. This equates as the end of the golden age of Osiris, when the former land of the gods comes to a sudden end as a consequence of perma ice. In Egyptian legend, all subsequent kings were the followers of Horus -trackers of the Sun. Gnostic Gospels refer to an 'Organization' that serves the Sun and its purpose is to initiate humans into knowledge and freedom, that ignorance is evil and that the Deluge subjects humanity to a life of toil and pre-occupancy with worldly affairs instead of pursuance of the quest for immortality. *Could this be the culmination of the truth of our genesis, in word and myth from every religion and society around the Globe? Symbolic keys to heavenly knowledge that will unite mythology and theology with one ultimate and supreme manifestation? Salvation of the soul can be attained through reasoning, experience and knowledge acquired during material existenc -Maat and Heka, the pursuance of eternal righteousness and fulfillment of the quest for immortality of humankind, as a species... the ideal path of the Sun in the battle of Armageddon between good and evil but who's who?*
Historically, beyond the Roman roads, wars have paved the way for events of quite a different nature to what was propagated. One wonders about the Falklands incident, when the Iron Lady engaged in a modern and sophisticated strategic war with Argentina. Patriotism aside, seemingly over a gateway to Antarctica... Likewise, one can only ponder on the true motives behind the antics of Bush by the Rivers of Babylon at the core of

the golden arc. Such political strategies are not in synchronization with the standard of evolution expected in our time, yet, this individual was democratically elected -twice (serving a double term) -oops! Elsewhere, fanaticism and indoctrination is rife too but let's stay with covert solar reverence. Wittingly cloaked or coincidental, thought provoking symbolism is found on American one dollar paper currency: the 13 layered pyramid and detached eye of Horus. In tandem with Stonehenge, the George Washington obelisk traces a concentric circle around the axis of precession. Stonehenge aligned with the Ecliptic pole some 9600 years ago, while straddling the precessional day/night divide. The Washington obelisk will align with the pole of the Ecliptic some 4800 years from the present, when the focus of the Sun will be situated on the Tropic of Capricorn, where it intersects the international longitude date line over the Pacific Ocean. This signifies the commencement of the critical quarter of precession. During the stable peak, Mt. Erebus, an active volcano in the vicinity of the U.S. Antarctic base, aligns with the pole of the Ecliptic. True to the legend, this location of the Greek god Erebus, is in a geographical struggle with twilight…

In the Southern Hemisphere, New Zealand was bisected by the pole of the Ecliptic some 11900 years ago. In Maori legend it is said: "that if the brothers Maui had not acted so deceitfully, the huge fish would have remained as a model for the rest of the Earth, for the present generation of men". It is regarded as 'the second evil', which took place after 'the separation of Heaven from Earth'. This will replay with a return in 14000 years from our present time. At the critical peak, Lake Eyre in Australia correlates with the precessional still point in heaven. The Ecliptic of the critical age also connects Easter Island and Great Zimbabwe, which significantly is associated with Horus bird-like symbolism. The tightly fitted stonework of the Great Enclosure is topped by double chevron pattern: tooth/thorn/nail/tepi –the wave of precession? The number 72 recurs in mythology and in dimension ratios of sites around the World. This also brings to mind the passage in the Bible dealing with the apocalypse, the downfall of evil and in its aftermath, a second coming –the return of Heaven to Earth. We read about the 'number of the Beast' in Revelation 13:18

'Let him that hath understanding count the number of the beast, for it is the number of a man and his number is six hundred and the count six'.

The chapter and verse in this case also provides an interesting derivation; 13 divided by 18 equals 0.72 (x100=72). The Old Testament incidentally comprises 39 Books; 13x2=26+13=39 divided by 2 = 19,5 (a Moon related figure). The so called 'number of the beast' also features in related mathematics; 13000 divided by 19,5 equals 666.666' –this number in turn, when multiplied by 39 equals 26000 and so on and so forth. While coincidence is favoured by odds, awareness allows one to investigate possibilities and is harmless as opposed to enforcing evil rule and control through fear and threat (land claims, rights and freedoms, passports, taxation). For ancient astronomers tracking the Sun would have been the primary objective although Earth's satellite, the Moon, would certainly have been closely monitored as well. Psalm 19:5 and the Book of Job 38:5 refer to measures of a Sun-Earth relationship and a division tilt. A Moon solstice occurs every 19 years. The waxing and waning Moon, to observant intelligence, would have been indication of the unique shadow characteristics associated with a spherical object under illumination of the Sun. Its proximity to Earth means the relative perpendicular relationship with the Sun to be virtually identical as that of the Sun and Earth and could be interpreted as: above, so below. By studying the day-night division line of the Moon it could be transposed to terrestrial orientation. There exists a coordinated network of monuments around the Earth and correlating to the sky. There is a third and smaller pyramid, that of Quetzalcoatl, who is associated with the figure Osiris, is also present at Teotihuacan the Mexican pyramid site. The site is laid out on a grid system and has a possible link to the Pleiades. Teotihuacan is 19,5 degrees north of the equator and an astronomical device, keeping count of doomsday; with its Pyramid of the Sun and the Pyramid of the Moon, from which extends the Way of the Dead (also referred to as the Way of the Stars). This avenue is set on an axis of 15 degrees 30 minutes West of South that targets Easter Island and the pole of the Ecliptic -at the commencement of the critical half of precession, with the Sun focus on Yonaguni. Yonaguni is a submerged site South-West of Japan (and 19,5 degrees East of Angor Wat) and incorporates a trench that aligns to the equinox. The site at Angor Wat, in Cambodia, incorporates a long causeway set at 0,75 degrees North of East –marking a precessional target.

At Chichen Itza on the Yucatan (on the same latitude as Giza -30 degrees North of the equator), where it intersects the two lands diagonal i.e. the axis of precession, there is a stepped pyramid, known as the temple of Kulkan. Its main axis is set at 38 degrees and targets the equinox. Yet another site at Nasca, in Peru also comprises many intriguing geometrical elements that align to the equinox and solstice. It ought to be a cause for concern that all these early civilizations possessed knowledge, which somehow, a later civilizsation -our civilization -had become estranged from...

What, where and now why has been answered. When, as we have seen, is determinable from this information, which leaves us still to contemplate who, which will reveal how. Two scenarios arise: humanity has been around for long and attained a level of evolution far beyond that imagined, then, through a catastrophic event regressed, or alternatively, there has been a probe from a civilization, from elsewhere... This may seem like nothing new in terms of speculative hypotheses but the difference is; it is uniquely and practically demonstrable –the evidence is tangible and irrefutable, yet sadly, humanity seems content to remain oblivious to these facts. If, as suggested by Sitchin, Earth was indeed occupied by extraterrestrials some 445000 years ago, the deluge and ice ages would have repeated 17 times since then. The appearance of mankind and myth merge into the most recent of the occurrence. Mayan and Andean records however, indicate human ancestry as having been subjected to it 4 times previously with expectations of the next due. Of concern to us, should be that these extremities have been monitored and recorded at a remote time, when according to our historic and scientific evolution, it was impossible, yet the evidence is overwhelming and echoes a grave warning: we have not yet grasped the complexity and consequence of precession! This information is latent in the geometry of the pyramids and stars, proving in the process, beyond any doubt, that their ingenuity cannot be attributed to anybody of any lesser stage of evolution to what our civilization has attained, but quite probably, far beyond... Earth's wobble causes a change in orientation of its axis. Orion thus rises and sets in lesser arcs above the horizon. Earth's axis at min inclination, some 2800 years BP, when Orion culminated on the celestial meridian in alignment with the KC South shaft and 13000 years later, at max. inclination the KC *North Shaft* targets Menkalinan on the celestial meridian (extant computer software lacks this knowledge, therefore cannot produce simulation).

Menkalinan's Earthly counterpart, we recall is the bent Pyramid, with its curious double slope. This, together with the Meidum Pyramid's original super structure requires some investigation. A superb intelligence devised a vertical sliding scale, so formulating a celestial meridian that Earth's pole targets at calibrated intervals while bobbing during a retrograde revolution. The motion that the Earth undergoes during a Great Year is 'concealed' within the equinoxes, as we understand them. The cycle of precession is in fact the Earth's primary action that has a bearing on all the other motions, namely: orbit around the Sun and rotation of the polar axis. The axis of precession is thus *not parallel* to the vertical 'z' axis but angled at around 24-26 degrees. The pendulum effect of the sky pivots on this axis, which means the circle traced out by the poles is not concentric to the pole of the Ecliptic and this is where the underestimation of precession lies: the pole of the ecliptic is not the centre point of balance. The off-set of this axis brings about the tilt of Earth's polar spin axis and during one quarter of the precessional cycle the poles are subjected to direct and prolonged Sun, without nights to cool...

Other than the gravitational effect of the Sun and the Moon, could this wobble have been induced by a glancing comet strike that wiped out most life and formed the Himalyan rim? We needed an accurate point of reference to realise the complete cycle and where we are in relation to it. It is a complex event to describe in words and required a medium, sufficiently robust for the message to survive the ravages of time. It was encrypted in the mythologies of antediluvian nations, waiting to be discovered -surviving in cultural practices -composed in word, song, architecture and scientifically, in astronomy and mathematics. In the Book of Enoch we read that God has put a chart on Earth and engraved in heaven to survive the Deluge and to keep count. The Biblical account of the Great Flood informs us that God will not destroy the world (mankind) in this manner again. This must mean it has been righted already, or, a warning has been left to aid us to overcome a grave fate. Perhaps a device that would enable us to avert this catastrophe -an 'ark,' so to speak, was incorporated at Giza [Did Moses carry a component from Egypt?]. Perhaps it's in self salvation -an opportunity to allow us to manage our destiny on this planet -when emotionally achieving a level of spiritual maturity and responsibility to be worthy of receiving it: when we are capable of soaring above degeneration, malice, hatred, cruelty, fear, affliction, jealousy and envy. Can our civilization meet the criteria to embark on action required to commence in this era?

PART II epilogue

In the summer of 2003, I was once again back on the North Coast of Kwa-Zulu Natal, where the first edition was printed and distributed six months earlier. After marketing to bookstores in Johannesburg and Pretoria over the past winter season, the warm Indian Ocean and a change of environment were welcoming. This time my objective was to create international awareness of my website and work. In the process of pondering on the 'why issue' and astronomical duality, the geographical geodesy relating to precession started revealing itself. In Lesotho I had seen a triangle in the sky, which I now projected on the World... I commenced with formulating my conclusion. The implications soon dawned, whereupon I **felt compelled to divulge my findings urgently to responsible parties** (from then, up to and including this edition, that's what I have been tirelessly occupied with but now tired of).
Correspondence was forwarded to the ambassadors in South Africa of: the USA, Britain, Germany, (no address for France), Russia, Japan, Egypt and Australia. cc: South African Ministry of Foreign Affairs. In the case of U.K and U.S.A. letters were delivered to the relevant Consuls in Durban by a commissioner of oaths. My request to the High Commissions was that this knowledge be brought to the attention of parties to whom it may be of concern –I envisaged these to include; Heads of State, research and development organisations, intelligence agencies, religious institutions and the academia. The South African Ministry promptly acknowledged receipt and indicated that it had been forwarded to the Department of Science and Technology. An automated email response by the Egyptian Embassy indicated it will be forwarded to the relevant person. Nobody has requested further details on the matter however (perhaps Dr. Hawass will make the announcement on live television soon!). The seemingly ignorant attitude of the political and scientific community is reckless and irresponsible, to say the least. It is a masochistic

infliction upon oneself to suggest any alternative interpretation to academic circles. This reaction was in response to a *one page* synopsis of my work:

----- Original Message -----

Sent: Friday, March 12, 2004 4:37 PM
Subject: Re: scientific find
You are an idiot and your theory is complete rubbish - do not waste my time with this tedious crap in future!

Dear sir
Among more than five hundred you certainly are the exception. My apologies for having upset you so much by merely trying to share knowledge -is it such a threat to warrant your reaction? On what educated basis may I ask is your opinion based? Have you studied my work to reach your conclusion? I can substantiate my claims -can you *prove* them wrong?
sincerely
H.G. Dirker

Sent: Saturday, April 17, 2004 1:39 AM
Subject: Reaction
Easily! and my quals are I have PhD in Egyptology - you are talking arrant, irrational nonsense but I have better things to do than waste my energies on you. Now go away and leave me off your lists in future.

----- Original Message -----

I obliged the gentle man from New Zealand and then commenced with mailing my findings to academies of science and astronomers -hopeful of presenting to a more receptive audience! Convincing the learned about the motion of our Earth was not going to be a sane task either, and for my own reference and an 'anchor to reality', I forwarded correspondence to a pshycologist in Cape Town. Then, scraping together last resources, I traveled to London in pursuit of endorsement and publicity.

With efficient assistance at Heathrow, I made a hotel reservation; a bed-sit with a telephone and shower cubicle in close proximity of Victoria station. Although it was incurring high costs (in my situation) it was centrally situated. Despite the convenience of a very efficient transportation system I did much walking, seeking out elusive agents and blisters soon slowed me down. In addition, a niggling toothache and a flu virus, probably owing to the confined space on the long flight from Johannesburg via Madrid began making a presence. None-the-less, I was making the best of an intriguing and exciting experience of discovery and enjoying the conscious thrill of an adventure. In summer, Britain is charmingly dressed in multitudes of bright colours, cascading from flowerpots on buildings and busy streets. With my scant funds, I was on a 19 day scheduled stay and had traveled there in the past, so all was not strange, my mission was… Hopeful of an opportunity to demonstrate my precession model, I ventured to the Royal Astronomical Society along Piccadilly. After being granted access, signing the visitors' book and without elaborating, I proclaimed to a fellow of the society that I had made an astronomical discovery "of the nature that evoked persecutions during the Middle Ages". I was reassured in good humour that persecutions don't take place any more and reporting of new astronomical phenomena, I learned, is to be made to the Central Bureau for Astronomical Telegrams (CBAT) in America (I did so repeatedly by mail, with no acknowledgement whatsoever). Still eager for strategic divulgement to officialdom, upon my departure, I noticed the door of The Geological Society in the courtyard. Perhaps due to intrigue or my foreign accent, after proclaiming an unusual situation with reference to my discovery over the intercom, I was let into a large and beautiful office. Perhaps somewhat bemused but refreshingly friendly, the nice lady informed me that the department head was on leave. She was very helpful however and took receipt of a complimentary copy and notes. Although only aware of the many tourist attractions in passing, the Shabaka Stone at the British Museum was a priority. I donated two complimentary books to curators at the Egyptology section. My situation straddled a paradox: publicity demands rhetoric and sensationalism while science relied on tedious facts, potentially insignificant to a population at large. The original intention had been to raise much needed capital –possibly through publicity in a newspaper. One noteworthy and agonizing telephone conversation was with a reporter, for *The Independent*, who humored my sensational claim and enquired: "which galaxy my pyramid builders were from". He requested that I send him a copy by 'second class' mail –I coughed up the extra for postage, thinking it deserved 'first class' travel ☺

Another indigenous splash of colour to express individualism, are the red, blue, green and of course black or white doors that adorn the rows of tenements on the streets of London. Undeterred and after being declined access to the office of a literary agent, in the absence of an appointment minutes earlier, I called from the public telephone on the nearby street corner, after which I was granted entry beyond the blue door in Covent Garden, to deliver a cover letter and sample copy of *Zep Tepi~The First Time*. Another meeting, with a 'pinstripe suited' literary agent, who collected me in a traditional London black Cab for a coffee, raised my hopes. The handsome advance accompanying such a deal would've rescued me but unfortunately it turned out that "it would be unethical for the publisher, the biggest buyer of this material, to do my project because they represent Bauval". With those hopes dashed, the situation called for new strategy. The dozen, or so books in my possession needed to be distributed over a diverse range and I went to London University, where I left a parcel for the Head of the Department of Astronomy and Physics. I attempted telephone calls to other institutions but inevitably, an astronomer was not accessible –what I had not kept reckoning with was that academic faculties were closed for the summer holidays. Hospitality extended by my friends in the North-West of

Britain provided the opportunity to prolong my stay in by 3 months, in an attempt to benefit maximum from the campaign. Short of having any opportunity for a live presentation, I proceeded with mailing hard copy information, as well as electronically, to astronomers with expertise in geodesy and Earth motion and strategically from countries around the World. Having the facilities at my disposal, I revised and updated the website, to which visitors were steadily escalating from an impressive list of countries. I was exhilarated to see among those, the USA Government and USA Military also. There had been no official or personal contact but I was hopeful for a thorough investigation of my work. Optimism reveals potential wherein perpetual motive for existence manifests; adaptation and humor are unique human qualities to manipulate time, opportunity and destiny. On clear nights I could observe the Northern hemisphere sky with Ursa Major, like a giant arm on a clock, slowly encircling Polaris -the celestial counter part of the Meidum Pyramid! In the meantime, clove oil and alcohol did not suppress my growing dental discomfort and I had to receive unplanned, costly treatment. Remaining constructive, I commenced blending a new edition of my work to incorporate the Conclusion Chapter. I again attempted to contact Robert Bauval through his webmaster, who acknowledged and forwarded the correspondence, to notify him of my work. Being able to communicate for all I wanted via email, I submitted my findings to the international academia and also had a guest article entitled *The Axis of Precession* published on Dr. Robert Schoch's website. At the end of what was also the wettest summer for Britons in as many years, I clocked up an uneventful 43. A strange thing there, come November, they turn back the clock and the Sun is in a different place in the sky! They brew good ale there but the call of Africa and a Sun in the right place lured me back to not greener, but cheaper grass… News of theft and vandalism involving the rondavels in Lesotho was disturbing and having risen, like the Phoenix from the ashes after the last incident, word was: "the vehicle went off the road in the mountains". Like I said, my friend Philip is a resourceful guy -it's ironic that his horse was named 'Rollover'. I love Africa but arriving back penniless and homeless was not an inviting prospect. In good spirit however and confident that it had been a good campaign, despite still being unpublished abroad, where it would really matter, it was not through lack of effort. I found consolation in the knowledge that what was required for the seeds to be sown, where they will receive certain rain, had been done and felt a sense of relief that an enormous objective had been reached: the task of compiling this information –oblivious of the immensity and difficulty of the journey that still lay ahead. Had I known it then, perhaps the task would have seemed insurmountable and unlikely, under different circumstances and commitments, would have tackled research on precession. All considered, relatively little time had elapsed since my arrival in Cape Town back in 2001, although in my own mind it seemed like 'forever'. Despite making some forfeits, *Zep Tepi ~ The First Time* was listed by leading bookstores in South Africa, within 2 years of making my initial discovery in Lesotho. Nearly 50%, of the 1000 copies that were printed, had sold over 6 months. It was only through my own restricted efforts in distribution and marketing however and without promotion or media coverage. Too few over too long, a small market and not a sustainable means but the show had to go on… driven by moral obligation and coming by almost solely on enthusiasm. Such an investigation could be all consuming and I still wished to live life. I obtained an estimate from a printer in Oxford but did not have the required capital, neither *one* publisher with vision and could not find *one* agent to make the bridge. There had still not been academic endorsement, or query about any component of my work. Perseverance requires an enormous amount of self-belief and a good sense of humour is obligatory. In an attempt of reassurance and self understanding, back on the farm next to the Suikerbos River, I began processing my memoirs in a non-technical philosophical shroud, relating my adventures and speaking my heart! Coinciding with this time, an Earthquake unleashed a devastating Tsunami in the Indian Ocean that crushed everything in its path. The high toll exerted on human life reinstates our helplessness to avert, or withstand natural disasters of magnitude. This tragedy will hardly compare to the havoc that lies unforeseen in man's future. Another year on, destiny led to the mother city of Cape Town once again, presenting new opportunity and a spiritual post mortem –the full circle. I developed art that reflects the essence of my research in abstract, lectured on my findings and continued with compiling my memoirs. More time, skills and experience enabled a more conclusive thesis with comprehensive illustrations. There are shortcomings, such as grammar but hopefully the reader will get the drift and if not, it doesn't matter -I am content in having given my best, obeying a calling and journeying on the river of life.

The ancients mapped the celestial expanse harmoniously and projected it geographically. The astronomical effect of this and selection of the site, in a Global context, is almost too fantastical to comprehend. Questions still remain: is it lost or undiscovered knowledge that the configuration of calibration and mapping of our Globe incorporate the cycle of precession? The Sphinx faces due East –tracking our source of light and life, the Sun, which is the actual cardinal that provides a directional constant. The true prime meridian delineates the longest river on our planet –the Nile and more importantly, the polar axis. Are our maps and projections as practical as scientifically possible, or are they 'upside down'? How do we determine the up or down side of a sphere that is enveloped by the Universe? Perhaps we need to rethink expressions relating to North and South. The orientation of the Poles will change in relation to the Sun, the Galaxy and the Ecliptic in an event that will unleash conditions, unlike anything we can come to imagine. Psychologically, we don't like changes. We prefer familiar comfort zones. Understandably, the obstacles would not be technological but rather mind set. Regarding our mystical genesis, if we wish to ever break free from the chains of oppressive and manipulated rule, we need to question aspects with minds of innocence. Not oblivious of contemporary persecution and subversion, however, if one does not have the freedom of pursuance of the truth it can take thousands of years to rediscover something that should never have been lost in the first place. Having cast a stone in the lake, ripples are a normal consequence but a point in case has been made, and reaction and criticism can be expected. I have lived through a few storms -not always pleasant, but have been blessed by the Universe!

Native Americans believe that 'a day properly lived is an achievement' –the journey is more important than the destination. Plato says: 'souls are made in equal number with the stars and each soul distributed to its several star… and he who should live well for his due span of time should journey back to the habitation of his consort star…'

Stars are at the epicentre of creation. They are almighty gods that contain all of the elements around a metal core (Pyramid Texts refer to the iron bones of the gods). It is indeed a sun to which we owe our existence -a sun that was sacrificed for us to live and that, warrants our worship. It started with air and moisture and then a super nova explosion that resulted in the birth of new stars and planets in a stellar nursery. Such an explosion was observed in 1987 for the first time. We are the children of a star, created in the remnant of an asteroid collision. We are also at the mercy of stars and our Sun, which has made existence possible on Earth, will also in the distant future, cause extinction. A comet can be the catalyst for the beginning of life, but there exists the danger of another catastrophe -one that can end human civilization -such as the collision, that is believed to have wiped out the dinosaurs some 65 million years ago. If this or any other, important information is contained in a cryptic message to us, should we not make it our quest to decipher it?

After leading a nomadic existence for several years, I yearned for a place of belonging and space to breathe… to reflect on events, refocus perspective and to harmonise. I returned to the magnificent mountains, where my adventure was interrupted and a special volume of leather-bound books of the 19th century discoverer explorers, complete with mapped routes. They were a gift from a Scottish mentor and friend, Ken McKeen and a great inspiration of facing challenge, endurance and determination. It has been my vision for them to gather dust in more meaningful context: in a lodge and the maps as décor for a cosy pub with an adjoining lounge and open fireplace, in honour of the spirit of adventure. I considered those travelers very fortunate, for having experienced the 'world of that time' and felt disappointed, thinking there was nothing left to be discovered… It may be encouraging for others with a similar passion, to know that there *is* an enormously great frontier and innumerable discoveries yet to be made. That frontier is space and the unfathomable Universe and of course, our evolution to a meaningful and responsible role of existence within it. We need an 'ark', a stepping stone in time and to spread our wings. Galactic travel capability requires electro-magnetic anti-gravity craft, not rocket thrust and there are some plans of 'my old man' that requires attention but time is a factor -perhaps with constructive collaboration by experts and a bit of magical *method* or *methodical* magic, we can reach the stars – that is the challenge! It is also time to move on, to close doors and for new ones to open.

For the attention of the Directorate of Science & Technology, CIA:

This is not a joke, nor a threat but a request:
take me to your leader

As you should be aware, I have tried to convey information via one of your consuls/embassies on a previous occasion. Whether they did the neccessary or not should reflect on your data bases, however, there was no follow up (of which I am aware or that involved me in person at least).
Whether that was per choice or negligence is not known and of no consequence actually, however, as a responsible citizen of this civilization I attempt once more to bring important information [to] the attention of parties that should be concerned.

The issue I refer to can be perused in this article:

http://sites.google.com/site/earthgyration/
and sub page
http://sites.google.com/site/earthgyration/Home/climate-change/

sincerely
Hendrik G. Dirker
26 December 2009

CIA automatic reply: Your question or comment has been successfully submitted. Your confirmation number is 5K9TCL1

APPENDIX

Westcar Papyrus c.1650BC item No.303, Antiquities Museum, Berlin
Prof. Adolf Erman –1st translation 1890 (in German)
Alan H. Gardiner , 1925 (in English) Dr. Miriam Lichtheim translation, 1975

Now **Prince Hardedef** stood up to speak: 'So far you have heard examples of the skills of those who have passed away, and one cannot tell the truth from the false. But there is a subject of your majesty in your own time, unknown to you, which involves a great magician.'

Said **his majesty**: 'What is this about Hardedef, my son?'

Said **Prince Hardedef**: 'There is a man named Djedi who lives in Djed-Snefru. He is a man of a hundred and ten years, who eats five hundred loaves of bread, half an ox for meat, and drinks one hundred jugs of beer to this very day. He can join a severed head. He can make a lion walk behind him, its leash on the ground. And he knows the number of the secret chambers of the sanctuary of Thoth.'

Said **his majesty**: 'You, yourself, Hardedef, my son, shall bring Djedi to me.'

Said **Hardedef**: 'O King, my Lord, I have brought Djedi' Said his majesty; 'Go, bring him to me.'

Said **his majesty**: 'How is it, Djedi that I never got to see You?'

Said **Djedi**: 'He who is summoned comes, O King, my Lord, I was summoned and I have come.'

Said **his majesty**: 'It was also said that you know the number of the secret chambers of the sanctuary of Thoth.'

Said **Djed**i: 'Please, I do not know the number, O King, my Lord, but I know where the place is.'…'There is a chest of flint in the building called "Inventory" in On. It is in that chest…'

'It is the eldest of the three children who are in the womb of Ruddjedet who will bring it to you…She is the wife of a priest of Re, Lord of Sakhbu, who is pregnant with the three children of Re, Lord of Sakhbu.
He has said concerning them that they will assume this beneficent office in this whole land, and the eldest of them will be high priest in On.'

Said **Djedi**: 'What is this mood, O King my Lord? Is it because of these three children? I say: first your son, and then one of the three children.'

Said **his majesty**: 'When will Ruddjedet give birth?'

Said **Djedi**: 'She will give birth on the fifteenth day of the first winter month.'

Said **his majesty**: 'Just when the sandbanks of the Two-Fish Channel are dry! I would have crossed over myself, so as to see the temple of Re, Lord of Sakbu.'

Said **Djedi**: 'Then I shall make four cubits of water over the sandbanks of the Two-Fish Channel.'

The anthropomorphic gods:

Iisis *(celestial counterpart: Sirius/Sothis)* original name: AST
Meaning 'seat'. Eldest daughter of four children, of sky goddess Nut and earth god Geb. Born on the 4th intercalary day. Married to brother Osiris. After their jealous brother Seth cut Osiris into fourteen pieces, Iis recovered all of the pieces except the phallus and through magical rites she had learned from Thoth, became pregnant with the seed of Osiris. She gave birth to their divine son Horus at Khemmis, on the West bank of the Nile. Her terrestrial association is with Heliopolis, which was the seat of a powerful priesthood, whose initiated members were the *custodians* of a *sanctuary* of *knowledge*, the Great Temple of Ra, the *Sun* God.

Osiris *(celestial counterpart: zeta Orionis)* original name: AS AR
The meaning of this name is uncertain, but has been interpreted as 'to create a throne' and as 'Seat' or 'Power of the Eye'. God of resurrection and after-life, he was worshipped throughout Egypt. Born five days before the summer solstice, on the first intercalary day, at Thebes, he is the eldest son of four children of sky goddess Nut and earth god Geb. Osiris was married to his sister Isis and they became the first rulers of Egypt. Osiris introduced civilisation in Egypt and *afterwards brought his teachings to the rest of the world*. He ruled by power of persuasion and not by force and brought Maat -a system of cosmic law and order. According to legend, Osiris was brutally killed on the 17th day of the month of Hathor (late Sept. or Nov.) in the 28th year of his reign, by his brother Seth, with the help of Aso, *a Queen of Ethiopia* and seventy two conspirators. He departed into the sky to establish a cosmic kingdom of the first time Duat among the stars of Orion, on the banks of the Winding-Waterway, the celestial Nile. The body of Osiris was cut into fourteen pieces and over the place where each was buried, Isis caused a sanctuary to be built.

Seth *(celestial counterpart~delta orionis)*
Born on the third intercalary day and married to his twin sister Nephtys, who was born on the fifth intercalary day. Although Nephtys, whose name means 'Lady of the House' (thought to be reference to the Palace of Osiris), was married to Seth, her loyalties were with Osiris.

Horus *(follower of the Sun)*
Son of Osiris and Isis -believed to be the first man-god to rule Egypt. Khem, also known as Assim, later called Letopolis, was the site of a temple which outdated the pyramids, and was closely connected with the Falcon god of the sky, Horus. Horus engaged in an epic battle with his uncle Seth over the throne of Osiris, during which Horus lost an eye and Seth lost his testicles.

INDEX

SUPPORTING MATERIAL

FIG. DRAWINGS & MAPS:

I.	Great Pyramid N-S cross section	43
II.	Upper chambers & star shafts	37
III.	Ennead of gods	56
IV.	Orion-Osiris-Horus Kings	59
V.	Nile Valley, Delta	70
VI.	Osiris-Horus tomb?	65
VII.	Sokar ship -departure of gods?	69
VIII.	Hermetic cycle of Duat?	73
IX.	Mnemonic message?	51
map [X]	(a) Two-Lands division (b) geographical Osiris/Orion figure.	93
XI.	Dahshur pyramids -offset	125
XII.	Pyramids=geometrical stars	136
XIII.	Pyramid & obelisk	149
XIV.	Gyro motion	185
XV.	Temperature graph	195
XVI.	Protractor	197

PHOTOGRAPHS: 93

Ph.1	Giza group	
Ph.2	Red Pyramid	
Ph.3	Bent Pyramid	
Ph.4	Meidum Pyramid	
Ph.5	Galaxy arms	
Ph.6	Duat projection	
Ph.7	Orion Constellation	
Ph.8	Giza aerial	
Ph.9	Orion's Belt	

DIAGRAMS 93

[A] ORION stick man, persona, constellation
[B] CELESTIAL ROSTAU ascending gods
[C] TERRESTRIAL ROSTAU
[D] TWO LANDS DIVISION

    HUB & CIRCLE

[E] SURVEY GRID
    CO-ORDINATES

[F] UNIFIED PLAN
[G] SACRED GEOMETRY
    Galactic orientation
    PRECESSION PHASES

[I] THE DUAT

[J] DUAT PERSPECTIVE
    ORION PERSPECTIVE

[K] PENTAGRAMS
    ORION & THE DUAT

[L] CELESTIAL PYRAMIDS
[M] Pi (π) in the SKY
[N] DUAT OBELISK

[O] PLANETARY PATHS + Comet Encke
    as above…
    …so below

[P] CELESTIAL DOME descending gods
    Celestial Pole star chart
    Gyration cone

[Q] CELESTIAL GLOBE divide
    GYRATION MODEL
    MICA star motion
    CLIMATE CHANGE ice extent & sea levels

    ORION PYRAMID secret chambers

GLOSSARY

References and further reading
Secret Chamber, Robert Bauval
The Orion Mystery, Robert Bauval & Adrian Gilbert
Keeper of Genesis, R. Bauval & G. Hancock
Fingerprints of the Gods, Graham Hancock
Rondebosch Library, Cape Town
Guide to the Pyramids of Egypt, Alberto Siliotti
The Riddle of the Pyramids, Dr. Kurt Mendelssohn
The Sirius Mystery, Robert Temple
Valley of the Kings, John Romer
Billions and Billions, Carl Sagan
The First Stargazers, James Cornell
The Death of Gods in Ancient Egypt, Jane B. Sellers
Atlas of Ancient Egypt, John Baines & Jaromir Ma'lek
The Pyramids of Egypt, Dr. I.E.S Edwards
Riddles of the Sphinx, Paul Jordan
Romer's Egypt, John Romer
Egyptian Mythology, Veronica Ions
The Phoenix Solution, Alan F. Alford
Giza The Truth, Ian Lawton & Chris Ogilvie-Herald
The Tomb of God, Richard Andrews & Paul Schellenberger
Private loan /donation
The lost Book of Enki, Zecharia Sitchin
The Cosmic Code, Zecharia Sitchin
When the Sky Fell, Rand & Rose Flem-Ath
Heaven's Mirror, Graham Hancock and Santa Faiia
Mysteries of the Earth, Jacques Bergier
The Mysterious Past, Robert Charroux
Simons Town / Fish Hoek Libraries, Cape Peninsula
A Little History of Astro-Archaeology, John Michell
Serpent in the Sky, John West
The eyes of The Sphinx, Erich von Daniken

Hall of the Gods, Nigel Appleby
Dome of the Rock, Jerry M. Landay
Guns, Germs, and Steel, Jared Diamond
The Great Pyramid Decoded, Peter Lemusirier
Tutankhamun The Exodus Conspiracy, Andrew Collins &
Chris Ogilvie-Herald
Bible Code 2, Michael Drosnin
Signs of the Gods, Erich von Daniken
The Atlantis Blue Print, Rand Flem-Ath & Colin Wilson
The Stargate Conspiracy, Lynn Picknett & Clive Prince
Meaning of the Dead Sea Scrolls, James van der Kam & Peter Flint
Odyssey of the Gods, Erich von Daniken
From Atlantis to the Sphinx, Colin Wilson
Before the Flood, Ian Wilson
The Book of Enoch, translated by R.H. Charles
The Templar Revelation, Lynn Picknett & Clive Prince
Rosslyn, Tim Wallace-Murphy & Marilyn Hopkins
Uriel's Machine, Christopher Knight & Robert Lomas

Quotes and other sources

Cosmographic Mystery, Johannes Kepler
On the Infinite Universe and the World, Dr. Giordano Bruno
(*Spaccio della Bestia Trionfante,* G. Bruno)

The Art Of Memory, Frances A. Yates
The Ancient Egyptian Coffin Texts, Philologist R.O. Faulkner
The Ancient Egyptian Book of the Dead, R.O. Faulkner
The Ancient Egyptian Pyramid Texts, R.O. Faulkner
The Egyptian Heaven and Hell, Sir E.A. Wallis Budge
(*Shat Ent Am Duat - The Book of the Duat*)

Ancient Egyptian Book of the Dead, Normandi Ellis translation
Myth & Symbol in Ancient Egypt, Prof. R.T. Rundle Clark
The Legend of the Phoenix, R.T. Rundle Clark

The Mythical Origin of the Egyptian Temple, E.A.E. Reymond
(*Specifications of the mounds of the early primeval age, Thoth*)

A Dictionary of Egyptian Gods and Goddesses, George Hart
Le Secret des Batisseurs des Grandes Pyramides; Kheops, G. Goyon

Hermes Trismegistus, *Asclepius III, Corpus Hermeticum*
Hermetic narrative; Isis to Horus, *Kore Kosmou*
Asclepius, *The Lament*
Plato, *Timaeus and Critias*
Herodotus, *Histories ii*
Diodorus Siculus, *Book 1*

Arch Bishop James Ussher, *Annals of the World, 1650*
Dr John Lightfoot, vice chancellor, Cambridge University, 1859
John Dixon letter to Piazzi Smyth, 1871
J.M. Keyness, The Royal Society, 1947
New Yorker 10 February 1997

Dr. John Billingham, NASA Ames Research Center, 1995
Professor Charles A. Whitney, *The discovery of our Galaxy*
Professor Carl Sagan, *Cosmos*
Dr. Peter Mack, *Night Skies*

Joseph Jochmans, *Time Capsule*
Joseph Ritman, *Bibliotheca Philosophica –Amsterdam*
Fred Pick & G. Norman Knight, *The Pocket History of Freemasonry*
Edgar Cayce; *Reading 378-16, Reading 281-42, Reading 5748*
William Kingsland, *The Gnosis or Ancient Wisdom in the*
                                                    Christian Scriptures

R. Cook, *The Pyramids of Giza*
Lucie Lamie, *Egyptian Mysteries*
R.A. Schwaller de Lubicz, *Sacred Science*
Miriam Lichtheim, *Ancient Egyptian Literature*

E.A. Wallis Budge, *From Fetish to God in Ancient Egypt*

Papyrus Westcar item No.303, Antiquities Museum, Berlin;
Professor Adolf Erman, 1890 German translation
Alan H. Gardiner, *Journal of Egyptian Archaeology*, 1925

Shabaka Stone, exhibit no.498 British Museum, London

Leiden Museum Payrus No.344 c.1990 BC

The Turin Papyrus c.1400 BC, Italy

Pyramid inscriptions:
{PT UTT. 261}
{PT UTT. 332}
{PT UTT. 669}
Pyramid Text lines:
{Pyramid Text 357}
{Pyramid Text 632}
{Pyramid Text 798-803}
{Pyramid Text 820-2}
{Pyramid Text 882-3}
{Pyramid Text 935}
{Pyramid Text 959-61}
{Pyramid Text 1014}
{Pyramid Text 1082-3}
{Pyramid Text 1716-17}
Coffin Texts c.2000 BC - 1800 BC:
{Coffin Text Spell 236}
{Coffin Text Spell 241}
{Coffin Text Spell 314}
{Coffin Text Spell 1035}
{Coffin Text Spell 1080}
{Coffin Text Spell 1087}

"...Heaven will not support the stars in their orbits,
nor will the stars pursue their constant course in Heaven...
But when all has befallen, Asclepius,
then the Master and Father, God,
the first before all,
the maker of that god
who first came into being,
will look on that which has come to pass
and
will stay the disorder
by counter working of his Will...
He will call back to the right path
those who have gone astray,
he will cleanse the world from evil...
Those gods who ruled the Earth will be restored..."

(Corpus Hermeticum -Asclepius III, Hermes Trismegistus)

www.ingramcontent.com/pod-product-compliance
Lightning Source LLC
Chambersburg PA
CBHW070530090426
42735CB00013B/2931